Carving Figureheads
& Other
Nautical Designs

Alan & Gill
Bridgewater

STERLING PUBLISHING CO., INC.
NEW YORK

DEDICATION

This book is dedicated to the memory of Alan's grandfather, Arthur Williamson—sailor and marine engineer—in remembrance for all those wonderful summers.

Acknowledgments

A big thank-you must go to our son Glyn, for his perseverance with the color photographs. A wonderful son.

Thank you for ferrying us on the Fowey River, Julian—another wonderful son—and thank you, Rachael, for the loan of Julian and the camera.

We would also like to thank the following manufacturers for their help:
Delta International Machinery Co.
Blue Bird Toys, for the Plasticine
Draper Tools Ltd.
Pebeo Paints

Library of Congress Cataloging-in-Publication Data

Bridgewater, Alan.
    Carving figureheads & other nautical designs / Alan & Gill
Bridgewater.
      p.   cm.   Includes bibliographical references and index.
    ISBN 0-8069-8706-5
    1. Wood-carving. 2. Figureheads of ships. I. Bridgewater, Gill.
II. Title. III. Title: Carving figureheads and other nautical
designs.
TT199.7.B727   1995
731.4'62—dc20   94-47294
                                            CIP

Edited by Laurel Ornitz
Layout by Joan Columbus

1 3 5 7 9 10 8 6 4 2

Published by Sterling Publishing Company, Inc.
387 Park Avenue South, New York, N.Y. 10016
© 1995 by Alan & Gill Bridgewater
Distributed in Canada by Sterling Publishing
% Canadian Manda Group, One Atlantic Avenue, Suite 105
Toronto, Ontario, Canada M6K 3E7
Distributed in Great Britain and Europe by Cassell PLC
Wellington House, 125 Strand, London WC2R 0BB, England
Distributed in Australia by Capricorn Link (Australia) Pty Ltd.
P.O. Box 6651, Baulkham Hills, Business Centre, NSW 2153, Australia
Manufactured in the United States of America
All rights reserved

Sterling ISBN 0-8069-8706-5

Contents

Color section follows page **128.**

Preface

When we first saw a carved wooden ship's figure-head in a museum, we were amazed. It was huge! Standing about 6 or 7 feet in height, it was a torso and head of a Mohawk warrior. The monolithic wood carving was described as follows: "a nineteenth-century ship's figurehead, laminated fir, painted, U.S.A."

As Gill and I were trained in the English arts and crafts tradition, and knew about church carvings, decorative furniture carving, nineteenth-century "art" sculptures, and the like, we were not only brought to a halt by the sheer size of the figure-head, but also by its powerful and primitive physical presence and the fact that it was painted.

Well, of course, from then on, we were hooked. Once our eyes were opened, we began to search out other figureheads and nautical wood carvings. Over the next few years, we saw figureheads in museums, walked around old sailing ships where we saw figureheads in situ, and even spotted a figurehead at an antiques auction.

We soon came to realize that nautical wood carving is a uniquely wonderful leftover from another era. As to how or why the craft survived and prospered in isolation, it's almost impossible to say. The feeling we have, however, is that ship carving—the techniques, size, and designs—bridged the seventeenth, eighteenth, and nineteenth centuries without being unduly affected by all the so-called "improving" academic art influences of the day. The more we dug and delved, it became increasingly obvious that American, European, and English ship carving appears to have drawn its inspiration, not as you might expect from architectural and furniture carving, but rather, directly from the medieval tradition of wood carving. That is to say, the forms are carved on a massive scale, the designs are refreshingly unencumbered by what has been described as "intellectual art," and, of course, perhaps most significant of all, the carvings are characterized by being brightly painted and gilded. It's not that the ship carvers of the eighteenth and nineteenth centuries went out of their

way to thumb their nose at high-art wood carving, but simply that they were happily in a world of their own, working as their fathers and grandfathers had done before them. Our intuitive impressions were borne out by a wonderfully peevish eighteenth-century academic's account that starts off by describing ship carvers as wayward geniuses and then goes on to describe ship's figureheads of the period as being "savage, barbaric, deformed, monstrous, unnatural, and perverse." We guess that he didn't much like them!

After a great deal of research, the time came around when we wanted to try our own hand at ship carving. What we needed, we decided, was a good fat how-to book. So, we made contact with various specialty publishers, phoned around to libraries, and generally went on a book hunt—but all to no avail. Yes, there are books that describe ship carvings—what they look like—and, yes, there are books that describe the tradition, but as far as we could ascertain, there wasn't a single book that actually described how to design, cut, carve, and paint a figurehead. The plain fact was that, if we wanted to carve a figurehead, then we had to study existing examples, analyze our findings, and then set to work carving one.

However, as a result, not only have we worked on all manner of ship carvings—everything from figureheads to name boards, banners, and scrolls—but, along the way, we have discovered all sorts of tricks of the trade.

So, there you have it. This book is, as far as we know, the only book on the subject of ship carving that actually tells you how to carve and decorate a figurehead and other nautical designs.

The book contains working drawings, inspirational designs, and in-depth detailed instructions on setting out the design, cutting and gluing the blank, modelling the carving, and painting the finished carving. Not only do we describe in detail how to carve and decorate 15 traditional designs, but we supply inspirational drawings, tips, notes, follow-ups, and much more. If you want to veer away from our designs and carve something of your own, then our inspiration designs will put you on course.

We have gone overboard—excuse the pun—with our inspirational color photographs. They are special, inasmuch as they show various views and details, so that you, the carver, can really see what's going on.

At the beginning of each project, we set the scene by telling you about the background of the piece, and then we go straight into the carving. With clear text, many detailed illustrations, and a number of step-by-step photographs, we tell you just about everything you need to know about making the project. If we make a mistake, then we tell you about it, and you learn from our mistakes. If we find out something special about a particular type of carving, technique, or tool, then we tell you about it, too.

Not to worry if you are a nervous beginner; we have included a good number of easy projects just to get you launched.

Figurehead carving is an amazingly vigorous and gutsy craft. The forms are large and bold, the techniques are adventuresome and expressive, the designs are strong and uninhibited, and the use of color is dazzling!

We invite you to roll up your sleeves, take up the challenge, and get started!

Best of luck!

Introduction

Of all the wood-carved images associated with the great days of the wooden sailing ship, the figurehead is, without doubt, the most romantic, evocative, and enigmatic. For many of us, the very mention of the word "figurehead" is enough to set our imagination soaring with all manner of images and words that have to do with the sea.

When I think of figureheads, I see in my mind's eye a glorious jumble of salty, stormy, sea-washed pictures: Spanish galleons, with their superabundance of painted and gilded carvings; Captain Drake and his ship, the *Golden Hind*; Nelson's *Victory*; Captain Ahab and his ship, the *Pequod*, with its carved Indian figurehead; and so the images roll by. I see Captain Morgan, *Treasure Island*, Lord Jim in the China seas, *Mutiny on the Bounty*. . . . Along with the images come the equally wonderful, and sometimes just as mysterious, words that have to do with wooden sailing ships: sloop, boom, bowsprit, bulwarks, scuppers, bilges, binnacle, cat-

heads, mainbrace, and all the rest. Of course, many of these associations come straight out of

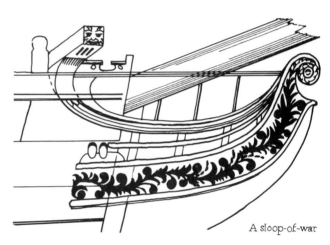

A sloop-of-war

American sloop-of-war—prow details showing the cathead, a fine scroll billet head, and the trail board.

Alan's childhood and from Hollywood epics, but the very fact that they linger bears witness to their importance and strength.

Figureheads are larger-than-life wood-carved figures that were traditionally mounted on the bow of the ship. The figurehead has its roots way back in the dim and distant mists of time, when the sea was an unknown place filled with dragons, monsters, and all manner of slimy horrors. When early seafarers—the Greeks, the Vikings, and the Chinese—first set sail, they had no way of knowing just what was waiting for them out there. Were there dragons? Were there cannibal isles and mermaids? Were there oceans where the water boiled and the winds raged? Was it possible to fall off the edge of the world? With all these fears, the best that these brave seafarers could do was to mount bold, larger-than-life images of power and defiance on the front of their ships and to cover the ships in authoritative and confident carvings, in the hope that the "spirit of the ship" would evade evil, lead the way, and maybe strike terror into potential enemies. And so it was that the Viking

Independence

A typical American mid-nineteenth-century bust figurehead, from the ship Independence—*note the way the bust is supported and bracketed by scrolls.*

ships were decorated with snarling figurehead dragons, the Greek ships had votive rams' heads set on the bow, the Romans painted the symbol of the all-seeing eye, and so on.

Gradually, over the centuries, as ships evolved and fashions changed, the serpents and dragons gave way to heraldic rampant lions, which in turn were replaced by the figures of mighty heroes, noble kings and queens, and proud ship owners. This evolutionary pattern more or less came to a halt at the end of the nineteenth century, when the shape and structure of the ship resulted in figureheads' being reduced to small stylized scrolls and badges.

With the figurehead being, as it were, the pinnacle of ship-carving achievement, we musn't forget that, to a great extent, all the exterior woodwork, from the stern and the rudder, to the side rails, trail boards, name boards, port holes, rope holes, and just about every other feature, was vigorously carved and painted. There were carved heads on rudder posts and carved name boards at various places around the stern and side rails, the rails were carved with stylized rope imagery, the stepped junctions along the rails were carved with all manner of fishlike beasts, the anchor cathead beams were carved with cat faces, the trail boards that led the way from the rails to the figurehead were carved with a frieze, the base of the mast was carved, the cabin doors were carved, various bits and pieces around the base of the figurehead were carved with scrolls and brackets, and, of course, the whole wonderful wood-carved extravaganza was topped off with the figurehead itself.

The uniquely remarkable thing about nautical carvings is that, for the most part, they were worked by naïve primitive craftsmen. By saying "naïve primitive," we in no way mean to deride the skills of these wood-carvers, but rather just the opposite. It was their lack of formal or classical training that resulted in the carvings being so wonderfully uninhibited and dynamic. Traditional ship carvings are characterized by being generous in scale, unbound by a sense of proportion, unrestrained in style, and usually brilliantly painted in bold primary colors.

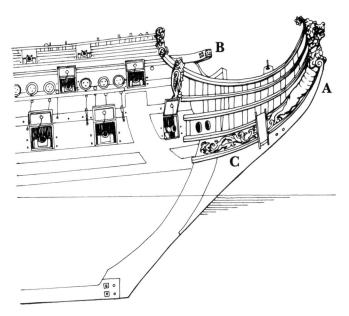

The stern and quarter galley of a model of a Dutch ship, dated from about 1660 to 1670, showing (A) the ornate carving over the stern, (B) the carving around the ports, and (C) the window or light details.

The prow of the same Dutch ship, showing (A) a lion figurehead in a characteristic springing-forward pose, (B) the cathead, and (C) the hancing piece.

Sadly, the great ship-carving tradition came to an end at the beginning of the twentieth century, when wooden ships gave way to iron-clad vessels that were leaner, tighter, and more functional. However, over the last few years there has been a resurgence in ship carving, with all manner of small vessels, boat clubs, and harbor-side dwellings being decorated and embellished by nautical wood carvings. As we live along the coast of Cornwall, England, we look out of a window and across the harbor to see a fishing boat with a small carved-and-painted trail board, a pleasure boat with a carved tiller, several yachts with carved name boards, an ancient cottage with a nineteenth-century figurehead mounted under the eaves, and a pub with a boldly carved-and-painted sign over the door.

Of course, we are never again going to see the likes of the old sailing ships with their glorious carvings, and the recent revival is no more than a small echo of what went before, but nevertheless the craft of ship carving still lives on in our hearts, minds, and collective folk memory. Ship carvings still evoke wonderful romantic images of exotic ports of call, the smell of the sea, and times past when sea voyages were a step into the unknown.

Tools, Techniques, Materials, and Terms

A–Z Guide to Ship Carving

Bench Clamp

A clamp used for holding down the workpiece. In use, the shaft is dropped into one of a number of bench holes, the workpiece is set between the swivel pad and the bench, and the screw is tightened up. The benefit of such a clamp is that it can be very swiftly released and relocated.

Billet Board

A small stylized scroll carving used at the head instead of a figurehead. Traditionally, such carvings are mounted on the stem head and under the bowsprit.

Blank

A prepared block or slab of wood that is ready to be carved. We usually get our wood from a specialty supplier or boat yard. We find that most boat yards are prepared to sell small pieces and scraps, whereas large mills are either unwilling or unable to handle small orders.

In the context of wood carving, ship carvings are unusual on two counts: they are out in all kinds of weather, and the finished carvings are usually heavily painted and varnished. Therefore, we tend to use a characterless, easy-to-carve wood like jelutong—it's inexpensive and wonderfully easy to carve—and build the blank up from small sections. This technique means that not only can we prepare the sections on the band saw, but, better still, laminated structures are more resistant to warping and splitting.

Bow Saw

If you don't have access to a band saw, then you could use a traditional hand-held bow saw. This

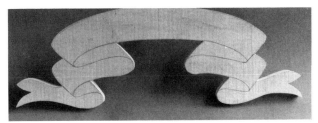

Blank—a prepared, ready-to-carve cutout, or blank. Note how important it is for the design to be arranged so that there is a minimum of short grain.

saw has a thin blade set in a wooden H-frame. The blade/handles can be rotated to enable you to clear the workpiece when cutting curves. A good saw for cutting thick slabs of wood.

Bowsprit

The long spar projecting from the front, or bow, of a sailing vessel that is used to carry the head stay forward as far as possible. Traditionally, small figureheads were slung under the bowsprit.

Carving in the Round

A three-dimensional carving that is worked and viewed from all sides, such as a figurehead.

Cathead

On old wooden sailing ships, the two timbers that project from either side of the prow to which the anchor can be hoisted and secured are known as catheads. The name has its roots in the ancient Viking tradition of having a carving of a lionlike beast mounted on the stem post. Although over the centuries such beasts evolved into stylized heraldic lions, and then later human figures and busts, the term "cathead" stuck. Almost without exception, ship carvers used cat imagery on the end of the cathead beam—no doubt the joke of having a cat's face on the end of the cathead beam seemed too good a chance to pass up.

Constructed, Laminated, or Built Up

This refers to a carving that is constructed or built up from a number of blocks or layers. For example, most of our figureheads are built up from a number of prepared $4 \times 4''$ sections. The advantages of this technique are that you can use small sections of easy-to-obtain wood, you can clear most of the waste on the band saw prior to carving, and, once made, the laminated structure is stable.

Cushion, or Bag

A leather or canvas bag loosely filled with sand or sawdust. In use, the workpiece is nestled by the cushion. It is especially helpful in carving large,

Constructed, laminated, or built up—a technique whereby the blank is made up of a number of glued-together pieces of wood. This technique not only enables you to use small sections of easy-to-obtain wood, but it also minimizes waste.

awkward, difficult-to-hold pieces that you can't easily secure in a vise.

Deep-Carved

In the context of ship carving, a carving that is deeply carved with surface hollows and undercuts. A figurehead could be deep-carved, whereas the motifs on a sea chest might be shallow relief–carved.

Dividers

A two-legged, compasslike instrument used for stepping off measurements. We favor using a large pair of engineer's dividers; they have a fastening screw, and they are more or less indestructible.

Figurehead

Of all the carvings found on traditional wooden sailing ships, the figurehead on the bow surely is the most dynamic, the most exciting to carve, and the most enigmatic. The very idea of having a larger-than-life figure to symbolize the spirit and authority of a ship is a uniquely wonderful anomalous notion.

Finish

Traditionally, ship carvings were sanded to a swift finish, given a thick undercoat of matt white lead,

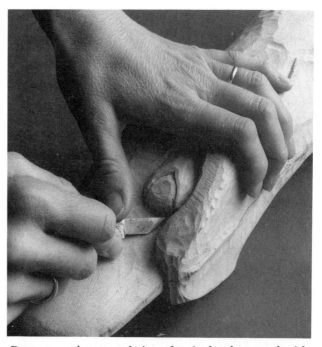

Deep-carved—a workpiece that is deeply carved with surface hollows and undercuts.

painted with bold primary oil colors, and then heavily varnished. We have modified the techniques somewhat by using water-based matt white emulsion for the undercoat and colored acrylics instead of oil paints. You might think that acrylics will let the weather through and start peeling off, but it's not so. If you lay the acrylics on in well-brushed, even coats, give the whole works a couple of coats of varnish, and then spend time each season keeping the varnish in good condition, acrylics will last forever.

Yes, you can use oil paints or enamels—the choice is yours. The only drawback is that you will have to allow for days instead of hours for the painting sequence.

Gouges and Chisels

For ship carving—meaning carving everything from name boards, scrolls, and billet heads, to rope twists, banners, and figureheads—you only need three or four basic types of tools: a flat chisel, a U-section gouge, V-section tools, and various knives. In this book, gouges are usually named according to the shape of their cutting edge rather than any number or code. For example, a gouge might be described as a "large U-section scoop gouge," with "large" referring to the width of the cutting edge. Chisels and gouges can be held in one hand and pushed with the other, or held in one hand and struck with a mallet.

Grinding

Using a grind stone to bring the bevel of a gouge or chisel to the correct angle and finish. See "Sharpening."

Grounding, or Wasting

Cutting away the wood in and around the design, causing the ground to be lowered and the design left in relief.

Incised

A shallow, knife- or gouge-worked V-section trench or scoop cut.

Jack Tar

Nautical terminology is full of references to "jack." for example, there is a small flag called a jack; a

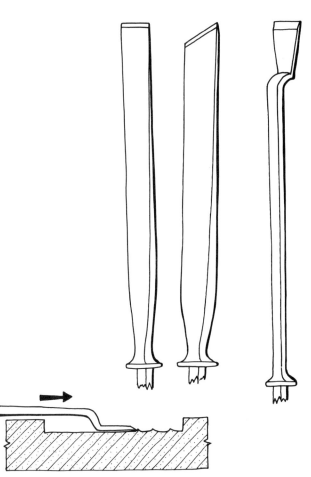

Quarter boards—usually referring to a name board that is attached to the aft quarters. Go for large, clear block letters.

Chisels. From left to right: Straight chisel, skew chisel, and dog-leg chisel. See how the dog-leg is used specifically for levelling lowered ground.

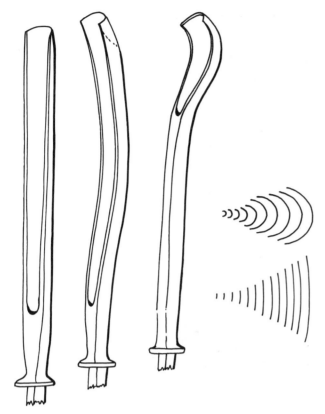

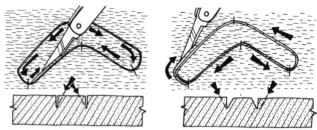

Incised. When you want to cut an incised line, first make a stop-cut straight into the wood and then make an angled cut at each side of the stop-cut to create a V-section trench.

Gouges. From top to bottom: Straight gouge, curved gouge, spoon-bit gouge. The shape of the blade in cross section is called "the sweep." We also sometimes use terms like "shallow-sweep" and "U-section."

jack knife, meaning a knife with a marlinespike attached; a jackstay, meaning a wire or rope to which the sail is fastened; and, of course, a Jack Tar, meaning an ordinary lower-deck seaman. As to why seamen were known as Jolly Jack Tars, it may have something to do with the easy-to-say alliteration as well as the popular romantic notion in times past that a sailor's life revolved around

drinking rum, dancing the hornpipe, singing sea shanties, and having girl friends in every port. In the late nineteenth century, Jack Tar figureheads were very popular in America and Great Britain.

Mallet

A wooden-headed hammer that is used with a chisel or gouge. Many carvers like to make their own mallet. One carver we know uses a cut-down baseball bat.

Plateau wood—a figurative term that likens high-relief wood to a geographical feature. A dog-leg chisel is a good tool for clearing up lowered ground.

Grounding, or wasting—cutting away the waste wood so that the design is left in relief.

Plateau Wood

In the context of this book, when a design has been ground—meaning cut away and lowered—the remaining high-relief feature is termed a "plateau." We tend to call details within a carving by terms commonly used for features within a landscape—hills, valleys, gullies, plateaus, and the like. So, for example, a stepped face between a lowered area and an area in relief is called a cliff and a V-section groove is called a furrow.

Quarter Boards

Name boards that are fastened to the four quarters of a vessel: one on each side on the port and starboard fore quarters and one on each side on the aft quarters. Some harbor authorities stipulate letter sizes, so check this out before you start carving.

Rail End

Traditionally, wooden ships had rail boards, or handrails, running forward from the stem through to the stern. As the various decks stepped down from the stern and then up to the head, the rails followed the levels and also stepped up and down. At each of these steps, the ends of the rail boards were brought to a fancy conclusion, with carved scrolls, dolphins, sea monsters, whalers, and other decorative forms.

Ribbon Ends

Board ends shaped like a folded or scrolled ribbon, resembling a banner or flag. If you want to see some stylized ribbon forms, visit a maritime museum.

Riffler Files

Small shaped files that are used for working tight, difficult-to-reach corners, holes, and valleys.

Roughing Out

Using the saw, band saw, or gouge to swiftly clear away the rough—the carving stage prior to modelling.

Riffler files. A knife-edge riffler file is a good tool for cleaning up deep creases. But be warned: Riffler files easily snap if they are dropped on a hard floor or are bent.

Roughing out—swiftly clearing away the waste wood prior to modelling. You could use the band saw before gluing up and then follow through with a large sharp gouge and a mallet.

Rubbing Down

Rubbing the wood down with a series of graded sandpapers so as to achieve a smooth, ready-to-paint finish. In marine carving, the wood needs to be smooth, but not so overworked that you blur the marks left by the cutting tools. With that said, some carvings—like, for example, the *Blazer* figurehead—are best selectively rubbed down so that there is a contrast between smooth and tooled textures.

Rudder Head

The rudder head is the top end of the rudder post to which the steering apparatus—a pulley and wheel or a rudder arm—is fastened. Traditionally, many wood-carvers enjoyed the joke of embellishing the head of the post with a fancifully carved head.

Sanding

Using sandpaper/emery paper to rub the wood down to a smooth finish. As wood dust can be

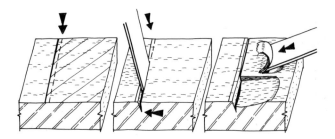

Setting in. To create a swift step, (left) mark the finished line and the cutting line, and shade in the waste; (middle) use a chisel to make a stop-cut that angles towards the waste; and (right) slice across the waste and into the stop-cut.

toxic, you might wear a cotton hat to protect your forehead and a respirator. When the sanding is complete, it's a good idea to brush yourself down, wipe the workpiece over with a slightly damp cloth, and move to a dust-free area that you have specially set up for painting.

Scroll

In a ship-carving context, a scroll is a carved motif that draws its inspiration from a scrolled or coiled roll—meaning, traditionally, a roll of parchment. The scroll—either carved in the round, like an S or C, or carved in relief—is one of the most commonly used maritime wood-carved forms.

Setting In

Cutting along the drawn lines of the design prior to lowering the waste. A design might be set in either before or after cutting the V-section trench; it depends upon the character of the carving. You could cut a V-section trench to the waste side of the drawn line, clear away the waste with a gouge, and then tidy up the drawn line with a knife or chisel. Or you could set the drawn line in with a stop-cut and then slide the gouge towards the stop-cut and skim off the waste.

Setting Out

This refers to transferring the design through to the wood as well as generally organizing the tools, wood, and working area prior to carving.

Sharpening

It's very important for wood-carving chisels, knives, and gouges to be kept razor-sharp. To this end, we have a sheet of fine-grade emery cloth

mounted on a 9″ disc of ½″-thick plywood. In the middle, there is a 6″-diameter disc of leather, flesh side out, and an even smaller disc of leather with the smooth side out of about 4″. It looks a bit like a target. The whole works is mounted and screwed on a faceplate on the outboard end of our lathe, but it could just as well be mounted on a bench motor or grinder.

To use it, we first stroke the blade on the emery cloth and then strop the bevel edge to a finish on the two inner leather discs. The entire operation is over in a few seconds. Chisels are held down flat on the grit/leather, while gouges are gently rocked from side to side so that the whole bevel comes into contact. The inside curve of the gouge is stroked with a small tapered slip so as to remove the edge-of-blade burr.

When it comes to sharpening the V-tool, you follow the same procedure as when sharpening a chisel—rub one side of the V and then the other—the only difference being that you have to adjust the bevel angle slightly so that you don't break through the point of the V.

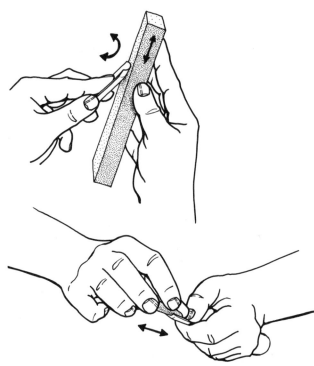

Sharpening. Top: When you are using a stone to sharpen the bevel of a gouge, stroke the bevel on the stone with an easy, rolling motion. If you hold both the stone and the tool up to the light, you will be able to judge the angle of the bevel by the amount of light shining between the two surfaces. Bottom: Use a shaped stone, called a slip, to remove the burr from inside the sweep.

Sizing

Using callipers, dividers, a template or whatever to transfer the various measurements from the working drawings and the maquette through to the wood. We usually make step-offs with a pair of dividers and measure widths with a pair of callipers.

Skew Chisel

A skew chisel has bevels on both faces and a cutting edge at an angle of less than 90° to the side of the shaft. It's a good tool for cutting V-section trenches and for clearing difficult-to-reach lowered areas.

Slips

Small shaped stones used for sharpening gouges. The stones should fit the various inside and outside sweep shapes and sizes of the gouges.

V-cuts. A knife is the ideal tool for making small controlled V-cuts.

Stop-cut. If you decide to make a stop-cut straight down into the wood without first cutting a V-section groove to the waste side of the drawn line, be very careful that the cutting edge doesn't run into the grain and split the wood.

Stop-cut

An initial straight-down cut, into which subsequent skimming cuts are made. A stop-cut acts like a brake; it literally stops and controls the cut. In some instances, where a straight-down stop-cut might split the wood, it's best to first run a V-section trench to the waste side of the drawn line and then make the stop-cut, so that the remaining rind of waste crumbles away into the trench. See also "Setting In."

Tool, Texture, or Tooling

In other words, the marks left by the tools. Some carvers like to remove most of the tool marks, while others think of the marks as a means of describing the form, like brushstrokes in an oil painting.

Undercutting

Lowering the waste so as to reveal a vertical face, and then scooping out the face so as to create a cavelike cavity. An undercut could be likened to a cave under an overhanging-cliff edge.

V-cuts

A V-section trench, as could be made with a knife or V-tool.

Workshop

For marine carving, your workshop can be just about any place, from your basement to a lean-to shelter out in the garden to a boat shed. All you need is a sheltered space with light and power. A benefit of working with traditional hand tools—a mallet, a knife, and various gouges and chisels—is that they create very little noise.

We tend to do the mallet-and-gouge carving in a garden-shed workshop; the cutting, sawing, drilling, and sanding in the end of the same structure; and the final painting in the house or under a covered porch. Ideally, ship carvers should have a series of separate rooms on the same level, so that they can easily move from one room to another as the work proceeds. Regardless of whether your workshop matches this ideal, try to keep the dust and paint apart and the workpiece moving to a minimum.

A–Z Guide to Wood Carving

Acrylic Paint

A plastic polyvinyl-acetate type of paint that is easy to use, water-based, and quick-drying. Acrylics are perfect for marine carving, since they can be used straight from the can or tube, the colors are bright and bold, and they dry fast. As ship carvings are exposed to all kinds of weather, it's vital that you protect the painted surfaces with two or more well-brushed coats of clear high-shine varnish. We usually varnish all surfaces—even the backs of boards—fasten the carving in place with brass screws and bolts or dowels, and then give the whole works another coat of varnish.

Band Saw

A power-operated tool consisting of an endless metal loop blade running over and driven by a number of wheels—the perfect tool for cutting small sections of wood in preparation for gluing up a blank. If you plan to do a lot of carving, a band saw ought to be well up on your tools-to-get list.

Bench

Although a wood-carver certainly needs a good bench, all that is required is a stable wooden surface that is strong enough to take a vise and a variety of clamps.

Brushes

Brushes come in many shapes and sizes. We prefer to use soft long-haired brushes, as used by water-color artists. If you use acrylic paint, then always wash the brushes immediately after use and store them bristle up.

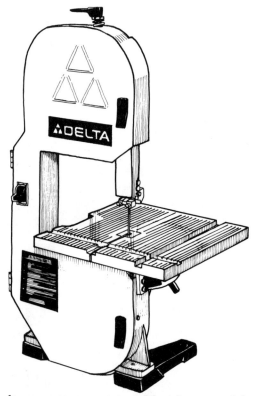

Band saw—a power-operated band saw used for making curved cuts in plank wood. Our saw has a 4" depth of cut. If you use a band saw, then be sure to follow the safety checklist as supplied with the machine. Be warned: Always keep your fingers away from the front edge of the blade, and never use the machine when you are tired or in a rush.

Callipers

A two-legged compasslike instrument used primarily for measuring widths and spans. A pair of callipers usually consists of two C-shaped legs that are pivoted at the crutch.

Clamps and Cramps

Screw devices for securing wood while it is being worked—variously called clamps, cramps, C-clamps, hold-downs, and any number of trade names. But, in the context of gluing up a number of band-sawn cutouts to make a large shaped blank—say, for a figurehead—we usually smear all mating faces with a generous amount of glue, lash the whole works up with strong rope, and then pull the binding tight by banging in a dozen or so long, thin wedges.

Clasp Knife, Penknife, or Hand Knife

Just about any fold-up or straight knife used for carving will do. We use a Northwest Indian crooked knife, a large jackknife, and a selection of small penknives. It's a good idea to start a collec-

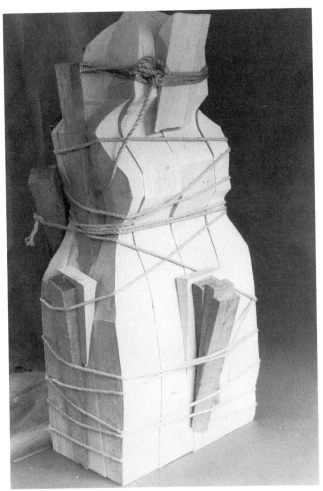

Clamps and cramps. Traditionally, ship carvers lashed the whole works up with strong rope—no doubt there was plenty of rope around and they were good with knots—and then clenched the binding by banging in long, thin wedges of waste.

tion, so that you'll have a knife to fit the task at hand.

Compass, or a Pair of Compasses

A two-legged instrument used for drawing out circles and arcs and for stepping off measurements. It's best to get a long-legged screw-operated type.

Coping Saw

A small-frame handsaw used for cutting thin, small sections of wood. The G-shaped frame allows the thin blade to be swiftly fastened and removed. A good saw for cutting curved profiles in small sections. If you plan on doing a lot of wood carving, then it would be a good idea to get yourself a coping saw, a scroll saw, and a band saw.

Designing

In the context of this book, this means working out a structure, pattern, or form by making drawings, sketches, outlines, and maquettes. If we see an unusual or exciting piece of ship carving—say, a figurehead in a museum or maybe a rudder handle in an old book or painting—we make sketches, build the form up swiftly from rough wood, and make a Plasticine maquette, all before we finalize the design and use special wood.

Dust-free

Before you start painting, always make sure that the workpiece is completely free from wood dust and debris. Sweep up the debris, vacuum the surfaces, wipe the workpiece over with a damp cloth, and then move to a dust-free area for painting.

We keep the carving area and the painting area completely separate. Our carving workshop is at one end of the garden, and our painting room is in the house.

Elevations

The drawn views of a wood carving—say, of a figurehead—are described as "elevations." A particular view, or elevation, might be described as "top," "end," or "side."

End Grain

Cross-section grain at the end of a piece of timber—the section seen when you make a clean cut through a tree. End grain is difficult to carve, so it needs to be approached with care. Be warned: If you drive a tool directly into end grain, there is a good chance that you will split the wood.

Finishing

This refers to scraping, rubbing down with sand-paper, painting, and varnishing a carving. For ship carvings that are out in all kinds of weather, it's vital that they be covered with several coats of varnish.

Glues and Adhesives

Although there are all manner of glues and adhesives—everything from animal glues to instant glues and resins—we favor using PVA (poly-vinyl acetate) for the projects in this book. PVA comes in an easy-to-use squeeze bottle and has a long shelf life. If you intend to mount the carving on the exterior of your boat, be sure to use a waterproof PVA glue.

Grain

The annual rings that run through the wood—all the lines, colors, and textures that characterize a piece of wood. Wood-carvers spend much of their time trying to work out how to approach the grain to best advantage. Will it cut? Will it splinter? Is it strong enough for the task at hand? However, one of the joys of marine carving is that, since most of the pieces will be painted, you can basically forget about good-to-look-at woods and concentrate your attention on woods that are easy to carve.

Green Wood

Wood that still contains sap—unseasoned wood. Green wood is wonderfully easy to carve; however,

once it has been worked, it continues to dry out, often causing the carvings to warp, split, and fall to pieces.

Gridded Working Drawing

A scaled, square grid placed over a working drawing. The object illustrated can be reduced or enlarged, simply by changing the scale of the grid. For example, if the grid is described as "one square to 1 inch" and you want to double the scale, then all you do is read off each square as being equal to 2 inches. When you come to transferring the drawing to the wood, simply draw out a grid at the suggested size and transfer the contents of each square. At four grid squares to 1 inch, you draw out a ¼-inch grid—where one square is ¼ inch. (You might also consider making use of an office-type photocopying machine that can enlarge or reduce the original. Then you simply transfer the sized drawing directly to the wood or use it to step off measurements to the workpiece with dividers.)

Hardwoods and Softwoods

Botanically speaking, hardwood comes from broad-leafed deciduous trees, while softwood comes from evergreens, usually pines. As hardwoods aren't necessarily harder in substance than softwoods, the terms are only meaningful in describing very general characteristics.

Inspirational Designs and Material

Meaning our sources—all the traditional nautical carvings that we've seen on old wooden sailing ships, in maritime museums, in boat yards, and in

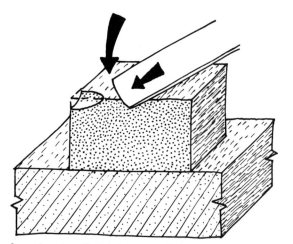 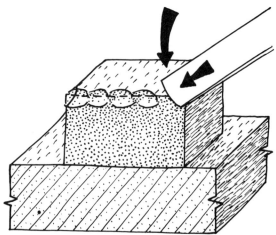

End grain. Avoid driving a tool directly into end grain. When you come to rounding over an end-grain edge, work with or across the run of the grain—that is, down, around, and over the end grain.

old books. It's a good idea to keep a sketchbook and make notes and sketches when you see something interesting. We've drawn most of our inspiration from American and European maritime originals.

We usually study forms and profiles as well as the painted finish, making notes about sizes and attachments, and then work out a variation on the original. Most clients of ours want a traditional carving. For example, a client might want a copy of a traditional figurehead, but with a slightly different costume and face.

Marking Out

Use a sharply pointed pencil/dividers to make guidelines.

Masking Tape

A general-purpose adhesive paper tape used to mark out midlines, measure around curved surfaces, and hold components while they are being sawn, glued, painted, etc.

Measure

This could be anything from a wood ruler or metal rule to a flexible tape or even a piece of string.

Modifying

Changing and redesigning a project so that it is bigger, smaller, worked from thicker or thinner wood, or whatever. Many traditional designs need to be modified to suit smaller, lighter boats or different needs. For example, you might want to carve a figurehead, not to mount on your boat, but rather to hang in your clubhouse or outside on your porch.

Paints and Painting

Before painting, always clear away bench clutter, wipe up dust, and carefully set out all your tools and materials so that they are comfortably close at hand. It's best if possible to do the painting well away from the carving area. We prefer to use acrylic paints protected with a couple of coats of clear varnish. See "Acrylic Paint."

Pencil-Press Transferring

Tracing a master design and then pencil-pressing the traced lines through to the wood.

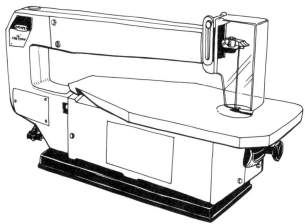

Scroll saw. A power-driven, fine-bladed bench scroll saw is a very good machine for cutting thin sections of wood up to, say, 1½" thick. Our saw is rather special, in that it is designed to take both super-fine blades and heavy-duty coping-saw blades.

Scroll Saw

A power-driven, fine-bladed bench saw that is sometimes called a jigsaw or fretsaw is used for cutting small sections of wood. In use, the workpiece is pushed across the worktable and fed into the blade. The blades come in many grades and are easy and inexpensive to replace. The super-fast, up-and-down jiggling action of the blade results in a swift, fine, safe cut. If you want to make, for example, name boards with fancy ends, flat scroll boards, or thin plaques, you need a scroll saw.

Tracing Paper

A strong translucent paper used for tracing. We usually work up a good design, take a careful tracing, pencil in the back of tracing with a 2B pencil, turn the tracing right side up and attach it to the working surface of the wood with tabs of masking tape, and then rework the traced lines with a hard pencil.

Work-out Paper

Inexpensive paper as might be used for initial roughs. It's best to use slightly matt white paper.

Vise

A bench-mounted clamp. Wood-carvers tend to use a large wooden vise called "bench chops" and/ or an engineer's swivel-mount vise with rubber muffles on the jaws.

A–Z Guide to Woods

WOOD BASICS

Most nautical carvings are worked with an easy-to-carve bland wood, like pine, basswood, jelutong, or lime, and then heavily painted and varnished. Therefore, it really doesn't matter whether or not the wood has an attractive color or figure because everything is covered by the paint. However, there are times and situations when you might want to use a fancy wood like mahogany or perhaps even a super-strong wood like English oak. You need to assess the situation and then ask yourself if you want the carving to be able to withstand a hundred years of weather, or is it going to be mounted in a dry boat house? are your funds limited? do you want the grain to show? and so on. It's best to go through a trial run with some easy-to-carve wood, and then take it from there. We often use lime or jelutong, since we like the traditional look of a brightly painted and varnished carving.

RECOMMENDED WOODS

Apple

A hard, dense, close-grained wood that comes in small sizes and carves well. This is a good wood for small exhibition work.

Basswood

Almost identical to English lime and also sometimes confused with canary whitewood, basswood is wonderfully easy to carve. This is a good wood for carvings that are going to be painted and varnished.

Canary (American Whitewood)

A yellowish soft wood, even-grained and knot-free. Very much like lime/basswood. A good wood for general carvings and carvings that are going to be painted and varnished.

Cedar

As cedar is sometimes used for the construction of light pleasure boats, there is a chance that you will be able to buy short ends from a boat yard. There are many varieties: western cedar, pencil cedar, Australian red cedar, and so on. It's best to try some and see how they carve.

Jelutong

A pale cream, easy-to-carve, inexpensive wood that can be carved and worked almost without regard to the run of the grain. If you plan on painting and varnishing your carvings, then we recommend using jelutong. Any straight-grained hardwood such as linden or maple is a good alternative where jelutong may be hard to come by (e.g., in North America).

Lime (American Linden and Basswood)

A close-grained, knot-free, easy-to-carve wood. The perfect wood for beginners. A bit like canary whitewood.

Pine

There are so many varieties of "pine" that the best advice is to try carving an easy-to-find type and then take it from there. Search around for a straight-grained, knot-free white variety.

Sycamore

A beautiful milk-white wood, with a close grain and a smooth, silky surface. Although sycamore was traditionally used for dairy and food bowls and general domestic wares, it is also sometimes used for cabin furniture and ship woodwork. Therefore, you might well come across some inexpensive short ends in boat yards.

Teak

During the nineteenth century, naval authorities in America and Britain used two woods for the highest quality work: English oak and Indian or Burmese teak. Although teak is extremely expensive and very difficult to saw, this is counterbalanced by it being relatively easy to carve and very durable. If you are intent on carving a masterpiece and have just come into a fortune, then go for teak.

TIMBER FAULTS

There is no such thing as a perfect wood; from piece to piece, a wood might vary from being wonderful to being unworkable. You can never be sure that a piece of wood is sound throughout. For

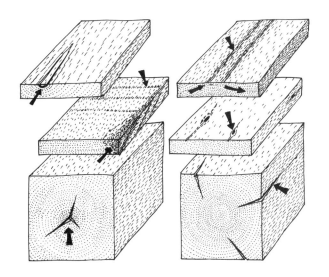

Timber faults. Being mindful that there is no such thing as a perfect piece of wood, be on the lookout for the following problems: (top left) cup shakes, a separation that occurs between the annual rings; (top right) undulating and streaked grain, which might result in the wood warping and twisting; (middle left) damaged, stained, and sloping grain, which can result in the wood splitting and/or crumbling; (middle right) dead knots, which are liable to fall out and leave you with a hole; (bottom left) heart shakes, shakes that start from the pith and run towards the surface, which can be a problem; and (bottom right) a star shake, which is usually the result of forced artificial seasoning and is best avoided.

example, in a couple of the projects, you will see that we started carving, only to find that the wood had a cavity or a split. The best you can do is go for a recommended wood and then work around any flaws.

There are many faults and flaws to be on the lookout for—everything from foreign bodies within the wood and hidden cavities, to stains, moulds, cup shakes, dead knots, unexpected grain twists, and wet sappy areas. Always start by checking the wood over for obvious problems, and then if you have any doubts, put it aside and go for another piece. If by chance you are well into a project and, say, a knot or split shows up, either modify the project to work around the problem *or* cut your losses and start over.

Blemishes

Meaning just about anything that is uncharacteristic. To one person, a knot might be beautiful; to another, it might be a blemish.

Checks

A check is a split or crack running down the length of the grain in a plank of wood. Since a check is an

indicator of possible larger problems, it's best to look for another piece of wood.

Decay

If the wood is soft, spongy, or crumbly, or it appears to be affected with worm holes, fungus, or white stains, then it's likely that the wood is starting to decay. If this is the case, look for another piece.

Knots

Knots can be dead, hollow, loose, spiked, encased, and so on. They are difficult, sometimes impossible, to carve.

Shakes and Splits

Separations that occur throughout the length of a log are called "shakes" and "splits." If, when you look at a log or plank end-on, you see a heart-shaped crack in the middle of the wood or star-shaped cracks around the end of the wood, then the chances are that there might be hollows, cracks, and splits within the wood. Always, but always, spend time looking the wood over for possible problems.

1626

1
Eagle's Head

Of all the wood carvings used on American ships, the bald eagle must surely be the most popular, the most dramatic, and the most handsome.

If old accounts are anything to go by—ships' logs, owners' diaries, shipyard records, old photographs, ship carvers' sketchbooks, and so on—the eagle was used variously as a transom ornament, as a full figurehead, on coats of arms, on the end of a billet board, on the end of the bowsprit, and in just about every other location where it was possible for such a carving to be mounted. One old account describes how the sharp eyes of eagle figureheads were constantly on the lookout for perilous shoals.

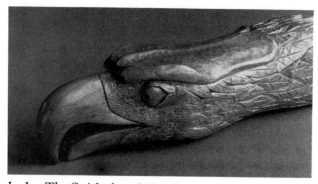

1–1 The finished eagle head.

Traditionally, the American eagle is portrayed in a proud, spectacular, patriotic pose—often as a freestanding figure and sometimes as part of a flags-and-trumpets relief—with a slightly open beak, a rather haughty arched brow, fierce eyes, and a long neck. As for texture and color, the feathers tend to be heavily stylized and arranged in much the same way as roofing tiles or shingles, while the finished carvings are usually painted white and/or gilded.

Our eagle (see 1–1) draws its inspiration from a huge eagle head that is now on view at the Mystic Seaport Museum in Connecticut. This strikingly bold carving—made in white pine and measuring about 60″ in length—is all that survives of a much larger figurehead that was made for the record-breaking American clipper ship *Great Republic*, built in Boston in 1853.

Bearing in mind that this head is as big as a man and not forgetting that, by all accounts, some part of it was lost in the fire that destroyed the ship, the sheer massiveness of the carving gives us a clue as to the size of other figureheads of the mid-nineteenth-century period. However, it's interesting to note that when the eagle was first mounted in place on the *Great Republic*, a contemporary account described the overall effect as being "plain and naked, with the figurehead adding nothing to the beauty of the ship's bow." It just goes to show that by the standards of the time, an eagle's head measuring over 60″ long was considered to be less than impressive. Amazing!

THOUGHTS ON DESIGN AND TECHNIQUE

Take a look at the working drawings (see 1–2) and photographs, and note how we have redesigned the head and greatly reduced it in size, so that it can be used in a modern pleasure-yacht context. For example, it could be mounted on the end of a bowsprit, attached to the stem post, or used as a rail end.

If you enjoy carving but aren't much into boats, the eagle's head could even be used as a feature in your house or on your porch; there are any number of possibilities.

Looking at the working drawings, you will see that, at a scale of two grid squares to 1″, our eagle has been cut from a 22″-long, 4 × 4″-square piece of jelutong. The actual head is about 13″ long, with the remainder of the wood being cut back so as to make a tenon. Our thinking was that the tenon would be further reduced when we finally mounted the head.

Wood-carving tip: On consideration, we saw that the end of the eagle's hooked beak was perhaps overly short-grained and fragile. But this wasn't a problem for us, because we intended to mount the

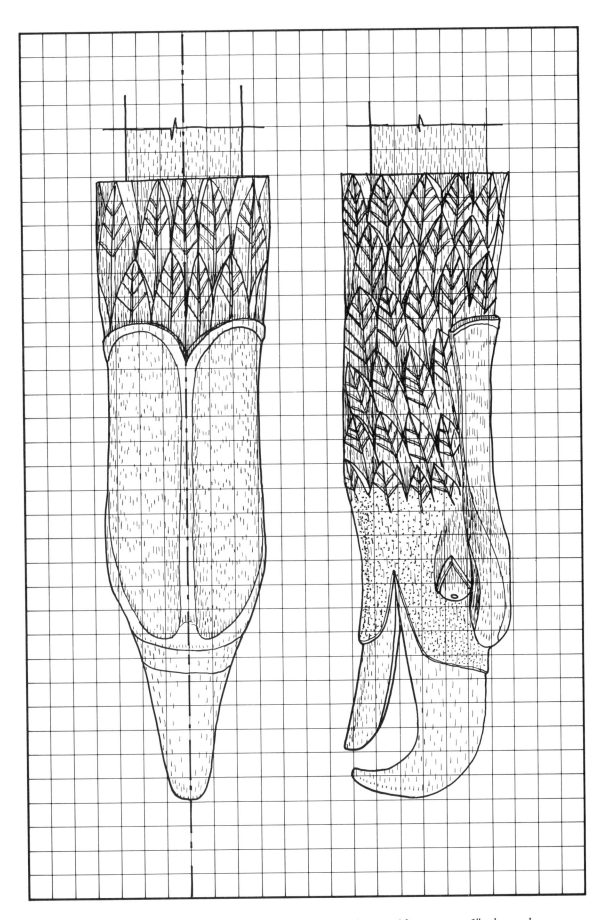

1–2 Working drawings, top and side views. At a scale of two grid squares to 1", the eagle measures about 13 to 14" from its crest through to the tip of its beak.

head high up on a beam end in our house. However, if you intend to, say, fasten the carving at the end of a bowsprit, meaning in a position where it is likely to get knocked, it might be best to use a more rugged wood and/or double up the size of the carving.

Study the project details and note how, because of the relatively modest scale of the carving, we were able to rough out the head on a band saw. However, if you do decide to go for a much larger head—say, one cut from a baulk of 8 × 8″-square wood—then you either have to use a big band saw or come up with another method of clearing the rough. A bigger carving isn't necessarily more difficult—just more effort!

Spend time considering how we have stylized the feathers in such a way that they can be more or less chip-carved with a knife. It's an easy technique—all you do is chip the shape of the feathers straight in with stop-cuts and then slide the blade at a flat angle in towards the stop-cuts, so as to clear the waste between neighboring feathers. It's a very uncomplicated procedure—you aren't so much carving the positive shape of the feathers as clearing the negative waste in between.

Now look at the finishing details and observe how the carving has been given a coat of matt white, painted with acrylic gold, and given a swift brush-over with a mixture of sepia and varnish, all before the final varnishing.

TOOL AND MATERIAL CONSIDERATIONS

This is a good project for beginners on several accounts: the finished carving is bold and eye-catching, the techniques are straightforward, and, perhaps most important of all, it can be managed with a minimum of tools. Okay, so we used a band saw and we do make mention of a small spoon gouge for the eyes, but, apart from that, all this project really requires is a couple of basic gouges and a sharp knife. If you don't have access to an electrical band saw to clear away the rough, you can get away with using either a good-size coping saw or a combination of a drill and a mallet and gouge. It's true that chopping out the profile with

Inspirational designs   Top: Billet head, by John Bellamy, U.S.A., late nineteenth century, painted blue and yellow. Middle left: Eagle figurehead, nineteenth century, painted pine. Middle right: Nineteenth-century American billet heads. Bottom: Decoration from volunteer fire-fighting wagon, U.S.A., nineteenth century, 28″ wide.

a mallet and gouge is a bit tedious, but it will get you there in the end.

We used a piece of prepared jelutong for several reasons: it's very easy to carve, inexpensive, and strong enough for what we had in mind. However, if you would prefer a more robust wood, then you could go for pine, lime, holly, English oak, or red or white American oak.

Wood-carving tip: If you live near a sawmill or perhaps a boat yard and are only looking for a relatively small piece of wood, you could arm yourself with a sharp gouge, visit the sawmill or boat yard, and try out a few remnants and blocks for size. Who cares what the wood is called! If it takes a smooth cut, is free from knots, is no more expensive than, say, white pine or basswood, then it's worth a try.

TOOLS AND EQUIPMENT

For this project, you need:
- a 1½″-thick slab of easy-to-carve wood that is 28″ long and 10″ wide, with the grain running along the length—we used a slab of jelutong
- a couple of straight shallow-curve gouges—a no. 06 or 07—one that's about ⅜″ wide and another that's about ¾″ wide
- a small straight deep-curve gouge—a no. 08 or 09—that's about ⅜″ wide
- a bent or curved gouge—a no. 06 or 07—that's about 1″ wide
- a scroll saw with a large-toothed coping-saw blade
- a small penknife
- the use of a workbench with a bench clamp
- a small block of Plasticine
- a sheet each of tracing and work-out paper—as large as the piece of wood
- a pencil and ruler
- acrylic paint in red and brown
- a can of yacht varnish
- a couple of soft-haired brushes: a broad and a fine-point
- a pack of graded sandpapers

PROJECT STAGES

Drawing Out the Design and Roughing Out

Having collected together all your tools and materials and as many magazine clippings of bald eagles as you can find, set your wood out on the workbench and give it a good long look-over—just to make sure that it's in reliable condition. It must be straight-grained, and it needs to be free from knots and splits—especially at the beak end.

Wood-carving tip: We like to use sawn or planed wood, for the simple reason that it's much easier to spot a flaw on a smooth surface. Certainly, you can use a piece of barked wood, but who knows what nasties might be lurking under the bark!

When you are confident that the wood is workable, decide which end is to be the beak, and mark the sides and faces accordingly. Set the top view out with an end-to-end central line. Draw the profiles up to size—the top and side views—and make clear pencil tracings. When this is done, carefully pencil-press-transfer the side view through to the wood. Rework the traced lines until they are clearly established (see 1–3, top).

With the image in place, take the wood to the band saw, position it side-up on the saw table, and

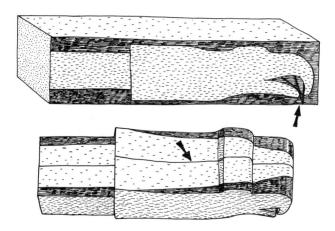

1–3   Draw the top and side views out on the wood.

set to work cutting out the side profile. If your saw is fitted with a wide blade, then don't attempt to saw around the curves—you will only break the blade or split the wood—but rather clear the waste by making repeated straight cuts. When you have achieved the side-view cutout, use a pencil, ruler, and a strip of masking tape to run a central line down and around the top end and bottom surfaces—that is, down the middle of the back, around and over the beak, and along the underside. With the line in place, pencil-press-transfer the top profile through to the top face of the wood (see 1–3, bottom). Now, being very careful so that the blade doesn't run out of control as it passes through the different thicknesses, cut out the profile, as seen in 1–4.

Then take the Plasticine, knock it into a block shape, and carefully make a model, or maquette,

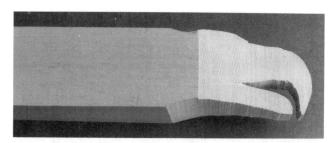

1–4   Saw off the waste, as seen in the side and top views.

of the head. Don't bother to detail the feathers—just go for the bold shapes: the beak, the brow, the shape of the eyeballs in the sockets, and so on.

Wood-carving tip: It's a good practice to make a maquette. You can make it to scale—say, half or quarter size—but it's best to make it full size.

Rounding Up

When you have made the basic cutout and the maquette, then comes the task of rounding up, or you might say, finding the form. It's a good idea at this point to sit back and compare the roughed-out block of wood with your various drawings, the maquette, and any magazine clippings that you may have gathered along the way. Spend time feeling the maquette with your hands and sketching in on the wood what you consider to be the primary markers and guides. You might mark in the eye sockets, the line of the brow, the width of the beak as seen in the working drawings, and so on. Draw in as many guides as you think necessary.

When you have a clear picture in your mind's eye as to what goes where, secure the workpiece with the clamps. Then take the 1″-wide bent gouge and start cutting away the sharp edges. Work towards a rounded form. It's pretty straightforward, as long as your gouge is sharp and you avoid running the blade into end grain. Work from the top of the head, out and around towards the cheeks, and out from the sides of the beak (see 1–5). You might make a few cuts, take another look at the maquette, make a few more cuts, maybe change the direction of your cuts, spend a few moments honing the blade, and so on. We sometimes use a mallet while, other times, work the gouge with a wrist-controlled scooping action. There's nothing complicated about it, as long as you take it at an easy, relaxed pace.

If you adhere to the following guidelines, you won't go far wrong:

• Remove the waste by making lots of small shallow cuts.

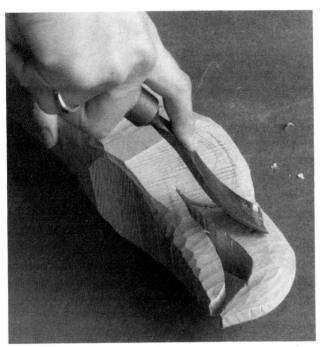

1–5 *Work from high to low wood, cutting away the sharp edges of waste.*

- Never bang the blade in at a sharp angle and then try to lever down on the handle.
- Work at a steady, even pace, all the while taking breaks to assess your progress.
- Try to bring the whole design to completion by moving backwards and forward over the entire surface.

Wood-carving tip: If a tool refuses to make a smooth, easy cut, then the blade needs honing and/or the wood is unsuitable.

And so you continue cutting back the waste, bit by bit, until the form gradually begins to look rounded and take on an eagle shape (see 1–6).

At this stage, don't try to take the small details to completion. Just concentrate your efforts on the big forms that characterize the eagle: the hooked beak, the heavy brow, and the balls that go into making up the eyes and the lids. And don't forget, you shouldn't be aiming for naturalistic realism, but rather trying to capture a naïve image that can instantly be recognized at a distance.

Modelling

When you have achieved a rounded form, with all the primary characteristics roughed out, take another look at your drawings and at the maquette. Then reestablish the central line and shade in the areas that need to be lowered. Being mindful that carving is a process of lowering the waste so that the detail that you are searching out is left in relief,

1–6 *Cut back the waste until the form gradually begins to look rounded and more or less shaped like an eagle.*

it's best to concentrate your efforts, in the first instance, on shading in the whole area in front of the eyes and below the ridge of the brows.

With the shading completed, take a small sharp knife and run stop-cuts along the underside of the brow, around the front of the eyes, and all around the stylized crest. Sink the cuts in to a depth of about ⅛″ (see 1–7).

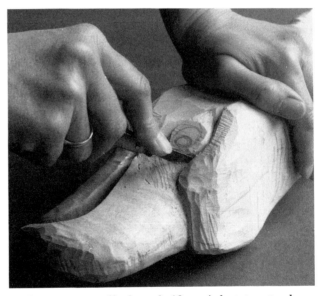

1–7 *Use a small, sharp knife to sink stop-cuts along the underside of the brow and around the front of the eyes.*

Using variously the knife and a small gouge and working on the area just in front of the eyeballs, cut at a flat angle, up from the beak and in towards the junction of the eyes and brow stop-cuts. Slice in, until a layer of waste falls away. Do this below and in front of both eyeballs. When, after a few repeated cuts, the eyes are left standing proud, deepen and define the initial stop-cuts and repeat the procedure, until the front of the brow and the eyes are left standing about ½″ higher than the

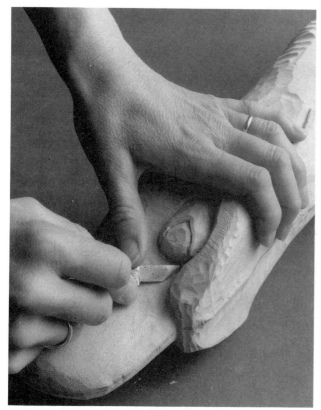

1–8 *Slice in and remove the waste so as to leave the eyes standing proud. Aim for having the eyes about ½" higher than the surrounding ground.*

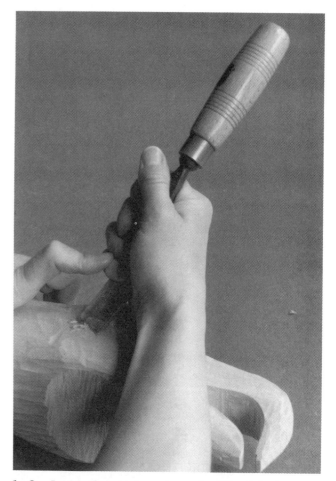

1–9 *Lower the wood on the underside of the brow and at the back of the eyes.*

lowered ground (see 1–8). Slice up from the sides of the head and over towards the crest and brow stop-cut, so as to leave the edge of the crest and brow stepped up. Make repeated cuts until the entire brow-and-crest feature appears to be sitting on top of the head—like a cap or beret. Lower the wood on the underside of the sides-of-head brow, at the point where it passes over the back of the eyes.

Wood-carving tip: I've got a feeling that I use a knife more often than most carvers. Most carvers tend to have a favorite tool. Gill likes using a shallow gouge, and I like a knife—it's just the way it is.

When the "cap" steps down to the eyes and the eyes step down to the cheeks, then make a stop-cut around the line where the feathers and beak meet. Cut in to a depth of about ⅛". Take the tool of your choice—I use a knife—and follow through, by making low slicing cuts across the surface of the beak and into the stop-cut (see 1–10). It's easy enough, as long as you keep a tight control over the knife so that it doesn't run past the stop-cut and damage another part of the carving, and be mindful that there will be times when you will be cutting more or less into end grain.

Wood-carving tip: If or when you come to cut directly into end grain, go at it with a lighter touch, and be very careful not to let the tool run into the grain. Work with a skimming, rather than a digging, movement.

To model the eyes, run the blade from the side

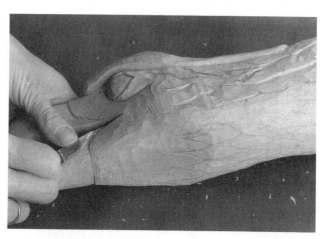

1–10 *Make low, slicing cuts across the surface of the beak and into the stop-cut.*

of the eye and over and around the front, so as to undercut the ball (see 1–11, top left). This is somewhat tricky, but only inasmuch as the front of the eye is made up from end grain. You have to watch out that the blade doesn't splinter the wood at the side of the eye (see 1–11, top right).

Having carved out the overall shape of the eyeball, take a pencil and draw in the line of the eyelid and the position of the pupil. Note how the edge of the lid is marked out as two parallel lines. With the lines in place, take a small penknife and set the line nearest to the front of the eye in to a depth of about ⅛". Still working with the knife, slide the blade over the eye and into the stop-cut, so as to create a step-up from the eye to the lid (see 1–11, bottom right). Set the other line in with a shallow incised V-cut (see 1–11, bottom right). Repeat this procedure for the other eye.

Draw a central line along the beak, and use the riffler file to sculpt the strong symmetrical curved shape (see 1–12 on page 30). Next, use a gouge to scoop-texture the top of the crest. Leave a central raised area (see 1–13 on page 30). Use a pointed tool—we used a V-tool and a drill bit—to peck-texture the area of fine feathers around the face (see 1–14 and 1–15 on pages 30 and 31).

The stylized feathers are easy to carve. All you do is draw in the pattern of the feathers with a pencil, set the drawn lines in with the point of the knife, and then slice the knife in at a low skimming angle, so as to lower the small triangle of waste between neighboring feathers. By working systematically along the rows of feathers, all the while removing the triangles of waste, you will gradually create the illusion that the lines of feathers overlap, like roof tiles. With the shape of the feathers in

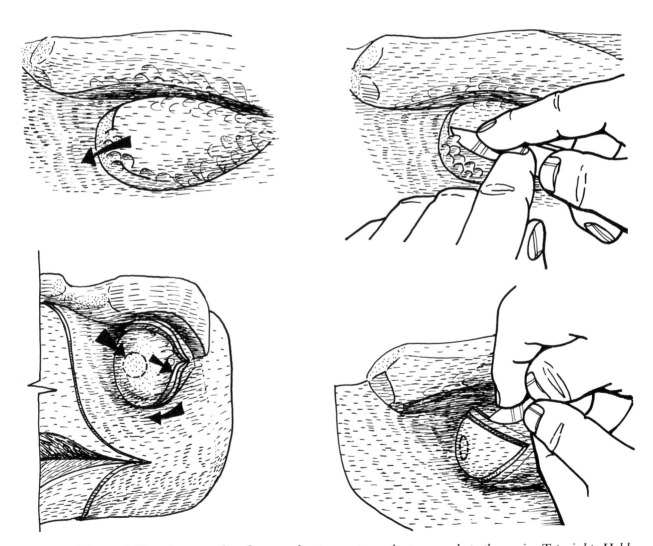

1–11   Top left: Modelling the eye—slice down and out so as to work at an angle to the grain. Top right: Hold the knife close to the blade so as to achieve maximum control, and remove whiskers of wood. Bottom left: Draw the pupil so that it is facing front, and cut in the stepped lid. Bottom right: Gradually deepen the cut, being careful so that the knife doesn't slip and do damage to the edge of the lid.

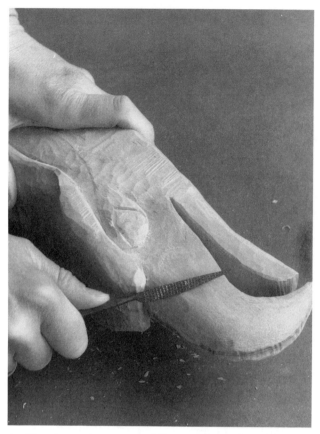

1–12   Draw in a central line, and use the riffler file to sculpt the strong symmetrical curve.

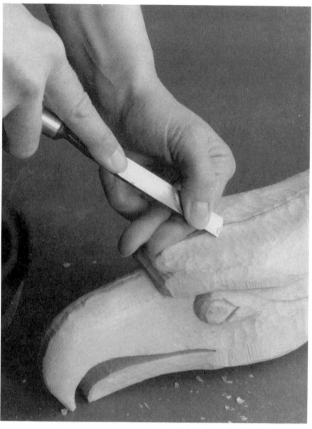

1–13   Use the gouge to scoop-texture the top of the crest. Leave a central raised area.

place, take a knife or gouge and cut all the little V-trenches that go into marking out the shape of the characteristic veins.

Finally, to cut the pupil holes, simply use a drill or use a small-width spoon bit gouge (see 1–18 on page 32).

Finishing

Having spent time with both the knife and sandpaper—tidying up details, crisping up the line of the beak, sinking the waste at the back end of the head, and so on—stand back and evaluate

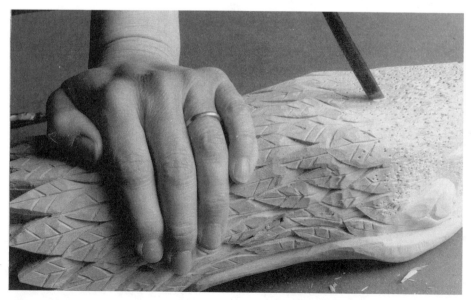

1–14   Use the parting tool to peck-texture the fine feather area.

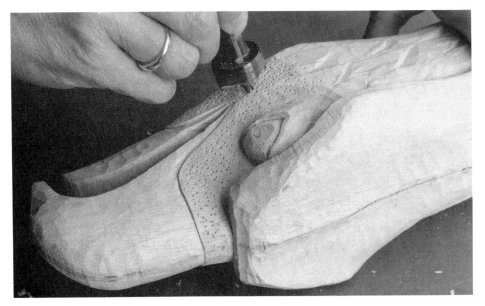

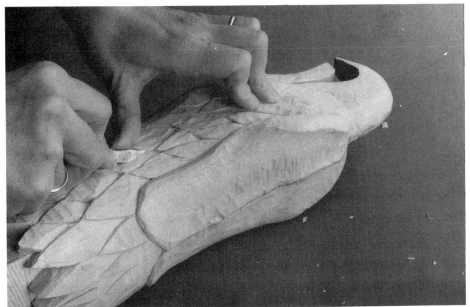

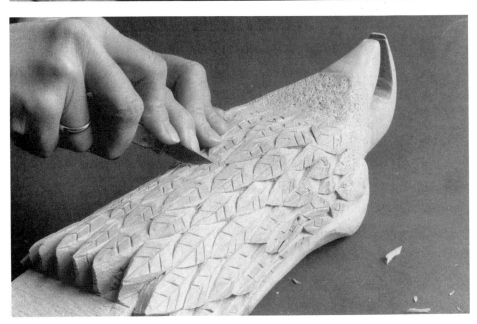

1–15 Use a pointed tool—a nail, spike, or whatever—to peck-texture the upper beak area.

1–16 Lower the small triangle of waste between neighboring feathers.

1–17 Cut in the little V-trenches that mark out the stylized shape of the feather veins.

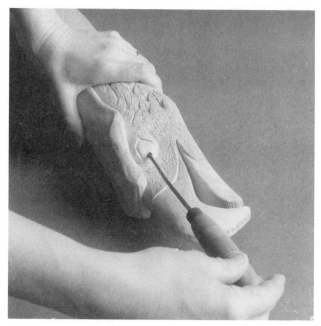

1–18 *Use a drill or small gouge to cut the pupil holes.*

the general effect. When the time is right, call a halt (see 1–19).

Wood-carving tip: As to when a carving is finished, it's not so easy to say. For example, I like to see lots of tool marks, whereas Gill likes to see a well-sanded finish. I guess I'm a bit sloppy when it comes to sharpening up the details, while Gill keeps fussing away! The best advice to follow is to call a halt when you are happy.

Having taken the carving as far as you want it to

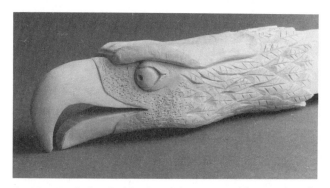

1–19 *Rub the finished carving over with a scrap of sandpaper.*

go, wipe away all the dust and debris and move to the clean dust-free area that you have set aside for painting and finishing. Start by sealing the wood with either a sealer or a thin coat of clear varnish. Once the sealer is completely dry, give it a brisk rubdown with the finest grade of sandpaper so as to remove all the whiskers and nibs.

Give the entire carving a coat of gold acrylic paint, wait for it to dry, and then lay on a coat of varnish. When the varnish is dry, mix a little of the sepia oil paint with a small amount of the varnish, and give the gold a swift brush-down so that the stain sits in all the cuts, dapples, and textured areas. Aim for a slightly soiled, worn, and weathered effect. Give the whole works another coat of varnish, and the task is done. Now you can socket the carving on the end of the bowsprit—or attach it in your home—and then sit back and enjoy the good feeling of a job well done!

TROUBLESHOOTING AND POSSIBLE MODIFICATIONS

- If you like the idea of the project but want it bigger, simply enlarge the scale.
- If you decide to go for a much larger carving, you might consider clearing some of the between-beak waste with a large-diameter Forstner bit.
- If you make a mistake and split off the front of the beak, simply glue it back in place and strengthen it with a dowel.
- Try to vary the textures so as to create a balance. For example, you could texture the feathers with V-cuts, dapple the top of the crest with a gouge, "peck" the front of the face with a punch or the corner of a chisel, and sand the beak smooth.
- When you are bringing the carving to completion, be sure to work with some sort of padding or protection between the workpiece and the bench/vise. Depending upon the size and shape of the carving, I either wrap the carving in rags and secure it in the vise or nestle it against a bag part-filled with sand.
- It's a good practice to keep cleaning up dust and debris so that you can see where you are at.

Three-masted schooner

2
Ribbon, or Banner, Stern Board

Ribbon, or banner, stern boards are simply carvings mounted on the stern or transom of a ship that are usually cut in relief to create the illusion of strips of cloth rippling and blowing in the breeze—like flags, ribbons, banners, or pennants.

It has been suggested that such carvings draw their inspiration from the ripples and folds commonly seen in medieval panels or the stylized ribbon and banner motifs on English and Continental heraldic coats of arms. However, to my mind, the ribbon ends are very much like the divided and forked ends of the long, tapered flags that were traditionally used on sailing ships as signals and wind indicators.

The rippled-ribbon motif enjoyed such popularity throughout the seventeenth, eighteenth, and nineteenth centuries that ship carvers tended to use it as a design "filler" on the stern, as part of figurehead drapery, as a running design leading up to the billet head, and so on. As to why the rippled ribbon was so favored, of course it is a beautifully flowing linkup motif in its own right, but perhaps more important than that, it is a carving that can easily be achieved with the minimum depth of wood and effort and expertise.

So, if you are looking to carve a striking relief design on a flat board—as a simple self-contained banner or maybe as part of a much larger scheme—you are going to enjoy this project.

THOUGHTS ON DESIGN AND TECHNIQUE

Take a look at the photographs and the working drawings (see 2–2 on page 34), and note how, at a scale of two grid squares to 1″, the carving measures about 24″ long and 10″ wide. See how it is cut from a 1½″-thick slab, with the grain running from end to end along the length. Consider how the ribbon is about 3″ wide at the top, tapering down to the forked ends at 1½″.

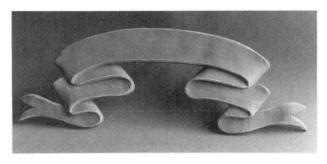

2–1   *The finished ribbon.*

The success of the carving has to do with the optical illusion that's created (see 2–3 on page 35). If you carefully study and analyze the curves and surfaces at the whiplash, you will see that the wood isn't actually cut down to the thickness of a ribbon, nor do the folds curve under each other—it's all a trick! Is it difficult? Not at all. Carving a banner is much easier than it looks.

If, after studying the design, you can't quite understand how the illusion of depth is achieved, then take a block of modelling clay—we used Plasticine—and make a maquette.

TOOL AND MATERIAL CONSIDERATIONS

This is an ideal project for beginners, in that it calls for a single slab of wood and a minimum of carving gouges. We did use a scroll saw to cut out the initial shape, but you could get away with using, say, a hand-held coping saw.

As for your choice of wood, you first need to decide whether or not the finished carving is to be painted or left natural and varnished. The choice is yours. If you want the finished carving left natural, then a wood like mahogany is a good choice. As we wanted our carving painted, we decided to use a slab of rough-sawn jelutong. But we could just as well have gone for, say, white pine, lime, or holly. The simple rule of thumb is to stay away

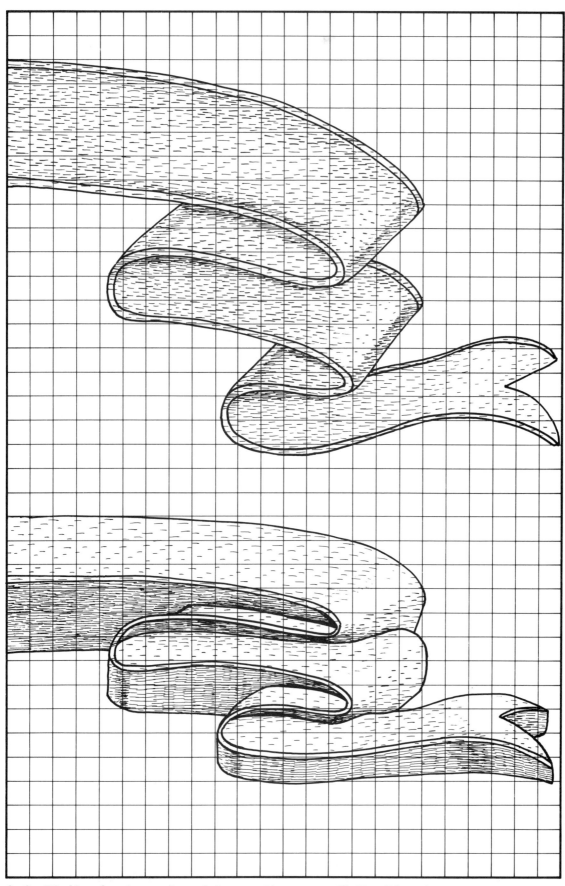

2–2 *Working drawings—the scale is two grid squares to 1″. Top: Plan view.*
Bottom: Diagrammatic drawing of edge-on view.

34

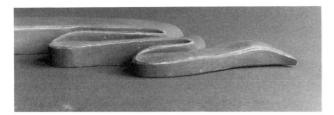

2–3 *Detail showing the depth of the various steps and planes needed to create the illusion of the ribbon folds.*

from coarse-grained knotty woods. Certainly, a lump of English oak might well last forever, but it will be hard on the muscles, leave your tools in a mess, and be murder to carve! If you have any doubts, ask your local wood supplier for advice.

Wood-carving tip: When you are ordering wood, be sure to get a written quote *before* the wood is sawn and prepared. Ask the supplier to specify exactly what it is that you are getting for your money! This is important, because we have found that some wood suppliers expect the customer to pay for the cutting waste, whereas others only charge you for what you take away. So, be specific and make sure all parties know what has been agreed upon before the wood is cut to size.

TOOLS AND EQUIPMENT

For this project, you need:
- a 1½″-thick slab of easy-to-carve wood that is 28″ long and 10″ wide, with the grain running along the length—we used a slab of jelutong
- a couple of straight shallow-curve gouges—a no. 06 or 07—one that's about ⅜″ wide and another that's about ¾″ wide
- a small straight deep-curve gouge—a no. 08 or 09—that's about ⅜″ wide
- a bent or curved gouge—a no. 06 or 07—that's about 1″ wide
- a scroll saw with a large-toothed coping-saw blade
- a small penknife
- the use of a workbench with a bench clamp
- a small block of Plasticine
- a sheet each of tracing and workout paper—as large as the piece of wood
- a pencil and ruler
- acrylic paint in red and brown
- a can of yacht varnish
- a couple of soft-haired brushes: a broad and a fine-point
- a pack of graded sandpapers

PROJECT STAGES

Setting Out the Design and First Cuts

Once you have studied the working drawings and photographs and have a clear picture in your mind's eye of just how the carving needs to be worked and managed—the size, the form, the number of ripples, and any design variations— then bring out all your tools and set them up. When this is done, set your wood down on the workbench and check it over to make sure that it's in good condition. Avoid using wood that appears to be split, stained, knotty, or damp.

Wood-carving tip: Always spend time choosing your wood. Why start with a piece of second-grade wood that's going to let you down when you are about three-quarters finished?

Having chosen your wood with great care, draw the design up to size, make a tracing, and pencil-press-transfer the imagery through to the working face. Being mindful that the overall image needs to be symmetrical and the grain must run from end to end through the design, work the lines until they are smoothly curved and clearly established.

With the imagery nicely set out, run the wood through the scroll saw, fretting out the entire banner shape. Try as much as you can to cut just a fraction to the waste side of the drawn line (see 2–4).

Making a Maquette

Before you go any further, take the block of Plasticine, roll it out until you have a slab about 1½″ thick, and then transfer one or the other of the ribbon-loop shapes through to its surface. You don't need the entire image, just a single loop at the bottom of the banner. Play around with the levels and the undercutting until you achieve a convincing form.

Wood-carving tip: If you have trouble visualizing the design, then drape a strip of heavy-duty fabric

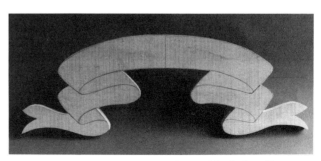

2–4 *The sawn cutout complete with design lines.*

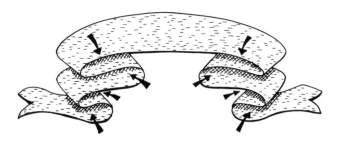

2–5 *Shade in the areas where the bottom edge of the ribbon appears to overlap the top edge of the loop.*

across the workshop and copy the imagery from life.

If you look at the various drawings and photographs, you will see that the illusion of depth is achieved by sloping the horizontal ribbon width down—from bottom edge to top edge—so that the lower edge is high and the top edge where it appears to go under the overlapping ribbon is low. You will see that it is the sloping and the undercutting that result in shadow, which in turn fool the eye into seeing greater depth.

Play around with modelling the Plasticine until you are confident that you know how the forms and planes relate one to another.

Lowering the Waste

Having fretted out the rough and made the maquette, take a pencil and shade in the areas where the top edge of the ribbon appears to be overlapped by the bottom edge of a loop (see 2–5). Now, with the wood secured down flat on the workbench, take the tool of your choice—we used a penknife and a ¾″-wide straight gouge––and slice and chop stop-cuts along the entire bottom edge of the ribbon (see 2–6). Don't go too deep in the first instance, about ⅛″ is fine. When this is done, take a straight flat-curve gouge and make a few slight cuts from the bottom edge of the ribbon up towards the stop-cut line (see 2–7). Continue until you get to know the "feel" of the wood and the character of the grain. When you are happy with the wood and the cutting movements of the tool, lower the forked end until you are left with a thickness of about 1″ (see 2–8).

The working order is: make a few light passes with the gouge so as to lower the wood by the depth of the stop-cut, make another stop-cut, skim off another layer of waste, and so on, all the while working across or at a slight angle to the run

of the grain. Every now and again along the way, stand back from the workpiece and assess your progress and technique. For example, you might decide to rehone the gouge, change your angle of approach, adjust the stop-cut line with the knife or gouge, and so forth. Carving is an ongoing procedure of looking, learning, and adjusting.

And so you continue sliding the gouge and/or knife across the width of the ribbon and down into the stop-cut, until the bottom edge of the ribbon is slightly undercut where it appears to overlap at the loop (see 2–9). When you have established the outline of the various steps that go into making up the loops, take a larger gouge and spend time lowering, finishing, defining, and shaping the ribbon form (see 2–10 on page 38). Repeatedly, stand back from the workpiece, assess your progress, shade in areas that need to be lowered, tidy up the angles with the penknife, and so on (see 2–11 on page 38).

When you come to the inside curve of the ribbon, at the point where the bottom edge of one

2–6 *Chop in stop-cuts to establish the ribbon edges at the folds.*

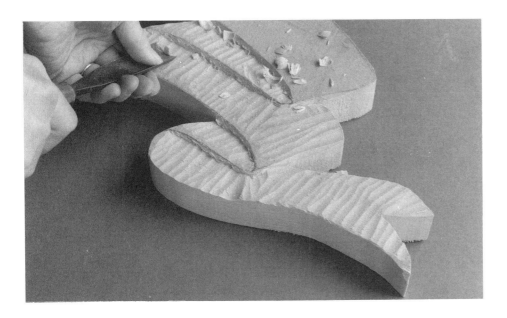

2–7   Lowering the waste wood—work towards the stop-cuts and across the run of the grain.

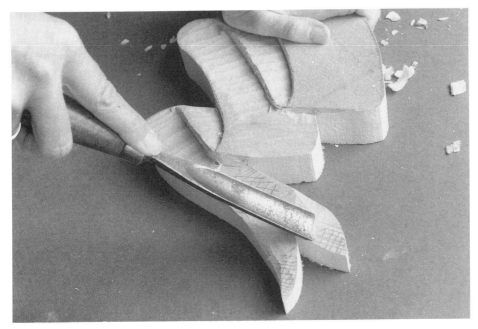

2–8   In lowering the ribbon ends, hold the gouge at a low angle to the surface of the wood. Work with care when you come to the fragile short-grained forked ends.

2–9   Slightly undercut the wood at the "turn" of the ribbon.

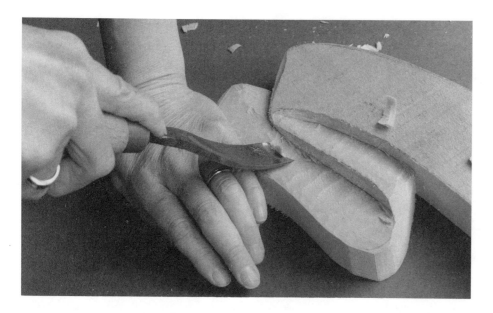

2–10   Use the large gouge to remove the bulk of the waste. (I'm using a bent gouge, but you could just as well use a straight or a fishtail.)

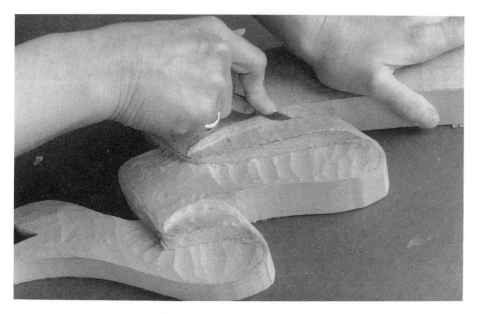

2–11   Trim and tidy the stepped edges with the knife. Slice downwards and at an angle, all the while being careful not to let the blade run into end grain.

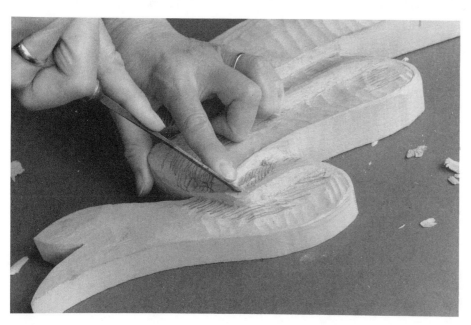

2–12   Move the handle of the gouge in an arc, so as to make a sideways scooping cut.

length of ribbon becomes the top face of the looped return, take a small gouge—one with a deep U-section blade—and work it with a tight scooping movement around the curve, so as to run the vertical "cliff" undercut in a smooth sweep into the horizontal surface (see 2–12). Try, as you are working, to keep the carving balanced and symmetrical. To this end, you might first work the left-hand bottom forked end, the right-hand forked end, and then the middle right-hand looped return. Never take a single detail to completion; always keep moving from side to side. Slant and angle the horizontal faces and the vertical planes, so as to leave a narrow strip or thickness that defines the ribbon edge (see 2–13).

It's all fairly straightforward, as long as you keep turning the workpiece and adjusting your angle of cut, so as to approach the grain from best advantage. You must always be sure to cut from high to low wood. Or, to put it another way, you must avoid cutting directly into end grain. With this being so, if you find that the wood is cutting up roughly, the chances are that you need to adjust your approach for a better cut.

Wood-carving tip: If the wood starts to cut up roughly, first try adjusting the angle of cut and then try honing the tools. I usually spend about five minutes in every 20 sharpening the gouges.

Final Modelling

When you have roughed out the entire ribbon, there will come a point when you feel that the roughing out has gone as far as it needs to go. When this stage is reached, hang the workpiece on a wall or stand it on a shelf and try to view it from as many angles and levels as possible. Then ask yourself the following questions: Are the curves smooth enough? Are the edges nicely defined, but not so thin that they might crumble away? Are the rounded horizontal surfaces—where the ribbon loops over to make the return—smoothly curved? Be as critical as possible.

With the roughing out more or less completed, take a soft pencil and spend time drawing in the curves, hatching areas that need to be refined, and generally marking out details that need to be adjusted and/or reworked. If you are a beginner, you will likely have trouble with the inboard curves of the loops and the thin band that indicates the edge or thickness of the ribbon. It's not that these areas are difficult but rather that you have to be constantly aware of the changing grain there. For example, if you cast your eyes over the inside-curve return loop nearest the forked end of the banner, you will see that, at the point where the thin edge runs into the horizontal surface, the flow of the grain will be such that you will have to change the direction of your approach for either side of the curve. You will have to work out and away from the forked end. And on the outside face of the same loop—where the horizontal surface of the ribbon curves over and under to become the vertical face—you will have to change the direction of the cut, so as to cut down towards the curve. You will have to cut towards the middle of the motif (see 2–14).

With all the inside curves of the loops nicely cut and worked, take a wider flat-curve gouge and set to work carving the various dips and ripples that give the ribbon character. In other words, if you

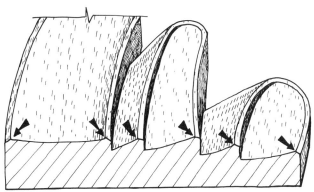

2–13 Slant and angle the horizontal faces and the vertical planes, in order to leave a narrow strip or thickness to mark out the ribbon edge.

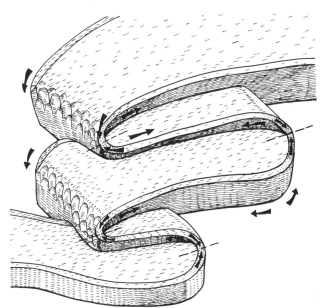

2–14 Be ready to change the direction of the cut at either side of the loop, to avoid cutting into end grain.

look at the outside curve where the horizontal face of the ribbon appears to wrap around and roll under itself, you will see that the ribbon has been slightly dipped across its width. This detail isn't essential, but it does help to convey the feeling that the ribbon is dynamic and alive—like a piece of fabric blowing in the breeze. These subtle curves or ripples are best achieved with a wide gouge—say, a bent or curved gouge that is about 1″ wide. Make repeated light skimming cuts across the grain, so as to roll the surface down, around, and under (see 2–15), while at the same time, dipping the ribbon across its width. Do this on all of the outside loops.

Take a small curved gouge and angle all the sharp edges—all around the ribbon—so as to give the edge a bevel of about a ¼″ width. If need be,

Inspirational designs   From top to bottom: Stern-board detail from the ship Prins Hendrik *(Maritime Museum, Rotterdam); stern-board detail from an eighteenth-century English ship (Norsk Sjöfartsmuseeum); gangway-board detail from the nineteenth-century U.S. Navy ship* Michigan *(The Mariners Museum, U.S.A.); and gangway-board detail from a U.S. Navy ship dated 1894–1899 (U.S. Naval Academy Museum).*

skim the vertical and horizontal sides just a little, until the edge is cleanly defined.

Painting and Finishing

When you have what you consider to be a cleanly finished carving, give it a swift rubdown with a

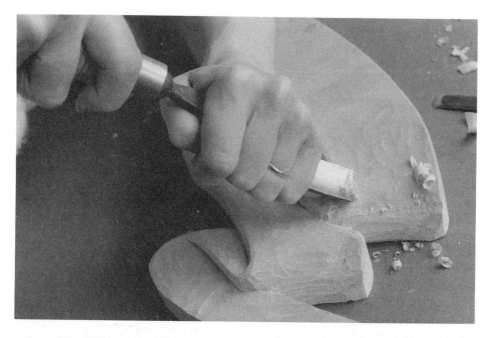

2–15 *Skim the surface at the outside of the loops, to create a slight hollow across the ribbon width.*

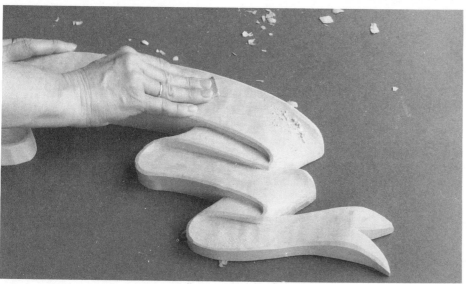

2–16 *Sand in the direction of the grain.*

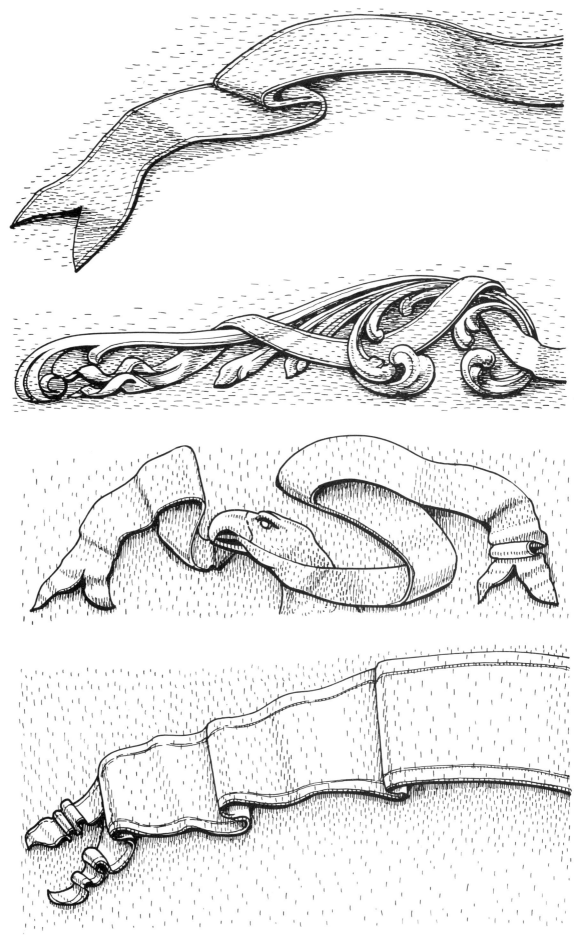

fine-grade sandpaper—just enough to remove loose wood and nibs—and move to the dust-free area that you have set aside for painting (see 2–16). Then wipe the carving over with a damp cloth and give the whole works a coat of red acrylic paint. When the paint is completely dry, go back to the workshop and rub the red paint through at the edges and outer curves of the ribbon. Don't overwork the sanding to the extent that the ribbon looks contrived or overfinished, but rather aim for a finish that suggests that the ribbon is catching the light.

Once back in the painting area, take the long-haired fine-point brush and the brown acrylic paint and paint in thin lines on the bevelled edges to give emphasis to the whiplash character of the carving. Keep the paint thick, so as to prevent it from bleeding into the grain of the wood. At this point, you will probably want to paint a name on the banner—look at other projects. Finally, give the entire carving a couple of generous coats of clear boat varnish and screw it to your boat, over your front porch, on the wall, or wherever.

TROUBLESHOOTING AND POSSIBLE MODIFICATIONS

• If you like the idea of the project but need a longer banner—say, for a big boat or maybe for a long name—there's no reason why you can't stay with the same ribbon width and number of loops and simply extend the middle section.

• If you want to go for a natural unpainted look, make absolutely sure that the wood is free from knots and stains.

• Don't be too slavish about following the design. If you want it bigger, or with more loops, or whatever, let yourself veer away from the design and modify the project to suit your own needs.

• If you become anxious about the carving, call a halt for a day or two and then go back to it with a fresh eye.

• Our tool suggestions are meant to be no more than a general guide. If you have, say, a totally different set of gouges, give them a try and see how it goes.

Whaler

3
Running-Rope Borders

Ropes and traditional sailing ships go together like . . . sun and sand, salt and sea, and wind and water. Ropes are the very stuff of sailing. Take a look at an old sailing ship, and you will see miles and miles of rope. Slender flexible ropes, huge ropes as thick as a man's arm, whipped ropes with fancy ends, ropes covered in canvas and tar—there are ropes of all shapes, sizes, types, and characters.

It follows that when a ship carver was searching for inspiration, he could not help but look to rope for design ideas—to the coils on deck, the fancy knotted work that made up the rigging, and the patterns made by the rope as it snaked through the various winches, eyelets, and blocks.

The ship carver used the rope motif on stern boards, around the base of the mast, on trail boards, and just about anywhere else that captured his fancy. In many instances, one can plainly see that he didn't bother to stylize the forms or in any way alter the imagery; he simply copied what he saw. When the carver was about to work a fancy border—on the edge of a board, around the transom, around windows, or for running rails—he often did no more than note the many instances where real ropes were used as decorative trims and fenders and then copy the idea directly in wood.

A simple carved-rope border can be an impressive treatment for the top edge of a board or rail, when you want to achieve a decorative detail without going to the trouble and expense of adding extra wood.

Sure, you could attach a length of real rope along the top edge of a rail, along a rudder arm, or wherever, but a run of rope is bound to take a beating. Not only is a length of rope carving durable, but it invites all kinds of questions and admiration, like: Is it real? how did you do it? was it difficult? that's amazing! and so on.

So, if you want to carve a fancy border and decorate your boat and at the same time pull a crowd, this could well be the project for you!

THOUGHTS ON DESIGN AND TECHNIQUE

Take a look at the working drawings (see 3–2 on next page) and the photographs, and note how we

3–1 Detail from the finished carving, painted and varnished.

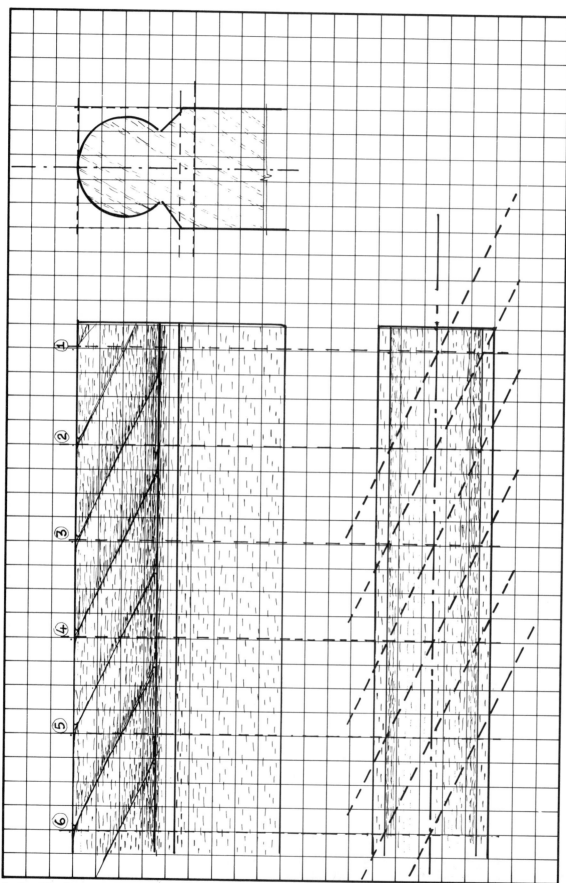

3–2 *Working drawings—the scale is four grid squares to 1". Left: Side view with alignment numbers and cross section. Right: Plan, showing strand lines.*

have used the rope technique to decorate the top edge of a tiller arm. Also, note how the carving relates to a module of 1″, meaning that the rope diameter and the horizontal distance between neighboring strands both measure 1″.

Wood-carving tip: If you want to change the size of the carving—bigger or smaller diameter—you still have to set the diameter of the rope and the distance between neighboring strands to the same module measurement—for example, both 2″, both 3″, or whatever.

Now look at the working drawings again, and see how we have worked the design on 1¼″-thick wood, with the 1″-diameter rope detail being arranged in such a way that it appears to be an actual rope that is inset and aligned with the top edge. Consider how the success of the carving hinges not only on the strands being carefully arranged so that the entire rope appears to be round in cross section but, also, on each individual strand being nicely plump and rounded. The rounded strands, the repeated rhythm, and the depth of the cuts between strands are all important in conveying the illusion that the carving is a piece of rope.

Although we have chosen to paint the carving in a red, white, and blue sequence—to emphasize the roundness and spacing of the individual strands—you could just as well paint it all one color, decorate it with gold leaf, or even leave it natural. There are lots of options.

TOOL AND MATERIAL CONSIDERATIONS

This is a good project for beginners, in that it requires a minimum of tools: a knife, a V-tool, and a couple of straight shallow-curve gouges.

Although we have used the rope technique to decorate a found tiller arm—a nice piece of old mahogany—this is not to say that you couldn't run the carving around the edge of a dinghy, along a rounded spar, around the edge of a chart table, or wherever. If the wood is round or can be cut so that it is partially round—as we have done in this project—it can be carved with rope imagery.

As to your choice of wood, you could go for jelutong, lime/basswood, pine, or anything else, as long as the wood is relatively straight-grained, free from knots, dry, and easy to carve.

Wood-carving tip: If you decide to use a wood from a local yard, make sure that it is well seasoned. It would be a shame to spend valuable time carving, only to find the piece warping and splitting.

TOOLS AND EQUIPMENT

For this project, you need:
- a 1¼″-thick board, or plank, of easy-to-carve wood at a length to suit the situation
- a drawknife or plane
- a metal straightedge and a couple of small clamps
- a ¼″-wide skew chisel
- a small V-tool
- a good sharp knife—we used a penknife
- a couple of straight shallow-curve gouges: ¼″ and 1″ wide
- a knife-edge riffler file
- the use of a workbench with a bench clamp
- a short length of 1″-diameter rope
- a roll of 1″-wide masking tape
- a pencil and ruler
- a pair of dividers
- acrylic paint in red, white, and blue
- a can of yacht varnish
- a couple of soft-haired brushes: a broad- and a fine-point
- a pack of graded sandpapers

PROJECT STAGES

First Steps and Roughing Out

Having carefully chosen your wood and the place on your boat where you want the carving to be situated, selected your tools, and generally prepared for the task ahead, give the wood a final look-over, just to make sure that it's straight-grained and free from splits and knots. Be especially wary about knots on the edge. Then study the working drawings (see 3–2) once more, and note the scale of four grid squares to 1″.

Assuming that your piece of chosen wood is 1″ thick, take a pencil and ruler and measure 1″ down from the top edge. Do this on both sides of the board. Secure the wood in the vise, and use the drawknife or plane to round over the top edge of the board. Aim for a nice and tidy half-circle of about 1″ in diameter.

Set the metal straightedge along the top side of this line—on the border to be carved—and clamp in place. If all is well, the straightedge should be covering part of the rope area. When this is done, take the skew chisel, spike the point down—so that the skew part of the blade is facing away from the rope and the vertical side is resting against the metal straightedge—and run it backwards and

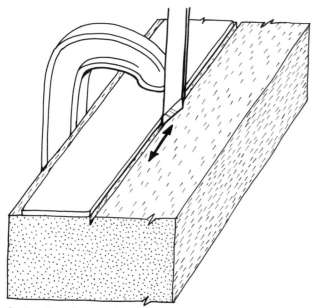

3–3 Set the metal straightedge on the border to be carved, and secure with a clamp. Run the skew chisel repeatedly backwards and forward so as to plough out a trench.

forward so as to plough out a trench (see 3–3). Continue until you have a triangular trench that's about ⅜″ wide and ¼″ deep. Repeat this procedure on both sides of the board, or plank. When this is done, move the metal straightedge so that it is on the other side of the guideline, and repeat the whole procedure until the top edge of the board begins to look more or less rounded. If need be, use the knife and one of the larger gouges to help achieve the shape (see 3–4).

Wood-carving tip: As you are aiming to cut a V-section trench, you could alter the technique and make the cut with a V-tool or a V-shaped scraper.

When you have what appears to be a board with a round rod or pole sitting on the top edge, remove the straightedge and swiftly rub the wood down to a smooth finish.

Setting Out the Design

Take a pencil and ruler, and run a central line along the top face of the rope axis, as seen in the plan view (3–2). When this is done, take the dividers, set them to 1″, and set the central line out with a series of 1″ step-offs (see 3–5). Number the step-offs 1 through whatever.

With the step-offs in place, take the 1″-wide masking tape, tear off a strip at about 8″, and, starting at number 1, roll the strip at an angle around the round wood, so that the edges of the strip pass through—just touch—the pair of odd numbers 1 and 3 (see 3–5, bottom). Repeat the procedure with the pair of numbers 5 and 7, 9 and 11, and so on, along the wood. Use the edges of the masking-tape strips to draw in pencil guidelines. Then repeat the process with the even numbers. If all is well, the wood should now be set out with each strand of the rope being about ½″ wide (see 3–6).

Setting in the Stop-cuts and V-cuts

With the position of the strands marked in with pencil guidelines, take the knife and very carefully set each line in with a stop-cut. Do your best to keep the cut clean (see 3–7). Take a sharp V-tool, and, being careful so that the blade doesn't run off and do damage to your hand and/or the main body of the workpiece, cut a V-section trench down, along, and around each of the stop-cuts, so

3–4 Use a large gouge to scrape and tidy up the trench.

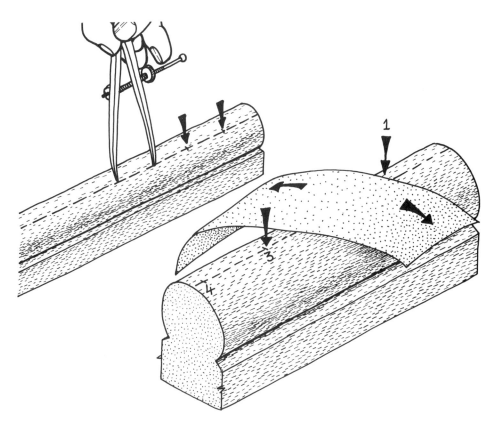

3–5 Top: Set the central line out with a series of 1" step-offs. Bottom: Hold the tape at an angle, so that the edges pass through odd numbers, and then roll the tape around the wood.

3–6 The wood set out with the ½"-wide strands.

3–7 Deepen the stop-cut, drawing the knife towards your body.

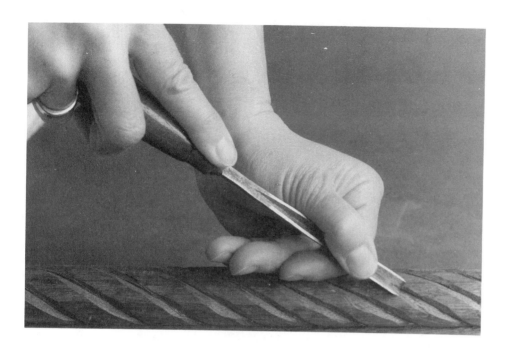

3–8 *Angle the tool so as to cut only on the right-hand side of the V-trench.*

as to establish the overall shape of the strands. Don't expect or even try to achieve the required depth with a single cut; it's much better to make repeated little-by-little cuts with the knife and V-tool until you are pleased with the effect. Be mindful that each strand needs to be smoothly curved along its length, parallel to neighboring strands, and half-round in cross section. It's all fairly straightforward, as long as the wood is smooth-grained and the tools sharp. With that said, and bearing in mind that you can only cut with the grain on one side of the V-trench, be prepared to approach the wood from another direction and/or bear down on one side of the tool, so as to approach the grain to best advantage (see 3–8).

Modelling

When you have run the V-cuts around the wood, then comes the task of bringing each strand to a convincing roundness. To this end, draw in a central line along each strand and then use the ¼"-wide shallow-curve gouge to carve from the central line high spot down and around and into the V-trench stop-cut (see 3–9, left).

Wood-carving tip: If you always work away from your body and on the right-hand side of the V-cut (or you could say the left-hand side of the strand), you will be cutting with the grain.

The procedure is as follows: round over the left-hand side of the strand, turn the wood around so that the other side of the strand becomes the left-hand side, and work this side in like manner (see

3–9, right). It's all pretty easy, as long as you keep your tools sharp and are mindful about the direction of the grain.

And so you continue working the strands a piece at a time, deepening the stop-cuts, tidying up the end of each strand, and so on, until the entire rope begins to take on a nicely rounded character.

When you have used the gouges to take the strands more or less to completion, use the riffler file and the sandpaper to clean up the workpiece. All you do is systematically work along and around the various strands until they appear to be part of the total rope (see 3–10). It's hard, dusty work, so take it slowly. If need be, fold the sandpaper around a flat metal ruler or a flat stick and work between the strands.

Finishing and Painting

Once the carving is done, give it a rubdown with the graded sandpapers. If you want to go for a painted finish—like our carving—move to the dust-free area that you have set aside for painting and give the rope a couple of coats of matt white paint. Work it well into the grain and between the strands.

Having waited for the paint to dry, use a fine-grade sandpaper to rub off all the nibs and then paint the strands the color of your choice. As we decided to go for a traditional red, white, and blue sequence, all we did was paint in all the red and blue strands and leave every third strand white.

Finally, when the acrylic paint is completely dry, give it another swift rubdown with the fine-grade

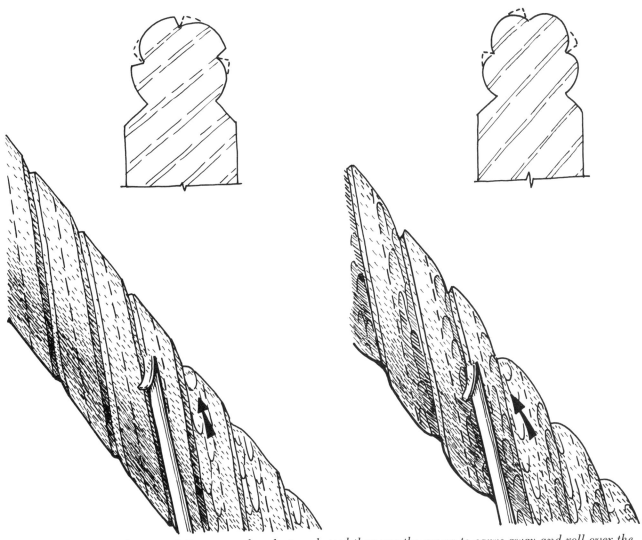

3–9   Left: Draw the central line around each strand, and then use the gouge to carve away and roll over the wood to the depth of the V-trench. Right: Turn the wood around, and repeat the cutting procedure on the other side of the strand.

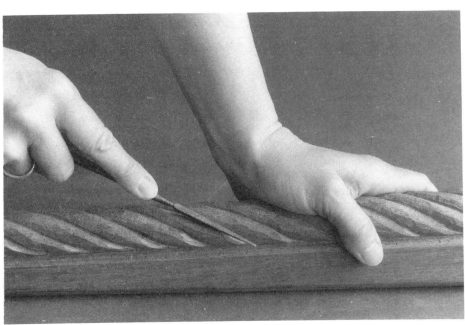

3–10   Use the knife-edge riffler file to clean up the strands and the trenches.

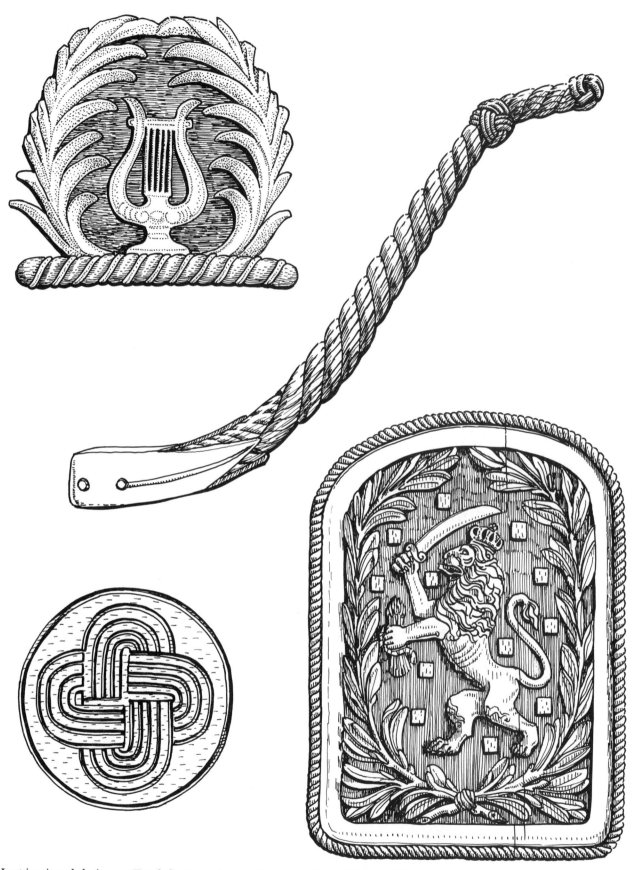

Inspirational designs   Top left: Stern board from a whaling ship, c. 1830, height 21″, painted and gilded (Bourne Whaling Museum, New Bedford). Middle: Tiller arm from the Prins Hendrik *(Maritime Museum, Rotterdam). Bottom left: Incised motif from a sea chest. Bottom right: Gangway board, end of the nineteenth century.*

sandpaper, lay on three or four thin coats of clear boat varnish, and then stand back and let everyone admire your (amazing and how-did-you-do it?) rope-trick carving.

TROUBLESHOOTING AND POSSIBLE MODIFICATIONS

- If you like the idea of the project but need a fatter run of rope, be mindful that the rope diameter and the horizontal spacing between strands need to be the same measurement.
- If you want to go for a natural unpainted look, there's all the more reason to make absolutely sure that the wood is free from knots and stains.
- As I dislike sanding and very much enjoy using a knife, I did a fair amount of the tidying up with a small penknife. I used it like a scraper.
- Choose your wood with care. Carving a rope border on a piece of soft lime is one thing, but trying to work a piece of knotty pine is quite another!
- As to how much sanding is needed and how smooth the carving should be, I prefer to see a carving with lots of tool marks and irregularities over a super-smooth mechanical-looking carving with all the character blurred out. Tool marks add character.

Clipper

4
Quarter Board with Incised Lettering

Sailing boats and ships were traditionally personified and given a name. The name of the vessel was set out on one or more boards, the letters being deeply carved and blocked in with a bold color. Then the boards were mounted variously on the stern, the quarters, and the bow. (See the next project.)

On the old wooden sailing ships, the ends of the boards were cut in an ornate profile and carved with a simple bold motif or pattern. The idea was that the name should be easily read at a distance, with the shape, size, and design of the letters and board helping to enhance the overall image of the vessel. The stern board might be beautifully arched with forked-ribbon ends, the quarter boards might be long and slender with the letters slanting forward, and so forth.

In much the same way as, say, car manufacturers now use names, logos, and lettering, and images to imply that such-and-such a car is wonderfully powerful, or fast, the ship carvers used the name, the lettering, and the shape of the board not only to decorate, embellish, and identify, but also to suggest that the ship was, for example, stately, fast, or belonging to a prestigious line.

THOUGHTS ON DESIGN AND TECHNIQUES

Take a look at the working drawings (see 4–2, A and B) and the photographs, and note how the board needs to be, at one and the same time, bold, ornate, and structurally sound. Or, to put it another way, it's no good if the board is fancy but so delicate that it breaks up under the force of wind and wave, the lettering so proud that it risks getting scraped off on the quayside, or the letters so fussy that the name can't be read at a distance.

It's probably fair to say that while ships' name boards are relatively easy to cut and carve, the design of the board and the spacing of the letters need a lot of careful consideration. If you study our board, you will see that we have opted for simple stepped half-circle ends, hex-star motifs, and naïve letter forms. The important thing to realize is that, while our letters are V-cut with serifs and the like, they owe very little to classical Greek or Roman letter forms. Our letters are relatively easy to cut, inasmuch as the chunky and playful forms allow for a fair amount of idiosyncratic carving. Or, as my grandpa would have said, "Our mistakes are easy on the eye." Note especially the fancy flourishes on the R, E, and L. The good news is, once the lettering and spacing have been worked out, the actual letters can be cut with nothing more complicated than a sharp knife.

Special tip: If you are looking for different letter forms, see our inspirational designs or see if you can get hold of a rub-on letter catalog as used by graphic designers.

TOOL AND MATERIAL CONSIDERATIONS

This is a good project for beginners, in that it requires a minimum of tools—not much more than a knife and a scroll saw. As to your choice of knife, much depends on your wood. As we decided to go for jelutong—it's wonderfully easy to carve and our workshop is full to bursting with the

4–1   The finished carved-and-painted board.

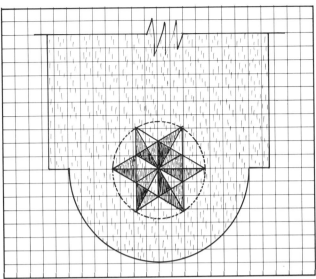

4–2, A   Working drawing—the end profile and star motif. The scale is four grid squares to 1".

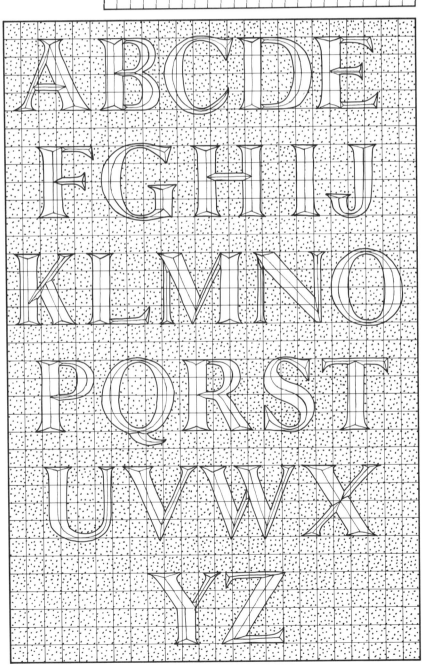

4–2, B   Working drawing—alphabet design, at a scale of four grid squares to 1".

stuff—I was able to use a small razor-sharp pen-knife. Then again, if you want to use a harder wood, like oak, you might well need to use a knife with a longer handle. The simple rule of thumb is: the harder the wood, the more leverage you need on the knife.

The length of wood will, of course, depend on the name you have chosen. We have allowed about 4″ for the board ends—meaning 4″ from the end of the board to the first and last letter—and 18″ for the seven-letter name, "Rachael." However, if you have in mind to give your boat or house a long full name—something like, for example, "The Good Ship Bonadventure Sunrise"—then you are going to need one long piece of wood.

TOOLS AND EQUIPMENT

For this project, you need:
- a 1″-thick plank of straight-grained, easy-to-carve wood that's about 4⅜″ wide and 27″ long
- the use of an electric scroll saw or a hand-held coping saw
- a good sharp knife—we used a penknife
- the use of a workbench with a bench clamp
- a pencil, ruler, and square
- a pair of dividers and a compass
- a sheet each of work-out paper and tracing paper to suit the length of board
- a can of matt white emulsion paint
- acrylic paint in blue and gold
- a can of yacht varnish
- a couple of soft-haired brushes: a broad and a fine-point
- a pack of graded sandpapers

PROJECT STAGES

Setting Out

Before you do anything else, take the pencil, ruler, and tracing paper and set out all the letters that make up your chosen name—see the working drawing (4–2, B). Set the letters along a 2¼″-wide track, so that there is a fair balance between letters and spaces.

Bearing in mind that the spaces are almost as important as the letters, spend time getting it right. If need be, draw the letters out on a board and live with it for a few days, just to make sure that you are happy with the overall effect.

Having meticulously drawn out the name and just as carefully chosen your 4⅜″-wide length of wood, take a soft pencil and a ruler and set the wood out with an end-to-end central line. When this is done, set your compass to a radius of 1¾″ and lay each end of the board out with a 3½″-diameter half-circle—see the working drawing (4–2, A).

With the half-circles in place, reset the compass to a radius of ⅞″ and set each half-circle end out with a 1¾″ circle. Now, working with the compass still set to ⅞″, step off around the circumference of the circle, drawing out the six arcs that go into marking out the six-point hex-star. Use the pencil and ruler to link up the circumference step-offs (see 4–2, A), so as to draw out the hex-stars. If all is well, each star will be made up of 24 identical triangles.

When you have clearly marked out the ends of the board, take your tracing, rework the back of the letters, and then tape it to the board. Now, just as you spent time fiddling around with the letters and the spaces, you need to make sure that the spacing between the first and last letters and the stars is nicely balanced. When you are certain that the positioning is right, use a rule and a hard pencil to press-transfer the letters through to the wood (see 4–3). Finally, press-transfer one or two of the more difficult letters through to a piece of scrap wood.

Cutting the Profile and Making Trial Cuts

With all the letters and motifs accurately set out, use the scroll saw to cut out the decorative half-circle ends. All you do is run the cut in at one side, follow around the half-circle, and then exit the other side. You won't have any problems, as long as you work at an easy pace so as to ensure that the sawn lines are crisp and smoothly curved and you run the cut a little to the waste side of the drawn line.

Special tip: A scroll saw is an easy and efficient machine to use, but only if it is in good condition, with a correctly set and tensioned blade and the teeth pointing down.

With the ends of the board cleanly fretted out, take your piece of scrap and have a trial run. You first sink the letter's central lines with stop-cuts (see 4–4, left) and then make slanting follow-up cuts at either side of the initial stop-cuts, so as to cut a V-section trench (see 4–4, right). Bearing in mind that the letters are made up from a series of straight and smoothly curved V-section trenches, all of a precise width and depth, spend time practising the differing strokes. Try out various hand holds, and see which ones work best for you. I

4–3   The board all ready to carve, with the motif and lettering carefully set out.

usually hold the knife with two hands—one hand holding and pulling, while the other is guiding and controlling.

To recap, the order of work is as follows: first make a single stop-cut down the central line or spine of the letter, and then make slanting cuts at either side of the stop-cut, so as to cut a V-section trench. Once the trench has been started, you then make successive cuts until the required depth and width have been achieved.

Cutting the Letters

If you take a look at the photographs and drawings, you will see that the letters are made up in the

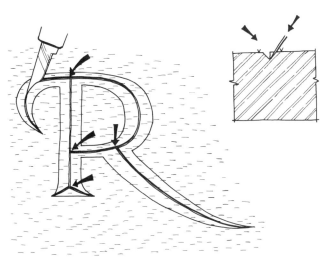

4–4   Left: Sink the central lines in with stop-cuts. Note how the depth of the cut varies, with the cut getting shallower as the end of the strokes tails out. Right: Cut towards the stop-cut so as to create a V-section.

main from four primary elements: straight wide uprights, straight thin horizontals, serifs, and tapered curves. The thing to bear in mind is that, while the straight lines are fairly uncomplicated—because they run with or across the run of the grain—the curves are more difficult, because you have to constantly change the direction of the cut to avoid cutting directly into end grain.

Once you have had a trial run on a piece of scrap, then comes the scary business of cutting the letters for real. In this process, there is very little room for error. If you make a mistake with one letter or even part of a letter, then you have to start all over again. See what I mean by scary! With that said, the rather loose and easy style of the letters does allow for some leeway. If, for example, a curve is a bit sloppy or a line is not quite straight, who's to say that you can't fiddle around with it a bit.

Start by cutting the first letter, the R. Make a single downward stop-cut for the main upright—a cut that starts and finishes in the middle of a serif triangle—and then make repeated slanting cuts until the full width has been achieved. When you come to cutting a curve—let's say the dramatic curve tail that runs down and forward from the R—the procedure is much the same. The only real difference is that you have to change the direction of the cut so as to work with the grain. If you look at 4–5 on the next page, you will see that the underside of the curve needs to be cut from top to bottom, while the top side of the curve needs to be cut from bottom to top. It's not difficult, but you do have to keep turning the board this way and that in order to accommodate the cut.

The C is particularly interesting, in that the curves run both with and across the grain (see

4–5 Cut in the direction of the arrows, turning the board this way and that for the angle of best cut.

4–6 The V-trench becomes shallower at the tails-off points.

4–7 For maximum control, support and guide the knife with both hands.

4–6). You first sink the central line with a stop-cut and then variously turn both the wood and the knife so as to cut with the grain (see 4–7).

And so you proceed by sinking a single stop-cut for the central line or spine, making slanting cuts at either side of the stop-cut, and then making successive cuts to bring the resulting V-trench to the desired width and depth. If you keep your knife sharp and only take thin skims or shavings, you won't go far wrong.

The junctions are a little bit tricky, in that while the width of the letter strokes varies, the bottoms of the V-trenches all need ideally to finish up at the same depth. For example, if you look at the H, you will see that while the uprights are more or less twice as wide as the horizontal crossbar, the depth of the Vs are the same.

I usually start a letter by establishing the wide upright, move on to cutting the horizontals and curves, and then finish up with the serifs.

Finally, when you have cut all the letters that make up your chosen name, stand back, assess the total image, and then use the point of the knife to sharpen up the serifs and generally perfect your work.

Cutting the Hex-Stars

Having used a compass, ruler, and pencil to very carefully draw out the two hex-stars, take a look at the working drawing (see 4–2, A) and note how each star is made up from 24 identical little triangular "pockets," or chip cuts. See the way that the triangular pockets are cut so that the right angle is achieved by making two stop-cuts.

The order of work for each triangular pocket is as follows: sink two stop-cuts to make the right angle in the middle of each diamond—where the deepest cut is (see 4–8, top right)—and then slide the knife in at an angle towards the stop-cuts, so that a small chip of waste falls away (see 4–8, bottom left). If you tackle one point of the star at a time—meaning one diamond, or lozenge, made up from four triangles—and cut out opposite triangular pockets within the form, you will find that once you have cut the first two pockets, the other two can be cut using existing stop-cuts (see 4–8, bottom right). The challenging part about cutting hex-stars is that, as you work around the star, each of the 24 pockets is set at a slightly different angle to the grain. But it's all fairly simple, as long as

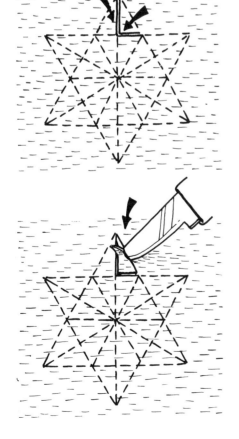

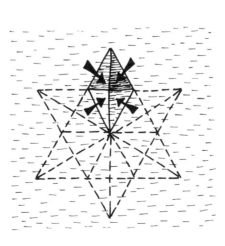

4–8 Top left: Sink two stop-cuts to make a right angle. Top right: Note that the middle of the diamond, or lozenge, needs to be cut the deepest. Bottom left: Slide the knife in at an angle and towards the stop-cuts, so that a small triangular chip of waste falls away. Bottom right: To complete the diamond, remove the other two triangles using the existing stop-cuts.

Inspirational designs   From the top: Nineteenth-century name board (Norsk Sjöfartsmuseeum); name board from the four-masted German schooner Teie, *built in Tonsberg in 1819 (Handels-og Sofartsmuseum, Paa, Kronsberg Hooge, Germany); and three trail boards from nineteenth-century American ships (Maryland Historical Society).*

4–9 The completed carving, ready for painting.

your knife is sharp and you keep your eyes on the run of the grain.

Finishing and Painting

When you have tidied up all the letters and the two stars, then comes the satisfying task of finishing and painting. Start by giving the whole workpiece a rubdown with the fine sandpaper. When this is done, wipe away all the dust and move to the area set aside for painting (see 4–9).

Begin by giving the entire sign a generous coat of matt white emulsion. When the white emulsion is dry, give it a swift rubdown with the finest grade of sandpaper and wipe away the dust. Next, being sure to slightly overlap the edges, block the letters and stars in with gold paint and leave them to dry.

Painting tip: Always use a light color for the letters. Light colors cast shadows, whereas dark colors look flat and dead.

Once the gold paint is dry, paint the face of the sign blue. Use a broad brush to lay on the large areas, and then use a fine brush to cut in the edges of the letters and stars. Finally, give the whole workpiece a couple of generous coats of varnish.

When the varnish is good and dry, mount the sign on your boat, over the porch of your house, over the mantelpiece, or just about anywhere where it can be easily seen and admired!

TROUBLESHOOTING AND POSSIBLE MODIFICATIONS

- If you like the idea of the project but need a wider sign with bigger letters, then stay with the same proportions and scale the letters and spaces to suit your needs.
- On consideration, I think that the first A in Rachael could perhaps be slightly wider at the base. What do you think?
- If you want to go for a natural, dark wood look, an old piece of mahogany with gold letters will stand up well and look great as is.
- Be warned: Carving a sign is no fun if each and every letter has to be cut through a knot! Choose your wood with care.
- If you can afford the cost, then it's best to use gold leaf for the letters.
- When you come to mounting the board, be sure to use brass or stainless-steel hardware.

Barquentine

5
Name-Board Shells

In the nineteenth century in America and Britain, every documented sailing ship was required by law to carry her name in large, clear letters. This was achieved by having the name carved directly into the stern planking, or more commonly carved on boards that were fastened below the side rails.

Although it was only strictly necessary to show the name on the stern, a good many ships carried at least four carved and decorated name boards: one on each side on the fore quarters and one on each side on the aft quarters.

Name boards give wood-carvers yet another good chance to show off their skills. Not only are the individual letters deeply carved and painted—this is a challenge in itself, as can be seen in the preceding project—but the ends of the boards are usually set out with fancy motifs.

Traditionally, board ends were carved with all manner of decoration: everything from scrolls and acanthus leaves, to stars, dolphins, whales, and shells. As you might well expect, shell motifs were frequently used by ship carvers. They carved periwinkles, whelks, mussels, oysters, and just about every common, exotic, or fantasy shell that you can imagine.

One of the most interesting shell motifs is the flat fan *Pecten maximus,* more commonly known as the Great Scallop. The scallop motif was a great favorite with wood-carvers throughout the eighteenth and nineteenth centuries, being used as side decorations on figureheads, as cabin decorations, on furniture, and, of course, on board ends. If you are looking to carve a stylized board motif, one that can be swiftly carved in a few hours, a motif that has about it all the salty freshness of the sand and sea, you can't do better than this scallop shell.

THOUGHTS ON DESIGN AND TECHNIQUE

Take a look at the working drawings (5–2), and you'll see why, at a scale of four grid squares to 1″, we decided to concentrate our efforts on carving a small number board. At about 1¼″ thick, 14″ long, and 4½″ wide—with the shells taking up most of the space—our board is just perfect for carrying a mooring number. However, if you would rather carve a long name board, then all you do is stay with the shell sizes and board width and simply increase the length to suit the name.

We studied an actual scallop shell and then reduced the design to a simple, stylized, easy-to-carve image. See how a good part of the shell has been modified so that it can be drawn out with a ruler and compass. For example, the small arc within the shell is drawn with a compass, the shape of the rounded ends are based on a half-circle, and so forth. As to the actual shape of the shell—meaning the hollows and dips—all we did was study the shell and then draw out the various dips and hollows so that they could be swiftly cut with the minimum of effort.

Bearing in mind that ship carvers often needed to cut four or more boards, all with more or less identical ends, it's plain to see that the design needed to be kept simple and easy to cut.

Therefore, trying to keep our design as simple as possible, we shaped the hinge end of the shell so that it could be swiftly cut with our ½″ shallow-sweep gouge, and we sized the ripples to fit our smaller U-section gouges. We designed the curves and hollows in light of our tools. If you are a beginner with a minimal tool kit, you might want to play around with your tools, noting the shape,

5–1   The finished board.

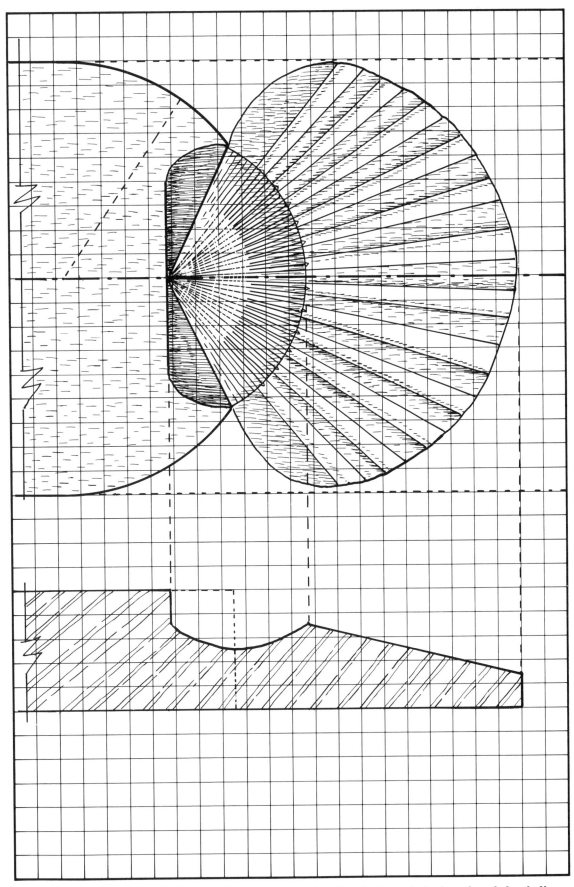

5–2   *Working drawings—front view and cross-section detail, through the board and the shell. The scale is four grid squares to 1″.*

depth, and character of the resulting cuts. Then you can design or modify the shape of the shells accordingly.

TOOL AND MATERIAL CONSIDERATIONS

This is a good project for beginners, in that it can be swiftly cut and worked with a minimum of tools and time. All you need are a knife, a V-tool, a couple of shallow-sweep gouges, and a length of easy-to-carve wood. After five hours or so of concentrated carving, the board will be ready for painting.

Regarding your choice of wood, much depends on what you have in mind. If, for example, you want the board to last a lifetime, then go for a piece of well-seasoned English oak, or maybe a piece of teak, which will outlive you and your boat. But if you simply want to get the job done quickly and with minimum cost, then go for pine, lime, or jelutong. Don't worry too much about the color or the character of the wood, because, after all, the finished project is going to be painted and varnished. Just make certain that the wood is smooth-grained and free from splits and knots.

TOOLS AND EQUIPMENT

For this project, you need:
- a 4½″-wide and 1¼″-thick plank of prepared easy-to-carve wood at a length to suit your envisioned name or number board—ours was 15″ long
- the use of an electric scroll saw or a hand-held coping saw

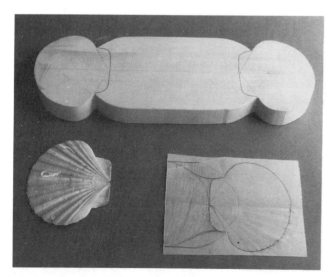

5–3 Fret out the fancy ends on the scroll saw. Note that the design on the tracing paper shows an alternative shell-board linkup design.

62

- two shallow-sweep straight gouges: ¼″ and ½″ wide
- a ¼″-wide U-section gouge—either straight or bent
- a small V-tool or veiner
- a good sharp knife—we used a penknife
- the use of a workbench with a bench clamp
- a pencil and ruler
- a pair of compasses or dividers
- a pack of graded sandpaper
- a small quantity of matt white emulsion or under-coat paint—we used ceiling white
- acrylic paint in green and gold
- a small tube of sepia artist's oil paint
- a can of yacht varnish
- a soft-haired brush

PROJECT STAGES

First Steps and Setting Out

Having carefully chosen your wood, sorted out your tools, and sized up your working situation, draw the design up to size and make a clear tracing. Make certain that the shell shape is symmetrical, with the design being reduced to a few clearly defined lines. Be sure that the characteristic ripple-fold arrangement is organized in such a way that the fan is well balanced.

When you have everything sorted out so that you have a sense of how the image needs to be worked and carved, set your chosen length of wood out with an end-to-end central line. When this is done, carefully pencil-press-transfer the image through to the wood.

Wood-carving tip: It's important to realize that the success of the carving hinges on the amount of time and effort you put in at the designing and setting-out stage. You can't just pick up a piece of wood and start hacking away; you need to think it through. Ask yourself: Is the wood sound? are the lines clearly established? do I have enough tools for the task? should I simplify the shapes to suit my tools? and so on.

First Cuts and Clearing the Rough

With the wood crisply set out and all your designs and inspirational material close at hand, pass the wood through the scroll saw and fret out the fancy ends (see 5–3). Go at a nice easy pace, trying, all the while, to achieve a clean, smooth cut that is ever so slightly to the waste side of the drawn line. If need be, tidy up with a plane and sandpaper.

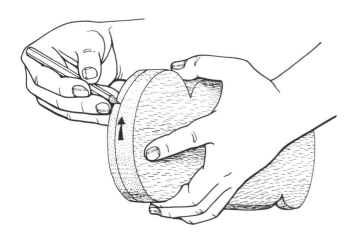

5–4 *Hold the pencil along one finger, rest the pencil and finger on the edge of the board, and draw the line around the edge and towards your body.*

Having cut out the profile and cleaned up the faces and edges, use a mallet and gouge to set the shell-board line in with a stop-cut—meaning the line that marks out the hinge of the shell. Don't, in the first instance, go deeper than about ⅛″, and be careful, where the line curves around and exits at the edge of the profile, that you don't split the wood.

Take a pencil, hold it hard up against your finger (as illustrated in 5–4), and run a line around the sawn edge of the shell. Set the line about ⅜″ down from the front face. With the guideline in place, take a shallow-sweep gouge and swiftly lower the face of the shell to the depth of the ⅜″ line (see 5–5). The procedure is as follows: skim off the waste to the depth of the stop-cut, reestablish the stop-cut, skim off another layer of waste, and so

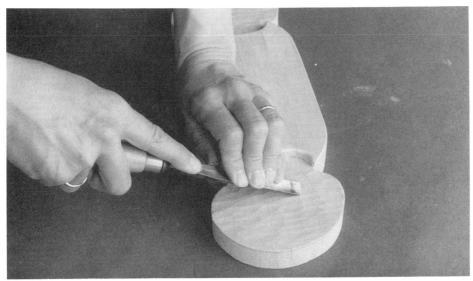

5–5 *Use the shallow-sweep gouge to lower the face of the shell to the depth of the ⅜″ guideline.*

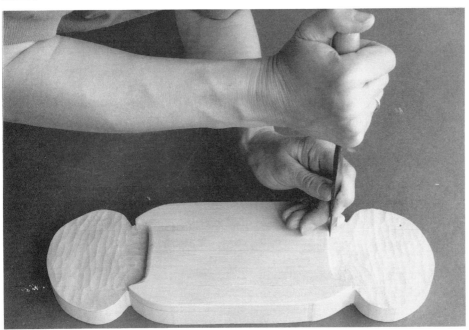

5–6 *Reestablish and deepen the stop-cut, and carefully slice down so as to clean up the edge.*

on, all the while being very careful not to overshoot the stop-cut and damage the end-grain stepped face. (See 5–6 on previous page.)

On approaching the ⅜″ line, ease back on the depth of cut and skim the face to a smoothly tooled finish. When you have lowered and skimmed both shells, first clean up the stepped edge with a gouge and then use a scrap of fine-grade sandpaper to rub the stepped edge and face down to a smooth finish.

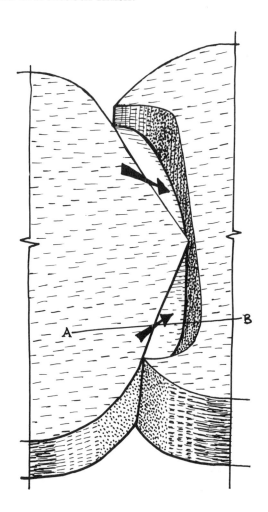

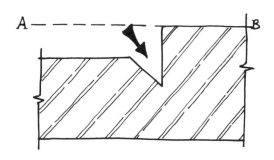

5–7 Slice away the valley at either side of the angle—between the bottom of the shell and the board. Top: Cut in the direction of the arrows. Bottom: Cross section of A–B.

Modelling the Shells

With the rough out of the way and having rubbed the sawn face and edge down to a good finish, take a pencil, draw a clear central line, and run another depth line around the edge of the shell. Repeat the procedure as already described, only this time set the line about ⅜″ up from the back face.

Stop awhile, and refresh your eye by checking with the working drawings. Note how the two straight lines that angle towards the bottom of the shell and the arc that delineates the depression relate to the central line, and then mark out the lowered face of the shell accordingly.

Rework the shell-hinge line with a stop-cut. Just as before, chop the line in to a depth of ⅛″. Take the ¼″ shallow-sweep gouge, and make a sliding cut down from the angled line and into the stop-cut. Carry out this procedure on both sides of the angle, so that there is a deep, clean-sided valley at either side of the angle—between the bottom of the shell and board (see 5–7).

Take one or the other of your small U-section gouges, and scoop out the quadrant between the angled line and the arc. Aim for a smooth depression. Next, take a wider gouge and slice down and out from the arc line—towards the outer edge of the shell—so as to angle the fan part of the shell down towards the edge-of-wood guideline (see 5–8).

When you have achieved a nicely sloped fan area, use a pencil and ruler to set out the dip-and-rise ripples that characterize scallop shells. It doesn't matter if you want to reduce the number of ripples, as long as you make sure that the fan is balanced. See to it that, as you swing around from one side of the shell to the other, the design starts and finishes on a dip. Shade in the dips.

Select a small U-section gouge—straight or bent—and gently scoop the waste out from each dip (see 5–9). One dip at a time, and starting at the arc line, run a wedgelike furrow, or channel, from the central point down towards the outer edge of the shell. Work backwards and forward around the fan until you achieve the rippled effect.

Wood-carving tip: Be very careful, when you are running the gouge down the channel, that you don't dig into end grain. If need be, change the direction of cut and, as it were, run the tool uphill.

Finally, take either the V-tool or a small U-section gouge and run a fan of small V-section furrows from the arc line into the depression (see 5–10).

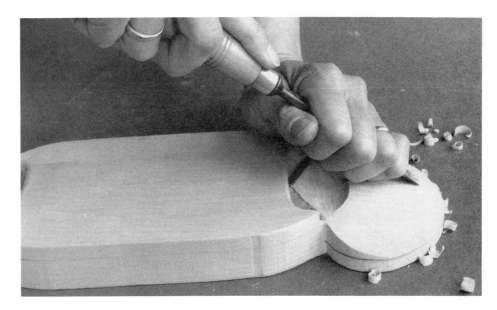

5–8 Slice down and out from the arc line, towards the outer edge of the shell.

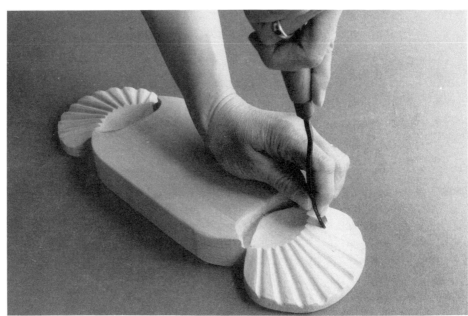

5–9 Scoop away the waste wood on the shell surface, keeping a strong furrowed look.

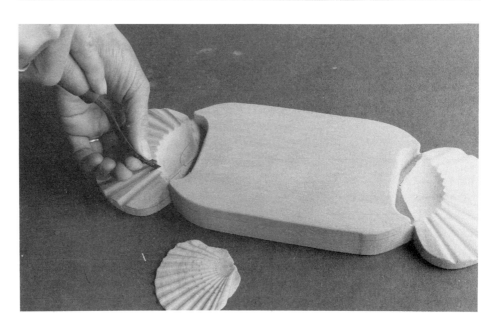

5–10 Run a fan of V-section furrows from the arc line down into the depression.

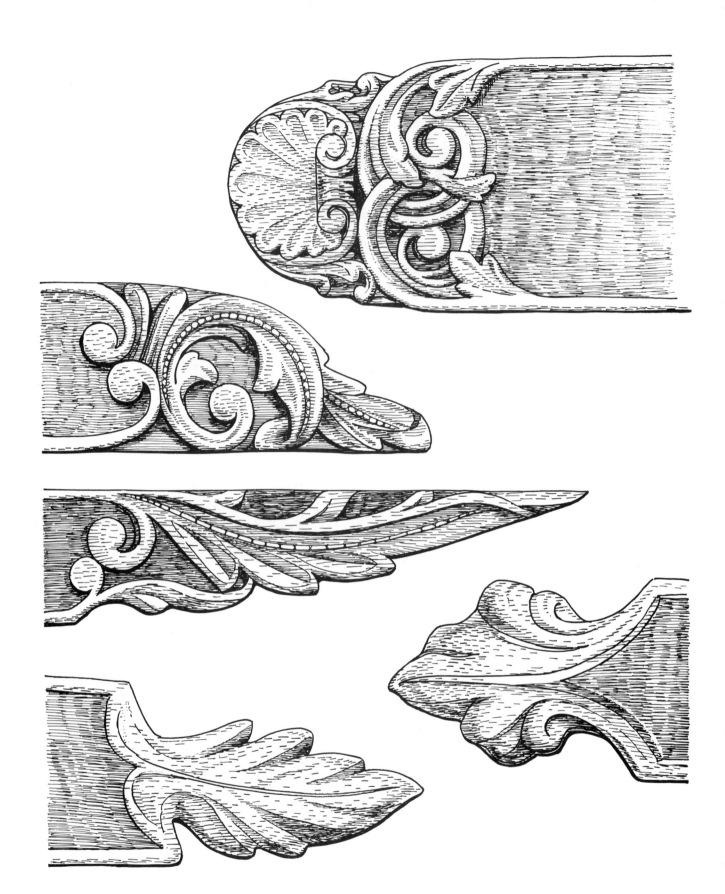

Inspirational drawings   Top: Name-board end from the four-masted German schooner Teie, *built in Tonsberg in 1819 (Handels-og Sofartsmuseum, Paa, Kronsberg Hooge, Germany). Middle two: Name-board ends from the three-masted schooner* Emanuel, *Thoro, 1880 (Handels-og Sofartsmuseum, Paa, Kronsberg Hooge, Germany). Bottom, left and right: Quarter board from an unknown ship, feathered-end detail, nineteenth century (Maryland Historical Society).*

Painting and Finishing

With all the dips and furrows established, go over both shells with fine-grade sandpaper, bringing them to a good finish. Smooth out the depression, tidy up the dips and rises so that they run smoothly into one another, rub the edge of the shells smooth, and so on. Continue until all edges and faces are clean and smooth to the touch.

Being well satisfied with the overall effect, wipe away the debris and move to the dust-free area that you have set aside for painting. Start by giving the whole workpiece a generous coat of matt white. When the undercoat is crisply dry, give it a swift wipe-over with fine-grade sandpaper so as to remove any nibs and grain whiskers. Then paint the shells gold and the board green.

Painting tip: Although acrylic paint is water-based, it is wonderfully hard-wearing—but only if you cover it with varnish. Varnish all faces and edges, even the back of the board.

If necessary, lay on several coats of paint until you have a dense cover. Wait until the paint is dry, and then give the whole workpiece a couple of coats of clear varnish. While the varnish is still wet, mix a smidgen of sepia oil paint in with a small amount of varnish and stroke the whole board down with a dry brush so as to achieve a slightly grained patina effect. Finally, paint the name or number on the board, mount it on the side of your boat with brass screws, give it another coat of clear varnish, and . . . you are ready to cast off!

TROUBLESHOOTING AND POSSIBLE MODIFICATIONS

- If you like the idea of the project but need a longer board, then stay with the width and simply increase the length.
- Choose your wood with care. A knot or split at the end of the board might well result in a real disaster.
- If you need to carve more than one board, then carve all the boards at the same time—fret out all the ends, mark out all the shells, gouge out all the scoops, and so on. If you work in this fashion, you are more likely to achieve a matched set.

1566

6
Scroll

One look through a collection of old wooden sailing-ship designs, a visit to a maritime museum, or, better yet, a walk around an old surviving ship will confirm that one of the most beautiful and indeed one of the most common motifs traditionally used in ship carving is the scroll. There are scrolls just about everywhere. Full figureheads are often standing on scrolls, three-quarter figureheads—like our Jenny Lind—are usually part scroll, small bust figureheads are presented on scroll-like shelves, there are sometimes scrolled forms at the end of stern boards, there are scroll brackets in cabins, and so on.

It could be argued that the history of the ship's figurehead—meaning the decorative carving at the head of the ship—starts and finishes with a scroll. The evolutionary sequence goes something like this: the first Viking ships are shown as having scroll-like forms at the prow, the scroll gradually changed to become a stylized beast mounted on a scroll, the animal and mythical creatures were then replaced by figures still mounted on a scroll, the figures gradually came to be reduced in size until they were replaced by busts and heads, and so on . . . until finally the wheel turned full circle, with figureheads falling from favor, to be replaced by billet-head scrolls. The interesting thing is that, although figurehead fashions and forms have changed and evolved over the years, the scroll is nearly always featured in the design.

As to the various names and types, a billet head is a scrolled form with the roll going over and forward, whereas the fiddlehead is a scrolled form with the roll going over and back, like the scrolled end of a fiddle.

THOUGHTS ON DESIGN AND TECHNIQUE

Take a look at the working drawings (see 6–2) and note how, at a grid scale of four grid squares to 1″, our bracket scroll is characterized by having both billet-head and fiddlehead elements. That is to say,

6–1   Finished scroll.

the top curls over and back like the scroll at the head of a fiddle, while the bottom curls forward. Note, also, the way the stylized form is rolled over so that, when it is seen in front view, the ends stick out, like a scrolled roll of paper.

We have designed the scroll so that it can be used variously as a bracket under a shelf, a decorative feature that can be mounted in the top corner of a cabin doorway, a cornice in the angle between the cabin wall and ceiling, and so forth. This little beauty can be used as a decorative or functional feature in just about any situation where there is an angle to be filled. Or it can simply be used as a decorative piece, say, under a bowsprit or on the stem post.

A scroll carving tends to look extremely complex, but, in fact, the process is surprisingly straightforward. If you carve this project and show it to your friends, you are likely to get more compliments than you really deserve. Or, to put it another way, if you enjoy praise—"how amazing! what skill! what genius! how did you do it?"—then it's

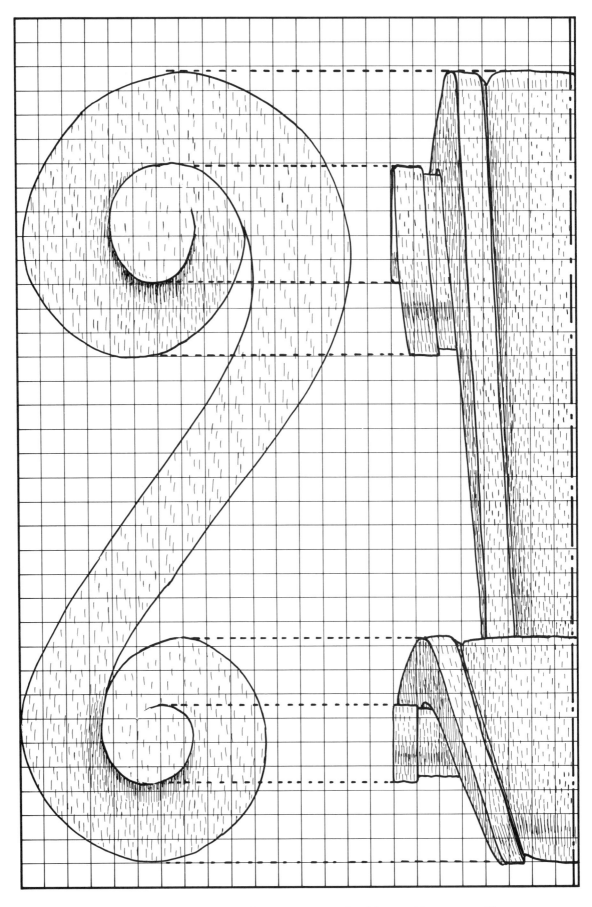

6–2 *Working drawings—front and side views, at a scale of four grid squares to 1″.*

best to keep the secret of scroll carving under your hat!

TOOL AND MATERIAL CONSIDERATIONS

This is the perfect project for beginners, in that, not only can the bracket be easily carved with a minimum of tools, but, better still, because the finished carving is designed to be painted, you can use just about any featureless easy-to-carve wood. With a scrap of jelutong or basswood and a shallow-sweep gouge and a penknife, you will be well on your way.

Although we used a band saw to fret out the blank, you could get away with clearing the rough with a saw, mallet, and straight chisel.

Wood-carving tip: If you plan on doing a lot of wood carving, it's best to get yourself a band saw. We use a Delta bench model with a 4″ depth of cut. Yes, you can use hand-held tools like a coping saw and a bow saw, but a band saw allows you to carve that much faster—without so much sweat.

TOOLS AND EQUIPMENT

For this project, you need:
- a piece of prepared 4″-thick wood that's about 10″ long and 5″ wide, with the grain running along the length—we used jelutong
- the use of a band saw
- two shallow-sweep straight gouges: ¼″ and ½″ wide
- a mallet
- a good sharp knife—we used a penknife
- the use of a workbench with a clamp
- a pencil and ruler
- a pair of dividers
- a sheet each of work-out and tracing paper
- a couple of soft-haired paintbrushes: a broad- and a fine-point
- a pack of graded sandpapers
- a can of matt white emulsion ceiling paint
- acrylic matt paints in red, black, and yellow-gold
- a can of high-gloss boat varnish

PROJECT STAGES

Drawing Out the Design, Setting Out the Wood, and Cutting the Blank

When you have sorted out all your tools and materials and generally prepared the workshop, take your work-out paper and draw the image out to full size. Draw out both the front and side views; see the working drawings (6–2). Having made sure that the scroll image is the right way around—meaning with the small end of the scroll facing the bottom front—play around with the S-shaped image until it nicely fits into a right angle.

Wood-carving tip: If you have doubts as to how the scroll looks in the round, then roll out a piece of Plasticine that's about ¾″ thick—like pastry—cut a 4″-wide strip, and have a trial run. See how the number of coils, the thickness of the coils, and the ratio between the coils and the length of the scroll determine its character.

Having achieved what you consider to be a good form, make a careful tracing. Pencil-press-transfer the traced image through to the side face of the wood, and shade in the areas that need to be cut away.

With the image in place, and having first checked to be sure that the band saw is in good condition—with a sharp, well-tensioned blade and all the guards in place—run the wood through the saw and fret out the S-shape (see 6–3). Make a series of tangential passes in order to cut as close as possible to the drawn line. Finally, take a sheet of coarse-grade sandpaper and rub the cutout down to a smoothly curved finish. The smoother the curves, the better the scroll.

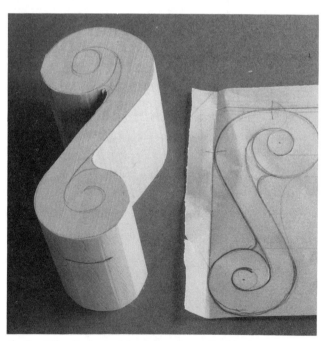

6–3 The S-shape blank cut from the block.

First Cuts

Take the cutout and very carefully run a central line down and around the whole form—that is, down the front face, around and under the small scroll, up the back face, and over and around the large scroll. It's vital that the central line is well

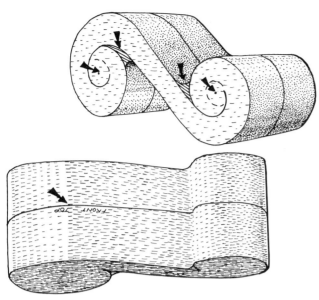

6–4 *Left: Run a central line down and around the entire form. Right: Draw in the inside of each of the coils as well as the midpoint, and shade in the V-section of waste where the coil winds back on itself.*

placed, so spend time getting it right. If need be, use a pair of dividers and/or a strip of masking tape to plot the position of the line. With a pencil, label the workpiece "front," "top," and so on (see 6–4, left).

Set the wood down on the workbench, so that one or the other of the side faces is uppermost, and reestablish the complete side image. Do this on both side faces. Make a special point of drawing in the inside of the coils and marking the midpoints. Shade in the little V-section of waste that occurs where the coil winds back on itself (see 6–4, right).

When you have drawn out a good, clear smoothly lined image on both side faces, use the mallet and gouges to sink the drawn lines in with stop-cuts.

Carving the Sides of the Scroll

Before you go any further, take a good look at the photographs and consider how, when seen from side view, the sides of the scroll could be likened to a road or track that winds down and around from a high point. Staying with this imagery, and starting at the big end of the scroll, the road travels around and down to a low point at the bottom of the small scroll and then winds slowly uphill to finish in the middle of the small scroll. The important point to bear in mind is that, if we compare the side view to a track and the middle of the scrolls to peaks or hilltops, then the two peaks are both at the same level. Or, to put it another way, when you are done

carving, the middle of the scroll should be the only part of the original face of the wood that remains uncarved. See the working drawings (6–2, front view).

Once you are absolutely clear in your own mind as to how the scroll needs to be worked, and having set the drawn lines in with stop-cuts, then it's time to get down to work. Take a shallow-sweep gouge, and starting on one side of the scroll only and at one or the other of the middle-of-coil high spots, skim back the waste so that the "track" begins to travel downhill. Don't rush or force the pace, but simply skim back the surface until neighboring winds of the scroll begin to be set at different levels. As you cut back the waste, make a conscious effort to angle the face of the track ever so slightly, so that it slopes out towards the outer edge.

As you cut the track lower and still lower—and having noted how the face of the scroll is revealed as the surface of the track is cut away—you will have to keep reestablishing the original drawn line, or track, edge with stop-cuts (see 6–5). Because part of the secret of carving a successful coil

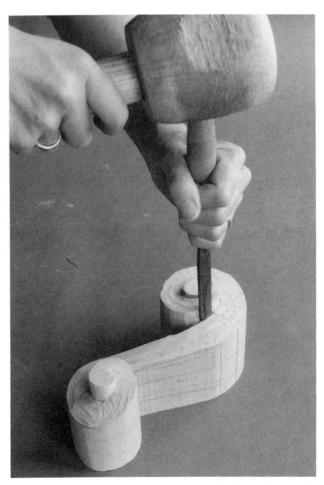

6–5 *Continue to make stop-cuts with the mallet and gouge, slowly reducing the waste wood.*

6–6 *Skim back the surface so as to create the winding downhill "track."*

6–7 *Transfer the level of the track, by taking a series of divider step-off points from the central line.*

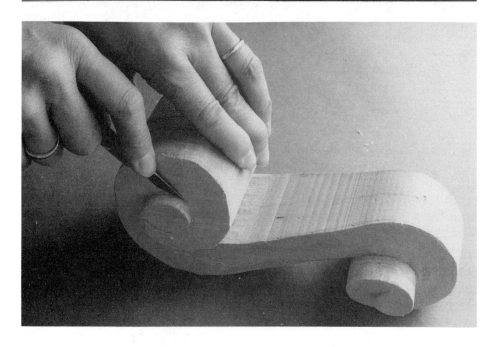

6–8 *Use a knife to clean and tidy up all the right-angle areas.*

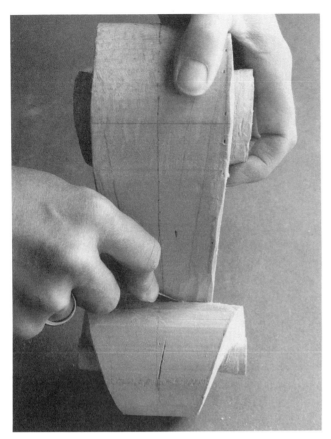

6–9 Use the knife to deepen the cleft where the scroll end appears to roll back over itself.

lies in your ability to ensure that the revealed sides of the coil remain more or less at right angles to the surface of the track, make sure when you are sinking the stop-cuts that you hold the tool upright.

Wood-carving tip: It's important when you are sinking the between-coil stop-cuts that you don't lean on the tool or hold the tool so that the surface

of the track is undercut. The little truth to remember is that, as the track winds downhill—to reveal a face that is at right angles to the track—the new face will carry the marks left by a badly delivered stop-cut. If you make a sloppy cut, the revealed face will show it.

Now continue defining the edge of the track with stop-cuts and skimming back the surface (see 6–6), until the lowest point of the track occurs at the bottom back of the small end of the scroll. Proceed until this low point is about ¾″ away from the central line. When you are pleased with the overall look of one side face of the scroll, very carefully transfer the level of the track, by taking a series of divider step-off points from the central line (see 6–7), and then carve the other side of the scroll in the way described.

Carving the Face of the Scroll

When you have carved both sides of the scroll so that they are more or less mirror images—so that the form is symmetrical when seen from the front—use a knife to tidy up all the right angles (see 6–8). Have another look at the working drawings and photographs, and note how the face of the scroll has raised edges and a slightly convex, or cambered, middle section.

Take a knife and, one end at a time, deepen the cleft where the scroll end appears to coil over on itself (see 6–9). Slice the valley deeper, and tidy up the edges, until the crease is crisp enough to fool the eye into believing that the scroll does indeed coil around over itself—like a spring or spiral.

Take a soft pencil with a sharp point, and set the

6–10 Sink a stop-cut ¼″ and parallel to the edge.

face of the scroll out with a line that runs ¼″ in from the edge. By this, we mean a line on the face of the scroll that is parallel to the edge, or a line that starts at one end to follow the face of the scroll around so as to finish up at the starting point. Do this on both side edges, so that the scroll has crisply defined borders when seen from the front.

When everything is fine and dandy, take a sharp knife and slice the drawn lines in with stop-cuts (see 6–10 on page 73). Aim for a clean-lined cut at a depth of about ⅛″. Then take a shallow-sweep gouge and slice out from the middle to the side—that is, into the stop-cut—so as to create a smoothly curved face that runs down into the wood (see 6–11). Work right around the scroll and on both edges. Next, follow up with a sharp knife, skimming back the gouge marks in order to leave the curved face looking smooth and crisp—like a cambered road.

Continue cutting the stop-cut deeper, slicing down into it with the gouge, and skimming off and tidying up with the knife, until the central ground runs in a smooth convex curve down into the crease and the edge borders stand proud. Although the overall procedure is fairly simple, things do start to get a little bit tight when you come to the scroll ends, where the coil appears to roll over itself. If you look at the photographs, you will see that, at the point where the face of the scroll rolls around to disappear from view into the between-coil crease, there is a small angled wedge of face wood that is enclosed on both sides by the proud edge. The best way to carve this area is to

use the point of the knife and a scrap of sandpaper.

Finally, when you have worked the scroll to your satisfaction, use the knife and fine-grade sandpaper to bring the surface to a good finish.

Painting and Finishing

When you are happy with the overall carving, wipe away the dust and move to the area that you have set aside for painting. Start by laying on an all-over coat of matt white emulsion. When the white ground is crisp and dry, rub it down with fine-grade sandpaper so as to remove all the rough grain and nibs. Repeat the painting and rubbing-down procedure until you have achieved a smooth finish. Then study the painting guide (see 6–12).

Having once again wiped away the dust, paint the edges and sides matt black and the central face a good rich red. It is difficult to paint into a crease, so it's best to lay on the black first—with a small amount of overlap running into the crease—and then to lay on the red. By working in this order, you can use a fine-point brush to cut the red back into the crease.

Having waited until the black and red ground colors are completely dry, take a fine-point brush and the yellow-gold paint and paint in the decorative trim lines. Last, give the whole works a couple of coats of clear high-shine varnish—and the bracket is finished.

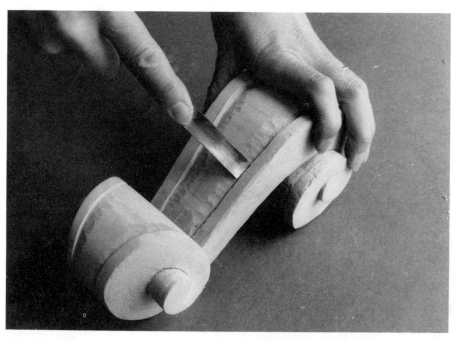

6–11 Make a series of shallow slicing or skimming cuts to create a face that curves down into the stop-cut.

6–12   *Painting guide.*

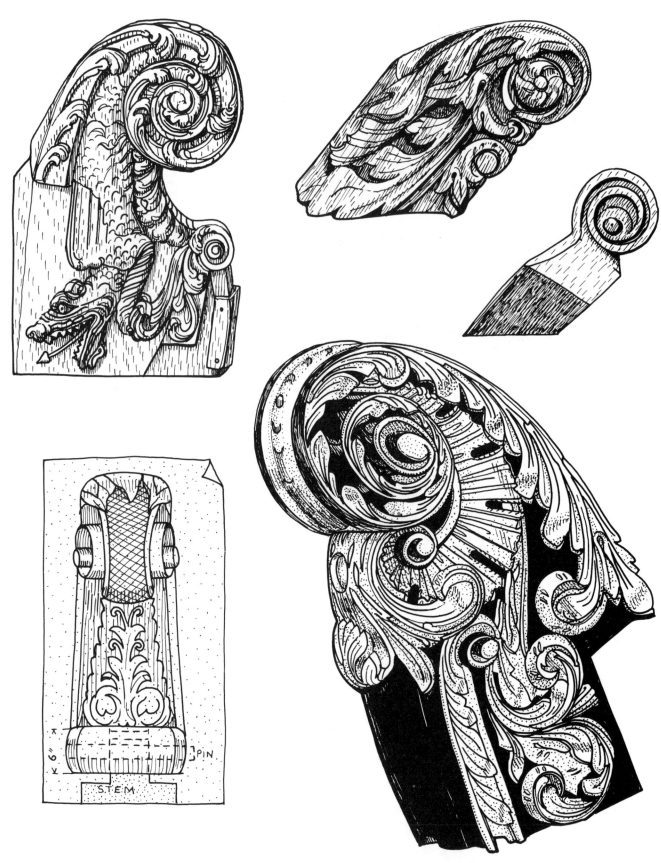

Inspirational designs   Top left: Billet head said to have come from the American frigate Constitution *in service in the 1812 war and removed from the ship in 1834. Top right: Two billet heads dated about 1860 and 1900. Bottom left: From a drawing (front view) of a billet head, dated 1874, from the schooner* A McNichol, *by Holman Chaloner. Bottom right: Scrollwork billet head from the ship* Award, *built in Quebec in 1859, painted and gilded (Valhalla Museum, Scilly Isles).*

TROUBLESHOOTING AND POSSIBLE MODIFICATIONS

• If you are going to carve a scroll bracket for indoors, then there's no problem. But if you are going to mount the scroll on the outside of your boat, be sure to protect it from the weather with extra coats of varnish. It's best to apply three or four coats of top-quality boat varnish and to situ-ate the carving under an overhang.

• When you are rubbing down, be sure to use fine-grade sandpaper and be careful not to blur the form.

• There's no denying that painting the scroll is tricky—it's difficult to achieve a clean-lined fin-ish. The best advice to follow is to rub down the workpiece well and then lay on the trim lines with a long-haired lining brush.

Sloop

7

Stem, Stern, or Trail-Board Acanthus Decoration

7–1   The finished acanthus section—painted golden yellow on a natural mahogany ground.

The grand wooden sailing ships of the seventeenth and eighteenth centuries—with their carved-and-decorated stern boards, rails, brackets, catheads, trail boards, billet heads, and fiddleheads—were designed primarily to convey an impression of stateliness, strength, speed, and power. The angle of the figurehead with its flowing swept-back forms, the sweep of the trail boards as they curved up to the figurehead, and the flourish of the stern boards were all carefully considered features that gave the overall impression of the ship surging forward.

Our acanthus leaf was inspired by a stern-board decoration from the American whaler *Eunice H. Adams*, build around 1845; see the inspirational designs (bottom).

Although the carvings were worked as individual pieces and then attached to the ship, the intention of the shipbuilder was to have the various pieces all tie in with one another, so that the ship would be seen as a single carved and decorated entity. The wood-carvers linked the individual carvings by running bands of secondary infill pattern from one primary feature through to another. One of the most popular design tricks, or ruses, was to carve a run of stylized and scrolled relief-carved acanthus leaf, and then to fill in the gaps with it where they occurred.

The acanthus leaf is a simple motif that can be traced back to classical Greek and Roman times. Although it is no more than a curved stylized leaf—an abstract form that has no symbolic or national significance—the clever thing is that it seems to fit most situations.

In the context of ship carving, the acanthus design was traditionally reversed and played around with in so many ways that it was used to decorate just about everything from corner brackets and catheads to cabin cornices and curved boards. If there was a gap in the running carvings or simply a blank surface that needed decorating, then it was more often than not filled in with an acanthus leaf.

If it's your aim to become an accomplished wood-carver, then you need to know how to carve this design.

THOUGHTS ON DESIGN AND TECHNIQUE

Examine the photographs and the working drawing (see 7–2 on next page), and note how, at a scale of two grid squares to 1″, the acanthus measures about 15″ long and about 5″ wide across the widest part of the leaf. Observe how we have simplified the potentially complicated bas-relief carving technique by eliminating the difficult and tedious stage of grounding, or groundwork. Instead, the acanthus motif is fretted out, mounted on a base

Inspirational designs (opposite)   Top: British Admiralty drawing of the stern decoration of the American frigate Raleigh—*launched in 1779. Middle left: Details from stern-board designs by wood-carver Edbury Hatch of Newcastle-Damariscotta, U.S.A., 1870. Middle right: Gilded pilaster capital from a ship cabin, c. 1880, from a collection in the Old State House, Boston. Bottom: Detail from a stern-board decoration, 84″ long, from the American whaler* Eunice H. Adams, *built in Newport, Rhode Island, in 1845.*

7–2 *Working drawing—the scale is two grid squares to 1″. Note the two fastening dowel pegs.*

board, and then carved and moulded. This method not only shortcuts the need to recess all the groundwork around the motif, but better still, it means that you can use a much thinner slab of wood.

Note how, for ease of carving and to minimize potentially weak areas of short grain, the motif is positioned so that the grain more or less runs through the length of the leaf. Mounting strength is achieved by having the cutout dowel-pegged as well as glued.

TOOL AND MATERIAL CONSIDERATIONS

This is a good project for novices and experts alike, because not only is it swift and easy to carve, but the technique is such that a bas-relief effect can be achieved with a minimum of time, sweat, and wood.

As you will be using thinner wood, it's all the more important for you to choose your wood with extra care. Ideally, the wood should be reasonably easy to carve, hard and tight-grained, as strong as possible across the short grain, free from knots, and warp-resistant. We chose maple, but you could just as well go for, say, oak, birch, beech, and even some types of pine. Much depends on where the carving is to be situated. If, for example, it's going to be outside in all kinds of weather—say, on the trail board—then it must be hard, dense, and resistant to warps. Then again, if it's going to be given wall space in a nice warm dry cabin, you don't have to be quite so choosy.

As for special tools, ideally you need to use either a band saw with a fine blade or a scroll saw.

Wood-carving tip: If you don't have access to an electric band or scroll saw, then you can just about get away with using a coping saw. Yes, it will be a long process, but it will get the job done.

TOOLS AND EQUIPMENT

For this project, you need:

• a 1″-thick slab of hard, dense wood that's about 15″ long and 8″ wide for the acanthus carving—if you want to make a run of carving, then select one or more lengths to suit
• a suitable backing board—we used a 1″-thick piece of mahogany, but you might want to mount the carving directly onto your boat or whatever
• a 6″ length of ½″-diameter hardwood dowel
• the use of a band saw or scroll saw
• a bench drill with a ¼″-diameter drill bit
• a coping saw
• a ¼″-wide parting tool
• a ¼″-wide U-shaped gouge
• a ½″-wide shallow-sweep gouge
• a good sharp knife
• the use of a workbench with a clamp
• a pencil and ruler
• a sheet each of work-out and tracing paper
• a soft-haired paintbrush
• a pack of graded sandpapers
• a quantity of PVA adhesive
• a roll of masking tape
• acrylic paint in yellow and gold
• a can of high-gloss boat varnish

PROJECT STAGES

Drawing Out the Design, Tracing, and Fretting

When you have gathered your tools, selected your wood, and generally decided how and where you want your carving to be set up, spend some time rehoning or sharpening your tools.

Wood-carving tip: It's a good practice at the beginning of a project to build up your feel-good-and-want-to-get-started factor by tidying up the workshop, rehoning the chisels and gouges, sharpening the knives, and setting out the tools so that they are comfortably close at hand.

Being mindful that our carving is no more than a demonstration piece—a small section that would in the normal course of events be repeated and reversed to make a long run—draw the design up to size and decide how it needs to be set out to suit your needs. For example, you might want a couple of leaves, an extra curve, a reversed design, or something else; refer to the inspirational designs for ideas.

Take a clear tracing from the master drawing, and then carefully pencil-press-transfer the traced outline through to your wood. Be sure that the

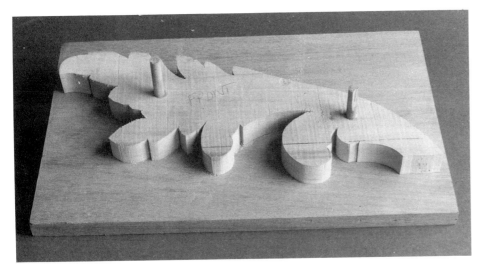

7–3 The sawn profile glued and pegged to the backing board. Note the grain match-up between the two pieces of wood.

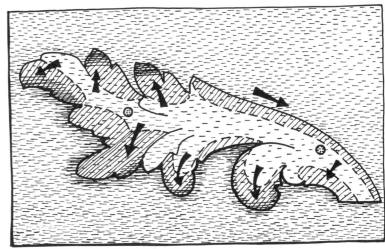

7–4 Right: Spend time shading in the areas that need to be lowered. The darker the shading, the deeper, or lower, the carving. Bottom: Set all the steps and overlap lines in with stop-cuts.

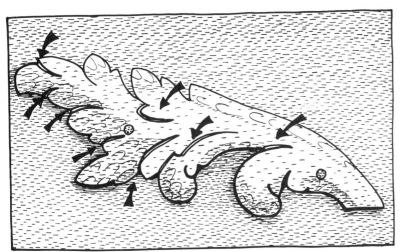

design is arranged so that the grain runs more or less from end to end through the leaves. Rework the profile outline so that it's clean and clear.

With the contour in place on your wood, run it through your saw, carefully cutting out the design. Feed the wood through at an easy pace, all the while making certain that the blade is presented with the line of the next cut. Being sure to run the line of cut a little to the waste side of the drawn line, aim for clean, smooth lines and crisp, sharp angles.

Mounting, Gluing, and Dowelling

Having achieved an accurate clean profile, swiftly rub the cut edges down with sandpaper. First remove any ragged nibs and splinters, and then rub down the whole underside until it's level and even.

Also, rub the backing board—your cut board or whatever—down to a smooth, level finish. Then position the cutout on the backing board and draw in a few alignment marks. Spread PVA adhesive evenly over both mating surfaces, set the cutout in position, and clamp up.

Mark out the position of the two dowel holes—as shown in the working drawing—and run them through with the ½″ drill bit. Go at least 1″ into the backing board.

Wood-carving tip: If you are going to attach the carving to your boat, you might as well leave the gluing and pegging until the carving is finished. You'll need at least two pegs for each carved motif.

Use the corner of a chisel to scratch a few furrows along the length of the dowels; then dip them in glue and tap them home (see 7–3 on page 81). When the glue is dry, cut the dowels back with a coping saw and chisel and rub the wood down to a smooth finish.

Setting Out and Roughing Out

With the cutout well mounted, fasten the tracing in place with tabs of masking tape and carefully pencil-transfer the traced lines of the design through to the wood. When you are happy that all is correct and as described, remove the tracing and shade areas that need to be lowered: where a leaf curls over and where one leaf is set slightly behind another (see 7–4, top, on page 81).

Wood-carving tip: If you are making a small exhibition sample—like ours—use a clamp to hold the work secure and protect the lowered ground from tool run-off with a piece of cardboard.

Take the mallet and the ½″-wide gouge, and set to work cutting back and rounding over the shaded areas. Cut from high to low wood—that is, from the middle of the waste down and out toward the edges of the cutout (see 7–5). And so you continue, cutting back little by little, until you have lowered and rounded selected leaves. Don't be in too much of a hurry. It's best to skim back a little waste, stand back and assess the cut, and so on, until the different forms and levels begin to stand out. Study the side view shown in 7–6 for a better understanding of the various planes, dips, and hollows. Notice how the top side and the tip of the leaf fall away at a very steep angle so as to finish about ¼″ up from the base, or ground.

Take a pencil and redraw where the individual leaves variously step down and appear to overlap. Take the mallet and small gouge or chisel, and carefully set the step and overlap lines in with stop-cuts (see 7–4, bottom). Set the lines in to a depth of no more than about ⅛″ (see 7–7).

With the stop-cuts in place, use the various sweep gouges to start carving back the different levels and curves that go into making up the individual lobes, leaves, and tendrils. Having noted how certain parts are somewhat hollow or concave while others are more rounded and convex, use your range of tools to carve the wood accordingly. To create the illusion that some leaves overlap others, you will have to keep lowering the stop-cut lines and skimming off, until the required depths and levels are achieved.

Aim to keep the surface lively and emphasize the rhythm by grouping and positioning the tool marks so that they run around the various curves in clustered sweeps. In other words, work with order and rhythm, so that the resulting tool marks add interest. However, don't overdo the tooling to the extent that the surface looks contrived.

Modelling and Finishing

When you have cleared away the rough and established the overall shape and level of the various leaves and lobes that go into making up the acanthus design, then come the physically less demanding and enjoyable tasks of modelling and finishing.

Spend time sanding and trimming back all the jags and rough surfaces. Make sure that the sawn edge of the profile is nicely tooled and finished. Then study the design, analyzing the shape and structure of the secondary veins, and draw them out accordingly (see 7–8 on page 84). Being aware that the run of the grain will inevitably tend to pull your lines off track, make a special point of seeing that the lines are smooth, curved, and flowing.

Use a good sharp knife to cut in the vein lines. With the knife held in both hands—one holding and pulling and the other steadying and guiding—set each drawn line in with two angled cuts, so that the waste comes away as a V-section, feather-ended sliver (see 7–9 on page 84). This is a tricky business, inasmuch as the knife will tend to keep running off track. But, on the positive side, by the time you've finished this procedure you will know all there is to know about going against the grain.

And so you continue . . . holding the knife at a low angle and doing your best to complete each vein with two sweeping, smoothly curved strokes.

Wood-carving tip: If you halt a vein in mid-cut, then the line will be broken and interrupted. It's

7–5 *Work systematically back from the edges, with a series of small scooping and skimming cuts to avoid tearing the grain.*

7–6 *Side view of the carving nearing completion—note the twists and curls of the individual segments, how the two bottom ones curl under, and the way some leaf areas are somewhat hollow.*

best to hold the knife at a low angle and make the dragging cut with your wrist on the inside of the sweep.

If, after making a twice-cut vein, you feel that the channel is a bit messy or not quite deep enough, then simply repeat the procedure. Once all the vein lines are in place, give the carving a swift rubdown with a sheet of fine-grade sandpaper.

Now for the big test! Stand back and give it the critical once-over. Ask yourself: Are the cuts bold enough? are the edges crisp and clean? do the vein lines help to give structure and emphasis to the form? is the whole carving a bit too blurred and bland? (See 7–10 on page 84).

When it passes your inspection, wipe it over with a damp cloth and move to the dust-free area that you have set aside for painting. Start by masking off the base board. That is to say, take a roll of masking tape and a scalpel and run a border of tape around the carving to protect the base from paint run-off.

Remembering to give it a light sanding between coats, lay on an all-over coat of matt white emulsion, followed by a coat of yellow paint, a coat of

7–7 *Set in a stop-cut where the overlapping segments need to be separated and lowered.*

7–8 *Mark out the veins with smoothly curved drawn lines that follow the sweep of the leaf.*

gold paint, and a couple of coats of clear varnish. Finally, give the carving a swift wipe-over with a sepia-stained varnish, and the carving is finished and ready for display!

TROUBLESHOOTING AND POSSIBLE MODIFICATIONS

• If you are going to carve an exhibition piece—say, to hang in the boat's cabin—then there's no

problem. But if you are going to decorate some part of the outside of your boat, be sure to protect the acanthus from the weather by using waterproof adhesive and three or four coats of top-quality boat varnish.
• When you are rubbing down, be sure to use a fine-grade sandpaper and be careful not to blur the edges of the cuts or scratch the base board.
• If you have any doubts as to how to fit several acanthus leaves together for, say, a run of pattern

7–9 *Draw the knife towards your body, using the index finger of your other hand to steady and guide it.*

7–10 The finished carving—see how, in this instance, the tool marks enrich the form and the gilded finish.

to fit a specific area, spend some time with tracing paper, measuring the area to be filled and playing around with different arrangements.

• Although the veins could be cut using a small parting tool, it is essential that the tool be razor-sharp. V-section tools are very difficult to sharpen—see Tools, Techniques, Materials, and Terms.

Barque.

8
Sea-Chest Panel

We all know about sea chests! Huge carved wooden boxes strengthened with iron straps, and with lots of boldly carved and painted imagery, such as a naïve motif, a set of initials, and maybe a date. For many of us, the very idea of a sea chest conjures up romantic flights of fancy that have to do with galleons, Long John Silver, pirates, pieces of eight, or *Moby Dick*. But, of course, the plain fact of the matter is that every sailor needed a functional chest for his clothes and personal possessions—a chest big and strong enough to be doubled up as a table or seat.

As to who carved and painted the imagery, the likelihood is that it would have been done by the sailors themselves. Just think of it: a voyage lasting a couple of years, very small, cramped quarters without windows, and only a few simple tools, like a jackknife, a gouge made from a barrel strap, and perhaps a paintbrush—what better way of relieving the boredom and tension than by decorating a chest with a carved-and-painted motif and maybe adding a set of rope handles!

Can you see in your mind's eye this candle-lit scene: a low cabin between decks, with a raggedy with a knife and gouge? As this self-taught carver sailor whittling and chipping away at his sea chest couldn't read or write and didn't have any pictures to copy, he undoubtedly would have chosen to carve a familiar image like, say, the ship and his initials, which would instantly identify the chest as his property.

The interesting thing about sea chests is that they are so personal, unpretentious, and low key. Of course, the sailor would have taken pleasure in his skills and wanted his carving, painting, and fancy ropework to be better than the next man's, but generally speaking, as he had very few preconceptions of how his artwork ought to look, he was usually able to achieve imagery that we would describe as being naïve and uninhibited. He had his tools, a predetermined space or panel to fill, and a lot of time on his hands—lucky man!

THOUGHTS ON DESIGN AND TECHNIQUES

Take a look at the photographs and the working drawing (see 8–2), and note how our panel mea-

8–1 The finished panel.

8–2 *Working drawing—at a scale of two grid squares to 1″, the panel stands about 18″ long and 12″ wide, with the grain running along the length.*

sures 18″ long and 12″ high. We copied the design directly from a sea chest made in Maine between the years 1840 and 1850. The chest is signed "Rufus Russell."

Consider how the design is achieved by lowering the waste ground so that the ship is standing in relief and then swiftly shaping up the profile so that the ship appears to be under full sail.

Having said that the design was more than likely carved by a seaman, we see that the masthead flags are pointing in the wrong direction. When a sailing ship is under full sail—with the sails billowing out with wind and the ship racing forward—the flags are also blown forward and away from the mast. So, does this mean that the chest was carved by a landlubber rather than a seaman? Then again, some old paintings with whaling ships show the flags pointing towards the prow. It's a bit of conundrum—is it not?

If you are interested in old ships, you could search old naïve paintings commissioned by owners, captains, and shipyards.

Finally, consider how the stylized ship looks all the more exciting and dynamic by being posi-

tioned slightly to the left, so that it appears to be racing forward.

TOOL AND MATERIAL CONSIDERATIONS

This is a good project for beginners, in that it requires a minimum of tools and expertise. All you need is a 1¼″-thick slab of easy-to-carve wood and a handful of tools, and you are ready to go.

Although we used a bench drill press and Forstner drill bits in various large sizes to lower the bulk of the unwanted ground around the ship—and it is a wonderfully swift and easy technique—this is not to say that you can't clear the ground with a hand-held router and/or a selection of dog-leg gouges and chisels. If you have both tool options, ask yourself whether you want a few minutes of swift and noisy drilling or would prefer to use a slow but silent hand-held tool.

Regarding your choice of wood, we used jelutong, but you could just as well go for lime, mahogany, or even a straight-grained pine. And, although we chose to carve a panel, you could search around for an old chest and carve the motif directly onto the front panel. By "old chest," we mean an ordinary 1930s type of pine clothes chest, as might be obtained from a junk shop or flea market for a small amount of cash.

TOOLS AND EQUIPMENT

For this project, you need:
- a 1¼″-thick board of easy-to-carve wood that's 18″ long and 12″ wide, with the grain running along the length
- the use of a bench drill with a selection of Forstner bits
- two chisels: ½″ and ¾″ wide
- a ¼″-wide V-tool or parting tool
- two shallow-curve gouges: ¼″ and ½″ wide
- a ¼″-wide U-section gouge
- a ¼″-wide skew chisel
- a ⅛″-wide bent or spoon gouge
- a ½″-wide dog-leg chisel
- a small pointed drift, or punch, to make the "gun" holes in the gun ports
- a metal straightedge
- a knife
- the use of a workbench with a bench clamp
- a pencil and ruler
- a pair of dividers
- acrylic paint in sepia, to stain the wood
- a can of wood sealer
- a soft-haired paintbrush
- a pack of graded sandpapers
- a can of beeswax furniture polish or dark brown shoe polish

PROJECT STAGES

First Steps and Roughing Out

Having carefully chosen your wood and/or a suitable chest, set out your tools so that they are comfortably close at hand. Study the working drawing (see 8–2 on page 87), and note the scale of two grid squares to 1″. Draw the design up to size. Take a clear pencil tracing, and then pencil-press-transfer the traced lines through to the working face of the wood. Spend time making sure that all the lines are cleanly and smoothly set out.

When you are happy with the imagery, move to the bench drill and use the Forstner bits to lower the waste ground. All you need to do is set the depth stop to about ⅜″ and then work through the drill sizes, from large to small. Continue until the bulk of the waste ground around the ship and in the spaces around the sails has been removed. Try to stay about ⅛″ to the waste side of the drawn lines (see 8-3).

With most of the waste cleared, work through the various straight and curved gouges, making stop-cuts around the entire design. In the difficult-to-reach areas—meaning the little pockets between the sails—use the skew chisel to slice down into the corners. Be mindful that you need to stay within the guidelines, and be careful not to slice into the edge of the design (see 8–4). Go at it slowly, all the while being very careful not to run the blades into end grain or a fragile short-grain detail. Pare back to the drawn line, so as to

8–3 Use the drill to lower the waste ground, setting the depth stop to about ⅜″.

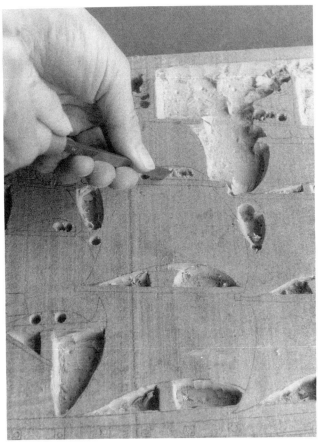

8–4 *Use the skew chisel for the small difficult-to-get-at areas, and slice straight down into the corners.*

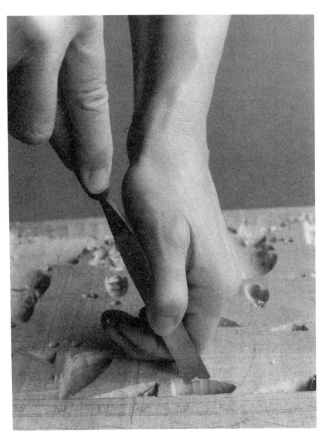

8–5 *Pare back to the drawn line, using one hand to guide the blade and the other to push and maneuver the handle.*

achieve a nice clean vertical face, or cliff (see 8–5).

Wood-carving tip: When you are working in small dips and holes, watch out that you don't lean on the shank of the tool so that it pries against the edge of the carving—you can do damage to both the carving and the tool.

Last, when you have worked around the image—so that the ship is raised up like a plateau—take the dog-leg chisel and systematically skim off the lowered ground so as to leave it looking clean and smoothly tooled (see 8–6).

When you are working in/on short-grain areas—like, for example, the ends of the spars and masts—be extra careful that you don't run the blade into the fragile grain. If you are a beginner, then be sure to hold the knife in a tightly controlled grip, while making the smallest of V-shaped cuts that follow and define the lines of the design.

Incising and Shaping

Once the profile is set out and the lowered ground tidied up, take the V-tool and outline the "waves." Don't cut too deep—about ⅛" is fine. Repeat the

8–6 *With a series of arclike movements—pushing the handle with one hand and guiding with the other—use the dog-leg chisel to gradually lower the ground until it looks clean and smoothly tooled.*

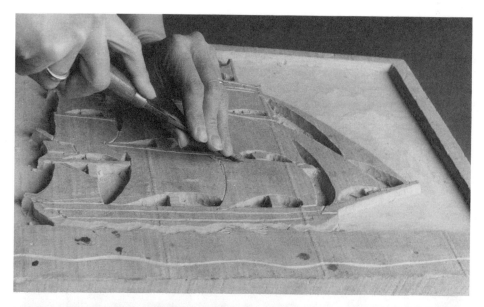

8–7   Use the V-tool to outline and define the sails and the drawn lines.

8–8   Having cleared the ground waste and outlined the imagery with V-cuts.

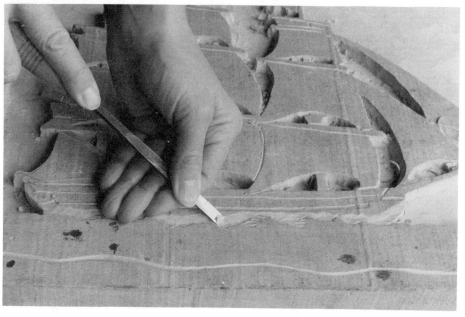

8–9   Reduce and shape the lower part of the hull, where it meets the line of the waves.

procedure so as to outline the individual sails, the spars (see 8–7), the gun ports, and all the drawn lines (see 8–8). When this is done, take a shallow gouge and reduce the lower part of the hull where it meets the wave lines and the leading edges of the sails (see 8–9 and 8–10). Being careful to work with or at an angle to the grain, lower the sails where they appear to overlap, the small parts of the mast that you can see between the sails, the flags, and so forth (see 8–11).

You won't have any problems, as long as the tools are sharp and you keep a close eye on the run of the grain. So, for example, when you are shaping the two sails that curve down from the front mast to the bowsprit—the spar that projects at the prow—you need to constantly change the angle of cut to approach the grain to best advantage. You work from top to bottom for the leading convex curves (see 8–12, left, on next page). Note how the sails are modelled—one edge sloping and the other curved (see 8–12, top right on next page). Go at it nice and easy, without forcing the tools, and if the grain begins to cup up roughly or if you can feel that the blade is running into end grain, then change the angle of approach. The simple rule of thumb is: if the tool slices through the wood and leaves a beautiful smooth surface, then you are doing it right—and if the surface appears rough and the going is difficult, then you are doing it wrong (see 8–12, bottom right on next page).

Continue until the ship stands out from the ground, the sails are rounded at the leading edge, the bowsprit is cleanly defined, and so on (see 8–13 on next page).

Modelling

Using variously the skew chisel, the knife, the dog-leg chisel, and the ⅛″ bent gouge, clean away the small areas of waste and tidy up the imagery. Chop

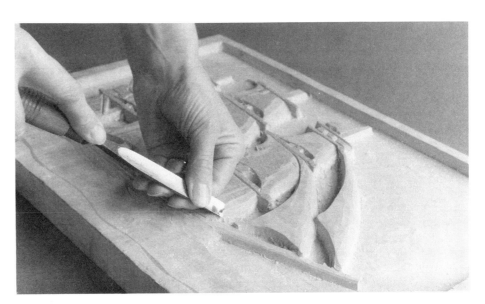

8–10 Round over the leading edge of the sails.

8–11 Be very careful, when you are lowering the ends of the masts and the flags, that you don't run the blade into the fragile short grain and split the wood.

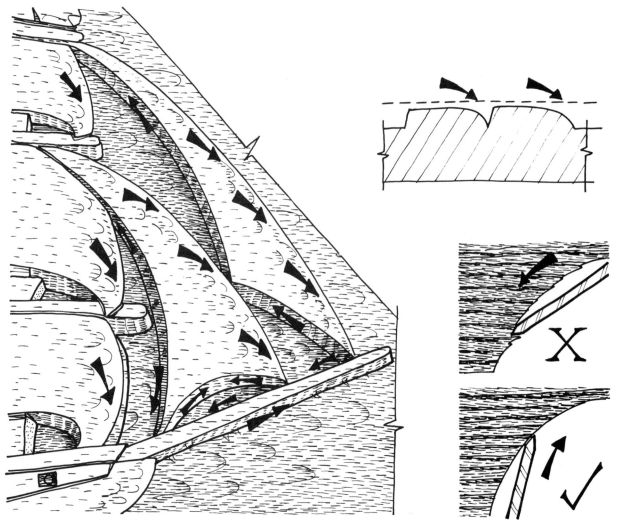

8–12   Left: When shaping the jib sails, work from top to bottom along the leading convex curves. Top right: A cross section through the two jib sails. Bottom right: The tool will leave a rough edge if you cut against the grain.

out gun ports, round over the crow's nests, and generally work the entire carving until all the surfaces have been tooled.

Wood-carving tip: It is very easy, when clearing the background, to do damage to the ends of the masts and the various spars. Be sure to angle away from the fragile short-grain ends and never try to undercut or slice directly into the end grain. A small piece of sandpaper folded into a point does a good job in these tricky areas.

Use the ¼″-wide U-section gouge to create the wave effect at the prow and stern and where the ship meets the sea and the sea meets the frame.

Having achieved what you consider to be a fair carving, then comes the tricky and somewhat tiresome task of cleaning up the ground behind the ship. The large areas are easy enough; you just take a piece of fine-grade sandpaper and rub away. But the small areas between the sails are a problem

simply because they are so small. You might try folding sandpaper into little points and wrapping it around the ends of sticks. It's not difficult—just frustrating and time-consuming!

Take a pencil and a short straightedge, and draw in on the lowered ground the small amount of rigging that occurs underneath the bowsprit. When this is done, use a small V-tool and/or a knife and straightedge to incise the drawn lines (see 8–14).

Wood-carving tip: Go over the whole works, making sure that all the spars and masts are straight. If necessary, use the rule and knife to slice away and adjust.

Work over the entire workpiece, modelling the masts and crow's nests, tapering and sloping the flags so that they run down towards the ground, and so forth. Finally, give the project a swift sanding with the fine-grade sandpaper.

8–13 *Leave the leading edges of the sails looking rounded, and make sure that the bowsprit is cleanly defined at the point where it slots into the bow.*

Finishing

Having sanded the carving until you are happy with the overall effect, wipe away all the dust and debris and move to the clean dust-free area that you have set aside for painting and finishing. Start by sealing the wood with either a sealer or a thin coat of clear varnish. When the sealer is completely dry, give it a brisk rubdown with the finest grade of sandpaper so as to remove all the whiskers and nibs. Use acrylic paints or a water-based stain to color the wood. Aim for a dark brown—like an old piece of oak or stained-and-weathered pine. When the stain is dry, take a scrap of sandpaper and rub through the color at wear areas. Concentrate on the sharp edges of the frame, the top edges of the waves, and the proud areas in the middle of the sails.

Give the entire carving a generous coat of wax polish, buff it to a high shine, and then hang it on a wall or fasten it to a chest.

8–14 *Top: The direction of the incised cuts. Bottom: Make sure all the spars and masts are straight—if need be, use a metal rule and a knife.*

TROUBLESHOOTING AND POSSIBLE MODIFICATIONS

- Your choice of wood is of primary importance. It has to be smooth-grained, free from knots and splits, and easy to carve. If you have any doubts at all, ask the advice of a specialist supplier.
- When you are rubbing down, be sure to use fine-grade sandpaper and be careful not to blur the edges.
- When your workpiece is in the vise or being held down with the clamp, watch out that you don't crush the wood. It's a good idea to place a clean piece of smooth scrap wood between the vice/clamp and your workpiece.
- Always have your working drawings and photographs in view; then you won't lose touch with the subject. Stop every now and then along the way, and sit back and appraise your progress. Don't be in too much of a hurry to finish.

Inspirational designs (opposite)   Top left: Design inspired by the mariner's compass, or wind rose, based on the original division of the circle into eight primary winds—a device which has its roots in ancient Athens. Top right: Relief-carved anchor motif from the lid of a chest—dated Maine, 1840–1850. Bottom: Drawing of Columbus' flagship, Santa Maria, *based on contemporary models.*

Whaler

9
Sea-Monster Rail End

9–1 The finished carving—gilded, stained, and varnished.

In days long gone, when the great sailing ships were entirely dependent upon the whim of the wind and weather, and the oceans were as yet unexplored, every mariner had a yarn to tell about the marvels and mysteries of the immeasurable seas. There were legends, fables, and eyewitness accounts that told of sea snakes, giant squids as big as ships, sea dragons, mermaids, and all manner of weird and wonderful deep-sea serpents and sirens. The sea was a place of wonder, where anything and everything was possible.

Inspired by the stories of sea serpents and the like, the wood-carvers drew pleasure from embellishing the ships with all kinds of hybrid birds and beasts, snakes with wings, and so on.

Our particular fabled beast was inspired by the figurehead of the English Royal Barge of Frederick, Prince of Wales, built in 1731 (see the inspirational designs, top). It is part dolphin and part human, with a couple of other unidentifiable bits and pieces thrown in for good measure. One of the most exciting things about traditional nautical carvings of this character is that the carver was

9–2 Working drawing—at a scale of two grid squares to 1", the carving measures about 15" in length.

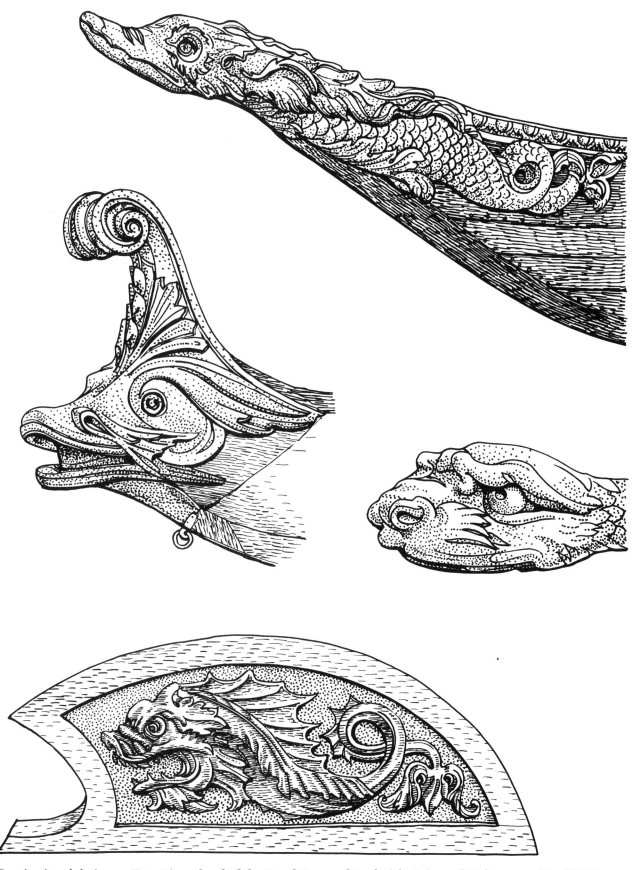

Inspirational designs   Top: Figurehead of the Royal Barge of Frederick, Prince of Wales, carved in 1731 by James Richard. Middle left: Figurehead of the Swedish Royal Barge Galten, *carved in 1787 by Johan Tornstrom. Middle right: Detail of a serpent figurehead from the American schooner/yacht* Phantom, *carved in 1865. Bottom: Rudder ornament, Dutch, early twentieth century.*

able to let his imagination run wild. Of course, he would have been given a brief with size specifications and whether it needed to be pierced and gilded or whatever, but, within those limitations, he was free to follow his own inclinations.

In the days when sailing ships had several decks, or levels, there were many locations where rails needed to come to a neat finish. Our carving is designed to bring an angle or step to a tidy, but dramatic conclusion. Such carvings can be seen as a finale—a climactic statement that brings a step or rail to an imaginative or graceful finish.

What else is there to say, except that if you are a carver who enjoys working on imaginative pieces, then this project is bound to be a whole heap of fun!

THOUGHTS ON DESIGN AND TECHNIQUE

Take a look at the photographs and the working drawing (see 9–2 on page 97), and note how, at a scale of two grid squares to 1″, the total rail ending—the beast and its surroundings—is cut from a 1¼″-thick slab of wood that's 18″ long and 6″ high.

Although we envision this carving as being placed on the end of the cockpit coaming, this is not to say that it can't be used in just about any situation where there is a right-angled step between a vertical and horizontal surface. So, for example, if you like the idea of the project but want a fancy detail for a hatch cover, a piece of trim for the side of a bunk, or something else, there's no reason why you can't change the scale and shape to suit your needs. If you do modify the shape, size, and wood thickness, you can still follow the same overall technique and procedure.

Study the various details, and see how the delicacy of the design has to do with the wood being pierced. In many ways this is a deceivingly simple project, because although the finished carving looks quite complex and detailed—almost carved

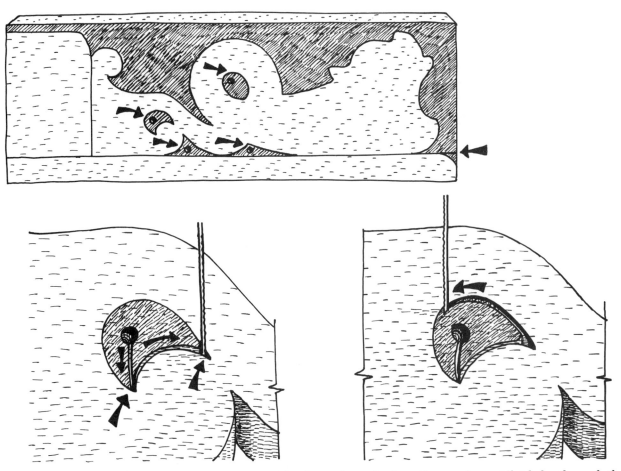

9–3   Top: Make a special point of using a straightedge to draw the base line, and run pilot holes through the four enclosed "windows" that need to be pierced. Bottom left: Pause at the corners, so as to make turn-around holes. Bottom right: Pivot the workpiece so that the blade is presented with the line of the next cut, and then proceed as already described.

9–4 *The completed cutout.*

in the round—it is, in fact, more of a flat plaque that has been relief-carved and pierced.

TOOL AND MATERIAL CONSIDERATIONS

For this carving, you do need to use a good range of tools, everything from a bench drill and a scroll saw to several fancy gouges. It's worth noting that if you decide to use a thicker wood or maybe carve a piece of wood that is part of your boat, you will have to forget about using the bench scroll saw and settle for doing the piercing with a hand-held coping saw and/or a selection of drills and a keyhole saw.

TOOLS AND EQUIPMENT

For this project, you need:
- a 1¼"-thick board, or plank, of easy-to-carve wood that's 18" long and 6" wide, with the grain running along the length.
- the use of a bench drill with bits of ⅛" and ¼" diameter
- three shallow-curve straight gouges for cutting the waves: ¼", ½", and 1" wide
- a ¼"-wide parting tool
- a ¼"-wide U-shaped gouge
- a ¼"-wide straight chisel
- a ¼"-wide skew chisel
- a ⅛"-wide bent, or curved, gouge
- a good sharp knife
- the use of a workbench with a clamp
- a pencil and ruler
- a sheet each of work-out and tracing paper
- a can of wood sealer
- a soft-haired paintbrush
- a pack of graded sandpapers
- a can of dark wood stain
- a can or tube of gold paint—we used acrylic
- a can of high-gloss boat varnish

PROJECT STAGES

Drawing Out the Design and Piercing

Having spent time making sure that your piece of wood is in good condition, check and hone your tools and arrange your working area so that everything is comfortably close at hand.

Now draw the design up to size, make a tracing, and pencil-press-transfer the main profile lines through to the wood. Make sure that the lines are cleanly established, and shade in the areas that need to be cut away. Make a special point of using a straightedge to draw in the base line.

With all the guidelines in place, run ¼" pilot holes through the four enclosed "window" areas that need to be pierced (see 9–3, top). When you are happy that all is correct, then move to the scroll saw. Start by cutting out the main profile, or outline. To cut out an enclosed "window," the working order is as follows: release the blade tension, unhitch the saw blade, pass the blade through one or another of the pilot holes, hitch up and retension, and fret out the enclosed piece of waste.

It's all fairly straightforward, as long as you make sure that the blade is well tensioned, the line of cut is a little to the waste side of the drawn line, and you take extra care when you come to a tight angle where you need to change the direction of the cut. The last point is especially important, because if you try to zoom around a sharp angle, then the chances are that you will break the blade. The best strategy is to slow down as you approach the corner, mark time on the spot—meaning on the corner—move the workpiece slightly until the blade has made a turn around the hole (see 9–3, bottom left), carefully turn the workpiece so that the blade is presented with the line of the next cut, and then continue on with the work (see 9–3, bottom right). Repeat the procedure with all four "windows" (see 9–4).

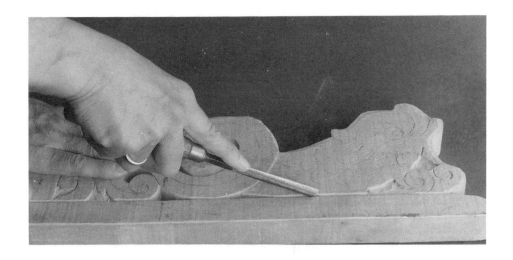

9–5 *Cut in, or sink, the drawn lines with the parting tool.*

Setting In the Stop-cuts and Roughing Out

Having fretted out the main profile and cut out the four windows, take the tracing and press-transfer all the other lines of the design through to the wood. Once again, make sure that all the lines are clearly set out and unambiguous. When you are happy that all is correct, take your V-tool/parting tool and painstakingly set all the main lines in with V-cuts (see 9–5).

Take one of your shallow-curve straight gouges, and swiftly work around the profile, slicing off the sharp edges. Don't fuss around too much at this stage; simply settle for rounding over the profile edge (see 9–6).

Position the workpiece down flat on the bench, and use a mallet and the various straight gouges and chisels to set the lines of the design in with stop-cuts. Concentrate at this point on the waves, the tail, the crossover in the middle of the body, the fringe of "gills" at the back of the head, the fin, and the lips. Chop the lines in to a depth of about ⅛" (see 9–7).

Wood-carving tip: Be very wary when you are chopping in the stop-cuts that you don't weaken the structure by overly working deign features that are aligned with the run of the grain.

With all the stop-cuts in place and the edges of the profile swiftly rounded over, it's time to lower the main areas of waste. Before you start, study the design (refer back to the working drawing) and see how the carving can be broken down into about four primary elements: the actual beastie, the four piercings, the lowered areas at the back of the tail, and the stylized waves at the head and tail.

When you have a clear picture in your mind's eye of how the design is to be worked, use the tools of your choice to lower and shape the wood accordingly. For example, you might use a shallow-curve straight gouge to lower the wood at either side of the crossover—the point where the beast coils around and crosses over itself (see 9–8 on page 102)—you might use a dog-leg chisel to lower the wood at the back of the gills (see 9–9 on pg. 102), and so forth. Be mindful that all you are aiming to do at this stage is to establish the various levels and begin the process of rounding over the edges.

The procedure is easy enough—all you do is lower the waste to the depth of the stop-cut and then repeatedly deepen the stop-cut and lower the waste until you reach the envisioned level. As long as you slice in a slow angle towards the stop-cut and make sure that you are working either across or at an angle to the run of the grain, then you won't go far wrong. The important thing to bear in mind is that the function of the stop-cut is to literally act as a brake to subsequent paring cuts. If you are doing it right, the force of your paring strokes will be contained and broken once the stop-cut has been reached.

Wood-carving tip: If you are a beginner and have doubts about how to make a particular cut, then set yourself up with a piece of scrap wood and have a trial run. If, for example, you are a little unsure of how to lower a small area, you might set a 1″ square in with stop-cuts and then experiment with your various tools to see how easy or otherwise it is to lower the ground within the square.

Modelling the Primary Details

When you have swiftly lowered the main areas of waste, then use the tools of your choice to model and shape the details that go into making up the design. Reduce the wood at the tail and either side of the crossover. Lower the main body area between the crossover and the back of the gills.

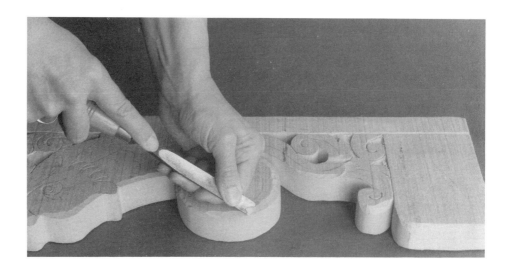

9–6 *Use the shallow-curve straight gouge to round over the profile edge.*

Model and round over the top of the head and the lips. Avoid cutting directly into end grain.

When you come to establishing the final rounded shape of the body, first draw a central line down and around the curved form and then shave out and down from either side of the line, so as to leave a spinelike ridge (see 9–10 on page 102).

You will find that the shadows cast by the spine strengthen the form, inasmuch as they imply that there is a force within the wood. The ridge breathes life into the carving by suggesting that the coiled form has an inner strength of sinew and muscle. This is a slightly tricky area to carve, in that as you work around the looped body, you have to constantly be aware of the direction of the grain in relation to your next cut. The simple rule of thumb to remember is that you must always be cutting from high to low wood—meaning, in this instance, that you must be cutting from the high ridge down, around, and under the curve of the body (see 9–11, top left on page 103).

If you find that the wood splinters or your blade is sliding into end grain, then the chances are that you need to change the angle of the cut.

Wood-carving tip: Don't try to cut all the delicate leaf shapes at this stage—it's best to cut the outer profile first.

To model the eye and the leaflike detail below the chin, start by enclosing the shapes with stop-cuts and shading in areas that need to be lowered. When this is done, carefully lower the area to the waste side of the stop-cuts, until the eye, brow, and mouth frills are left standing in relief. Once again, be careful that you don't overrun the stop-cuts and do damage to the eye. Work with very tight and restrained movements, all the while being prepared to pull back if you feel the tool running out of control.

Wood-carving tip: If you make a mistake and slice off an important detail that can't easily be modified—like, say, a nose or an eye—don't panic. Simply stick the wood back in place with Super Glue, and take more care the next time around.

When you are ready to carve the delicate leaflike shapes, be aware that the edges are very fragile and short-grained. They can easily be spoiled. The best procedure is to first carefully outline the de-

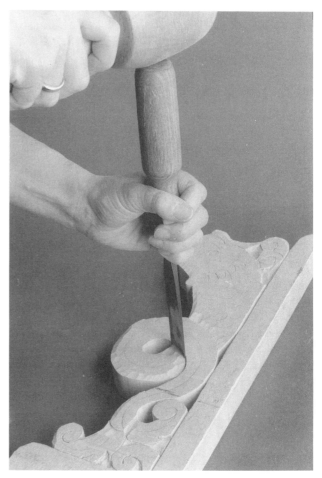

9–7 *Chop the crossover line in to a depth of ⅛".*

9–8 Use the gouge to reduce the waste, cutting at a low angle towards the stop-cut.

9–9 Hold the dog-leg chisel in both hands—one guiding and the other pushing—and pare away the waste wood.

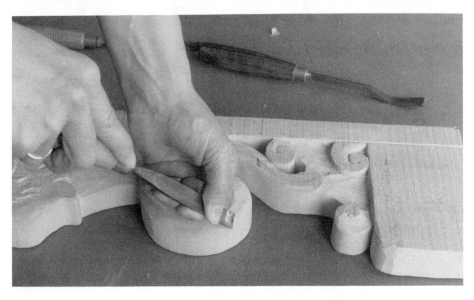

9–10 Shave the waste away from either side of the coiled body, so as to create a spinelike ridge.

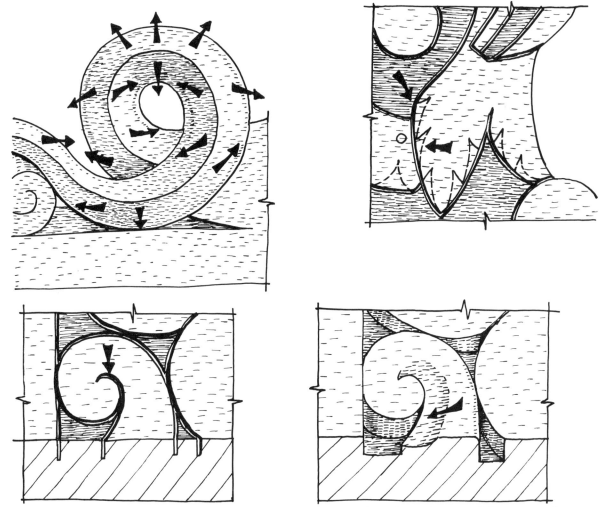

9–11 Top left: Cut from high to low wood and across or at an angle to the grain. Top right: Lower the waste, so as to leave the primary steps that go into making up the design. Bottom left: To carve the waves, use the gouge and the knife to set in the stop-cuts. Bottom right: Lower the surrounding waste, and use the knife or gouge to model the inner curve of the wave.

tails with V-cuts, then to use a knife to slice in stop-cuts, and finally to use the point of the knife to shave and lower the surrounding ground.

To carve the stylized waves (see 9–11, bottom left), start by using a gouge or knife to set in and define the scrolled shape with stop-cuts. Lower the waste from the surrounding ground. Repeat this procedure until the wave stands up in proud relief. When this is done, take a small gouge and carefully shave the waste from the inside curve. Slope the curve down so that the end of the wave—the little scroll detail—is left standing in relief. Once again, it's pretty straightforward, as long as you are mindful that the middle of the scroll becomes increasingly short-grained and fragile (see 9–11, bottom right).

The deepest areas—around the tail and below the chin—need to be lowered by between ⅜ and ½". Don't be tempted to lower the waste in a single cut; it's much better to work in a series of successive ¼" stages. Use the mallet and gouge to define the tail with stop-cuts, shave off the surrounding ground to the depth of the stop-cuts, make more stop-cuts, and so on, until you reach the required depth.

Final Modelling

Having used the gouges to define the outline of the eye, use the sharp knife to round over the edge. Work from the middle to the sides, until the eyeball stands up like a little rounded button. Follow the same sort of procedure for the lips. First define the shape of the lips with stop-cuts, then lower the surrounding ground so that the lips are left standing in relief, and, finally, model the curved edges round as the lips fall back to the ground.

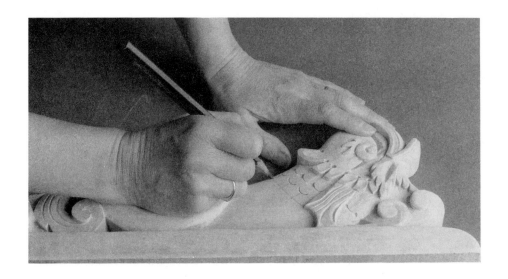

9–12 Draw in the guidelines so that they relate to your gouge sizes and sweeps.

To model the rufflike collar, or gills, first drill out the line of holes, then set in the petallike shapes with a sharp knife—to make stop-cuts—and finally slice away the small areas of waste between each pointed motif. Use the same technique to model similar areas, such as the eyebrows, the leaflike shape at the corner of the mouth, and the ends of the tail.

Wood-carving tip: When you come to carve the incised lines on the fin and tail, hold the knife with two hands. Maintain maximum control by holding and guiding the handle of the knife with one hand, while at the same time holding and guiding the blade with the other.

With the carving variously scraped, shaved, and sanded to a smooth-to-the-touch finish, then comes the very satisfying task of cutting in the scales. Start by using a pencil to carefully draw in the top three or four rows of scales that occur just below the collar. Relate the shape of the scales to

9–13 Use the guidelines to position the gouge, and then chop them in to a depth of about ⅛".

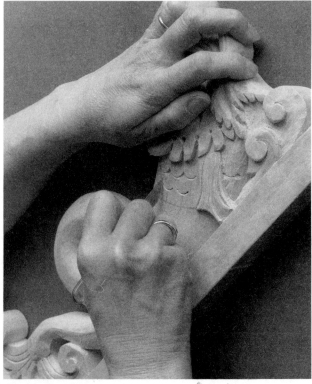

9–14 Remove the little triangle of waste from between each scale, link the gouge cuts with a stop-cut, and then slide the knife in at a low angle towards the stop-cut.

9–15 Rub the wood down to a smooth finish, and clear away the dust in preparation for painting.

one or another of your large shallow-curve gouges (see 9–12).

Use the gouge and mallet to chop the scale shapes in to a depth of about ⅛″ (see 9–13). Remove the little triangles of waste from between each of the scales (see 9–14). Set the pattern of scales in with stop-cuts, and then take a smaller gouge—one with a deeper U-section shape—and systematically remove the little scoop of waste from the middle of each scale. When you have carved the top three or four rows of large scales, use the smaller tools to cut the rows of smaller scales. Finally, when you come to the smallest scales, simply cut them in with a small gouge and leave them unmodelled.

Finishing and Painting

When you consider the carving done, use the knife and the fine-grade sandpaper to scrape and rub all the surfaces to a good finish. Pay particular attention to the eyeball, the lips, and the coiled part of the body. Continue sanding and working with the knife until you are pleased with the overall effect (see 9–14). Then brush away the dust and move to the area set aside for painting.

Give the entire workpiece a coat of sealer, let it dry, and then sand back all the nibs and whiskers of wood. Finally, stain the rail, give the beast a couple of coats of gold paint, give the whole works a couple of coats of yacht varnish, and WHOOPEE! the carving is finished.

TROUBLESHOOTING AND POSSIBLE MODIFICATIONS

- If you plan on carving an exhibition piece—like this project—then do as we have done. But if you are going to decorate some part of your boat, then decide whether or not you will be adding the carving as a piece of decorative trim or unscrewing or unbolting some part of the rail or whatever and carving that to shape. If you are going to carve a piece of your boat, much will depend upon the size of the piece to be carved and the type of wood. It will be great if you are going to carve a piece of mahogany, but heaven help you if you are going to carve a piece of knotty oak, or pitch pine!
- When you are rubbing down, be sure to use fine-grade sandpaper and be careful not to blur the edges of the cuts.
- If you have any doubts as to the shape of the project, make a maquette before even touching the wood.

Barquentine

10
Little Admiral Rudder Head

*10–1   The admiral rudder head—(A) front view,
(B) side view, and (C) top-front view, showing hat.*

Towards the end of the seventeenth century, the
solid stern sections of ships were gradually being
give a more open and decorative appearance.
With all manner of highly ornate stern galleries,
balconies, and colonnades being included in the
design, it became popular to run carved decorations all around the inside and the outside of the
stern area.

This desire for highly carved stern ornamenta-
tion found particular favor on small Dutch coastal
and inland vessels, where it became fashionable for
just about every part of the stern to be carved and
painted. For example, the helmsman's seats were
carved with biblical scenes, the rudder arm was
carved with lion and dolphin imagery, and the top
end of the tiller was carved with all manner of
highly dramatic lions, dragons, and dolphin

heads. Just about every surface was deeply carved and lavishly painted and gilded.

Of all the Dutch stern wood carvings, some of the most original—and certainly the most fun—are the figures that were traditionally used as crowns, or mounts, on the top end of the rudder post. Some of these rudder-post figures are truly amazing—lions, dogs, dragons, mythical beasts, bare-breasted women, soldiers with huge hats, characters part human and part animal—all deeply carved and gloriously painted.

I particularly like the portrait heads of captains and admirals. However, the term "portrait" should be used with some caution, since we don't know for sure that they are, in fact, portraits. But many of the figures are so personable and eccentric that the likelihood is that they were modelled from life.

THOUGHTS ON DESIGN AND TECHNIQUE

Take a look at the working drawings and painting grids (see 10–2, A, B, and C, pages 108, 109, 110), and note how, at a scale of three grid squares to 1″, the finished head stands about 10″ high and is a little less than 8″ in diameter.

Now take a look at the project pictures (see 10–1, A, B, and C), and consider the carving in terms of technique. It could be described as not so much carved in the round as a deeply cut, stylized relief that has been wrapped around the surface of a cylinder. However, the three-cornered hat could be described as being truly carved in the round, in that it is, albeit naïvely, a realistic three-dimensional rendition of a hat and feather.

If you are new to wood carving and interested in carving three-dimensional sculptural forms, then this project is a good gentle lead into the various in-the-round techniques. Although the finished carving looks relatively complex—with lots of details, color, and movement—the individual project stages are fairly simple and uncomplicated. For example, the wig and the ruff are really no more than a pattern of furrows and ridges. And, if you look at the front of the carving, you will see that the clothing details are made up from easy-to-cut bands of patterns.

All in all, the only slightly tricky areas to carve are the nose and mouth. As the grain runs up and down through the carving, both the nose and mouth are short-grained and fragile. You have to be very careful that you don't overrun with your strokes and slice off, say, the tip of the nose or the fullness of the lips.

TOOL AND MATERIAL CONSIDERATIONS

For this project, you do need to use a good range of chisels and gouges as well as a bench drill. Okay, maybe you could forget the drill and settle for clearing—with a great deal of sweat—the large amount of end-grain waste in and around the feathers with, say, a spoon gouge, but this will only add to the number of gouges you will need. If you only have a small tool kit, then it's probably best to get started and then revise the working methods to suit your tools. For example, you could get away with using a knife instead of a V-tool and a skew chisel.

With regard to the choice of wood, we have gone for jelutong, for the very good reason that our workshop is bulging with the stuff. Yes, jelutong is a good easy-to-carve wood, but you could just as well use lime, white pine, or just about any easy-to-carve wood that is straight-grained and free from knots. As to the size of the wood, we chose to laminate four prepared 4 × 4″ sections—finished at about 3⅞ × 3⅞″—because this is what we had. If you have a rounded section of a log of the right diameter, then give that a go.

Wood-carving tip: In our experience, it doesn't seem to matter how many sizes of wood we order; we are always looking for something different. Therefore, I usually order 4″-thick wood—in 4 × 4″ sections or as a 4″-thick plank—and then laminate or saw it down to suit the project at hand.

TOOLS AND EQUIPMENT

For this project, you need:
- four 9½″ lengths of prepared 4 × 4″-square jelutong
- a workbench with a vise or carver's chops
- a pillar/bench drill, Forstner bits, ½″ and ¾″
- a ¾″-wide chisel
- a 1″-wide straight shallow-sweep gouge
- a 1″-wide shallow-sweep bent gouge
- two U-section gouges: ½″ and ¼″ wide
- a ½″-wide dog-leg chisel
- a ¼″-wide V-tool
- a ¼″-wide shallow-sweep gouge
- a ¼″-wide skew chisel
- a small, sharply pointed knife
- a pencil and ruler
- a sheet each of work-out and tracing paper
- a pack of graded sandpapers
- a roll of masking tape
- a quantity of PVA adhesive

10–2, A   Working drawing and painting grid—front view. The scale is three grid squares to 1".

10–2, B   Working drawing and painting grid—side view. The scale is three grid squares to 1".

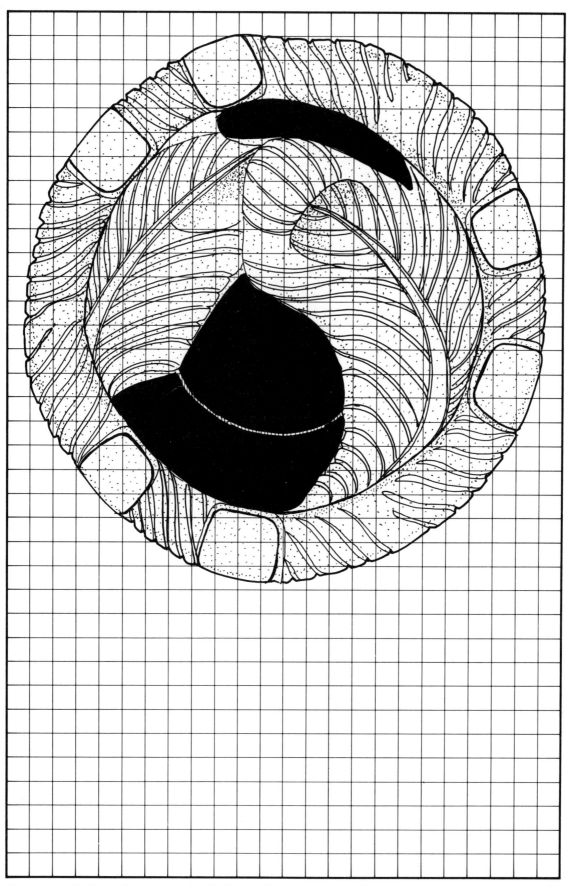

10–2, C   Working drawing and painting grid—plan view. The scale is three grid squares to 1".

- acrylic paint in black, red, pinkish-tan flesh tone, yellow, dark green, and gold
- a can or tube of matt white emulsion paint—as used for ceilings
- a can of clear high-shine varnish
- a small quantity of artist's oil sepia

PROJECT STAGES

Laminating the Wood and Setting Out the Design

Having studied the design, collected all your tools so that they are comfortably close at hand, and generally gotten ready for the task ahead, take your four lengths of prepared wood and glue them together, so that you have a block that's about 8 × 8″ square and 9½″ high. If the 4 × 4″ sections are in any way damaged or crushed at the corners, then make sure that the damage is contained well within the middle of the block or arrange it so that it will be cut away when roughing out. Strap the glued-up wood tight with rope or clamps, and put it to one side.

When the glue is dry, and having made full-size drawings and tracings of the front and side views, pencil-press-transfer the front view to one of the faces of the wood (see 10–3).

10–3   Pencil-press-transfer the traced image through to the wood.

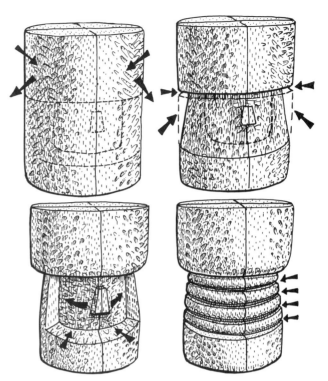

10–4   Top left: Remove the corners of waste, and carve to a cylinder. Top right: Sink a stop-cut around the bottom edge of the hat, and lower the waste below the line. Angle the surface into the stop-cut. Bottom left: Lower the entire face area so that the nose is left standing proud. Bottom right: Run four horizontal and parallel V-cuts around the wig area.

Clearing the Waste and Setting In the Design

Take the mallet and the 1″ gouge, and swiftly round off all the waste corners of the block (see 10–4, top left). Every now and again, call a halt to the carving and spend time reestablishing the lines of the design. Make sure that you have a good strong line at the bottom of the hat.

With the bulk of the waste cut away and all the primary lines in place, take a chisel and sink a stop-cut around the bottom edge of the hat. Now, working with the mallet and the gouge, cut up to the stop-cut, so as to lower the wood below the hat line (see 10–4, top right). Repeat the procedure until you have lowered the entire face-and-wig area to an overall depth of about ½″. Try to keep the cylindrical shape.

Select what you consider to be the best face of the wood, draw in the top-of-ruff line, and set it in with a V-cut. Use the tracing to transfer the placement of the nose. With all the lines in place, get to work lowering the entire face area around the nose, so that the nose is left proud (see 10–4, bottom left).

With the overall shape of the face more or less established, take the mallet and V-tool and run four horizontal and parallel V-cuts around the wig area (see 10–4, bottom right).

Roughing Out the Hat and Collar

Redraw the three-cornered shape of the hat, identify the shape and position of the three dips at the side, and then cut the dips back to a depth of about ½″ (see 10–5). Not forgetting about all the little decorative whorls—two at each peak—chop out the hat as it dips and peaks around the top edge of the brim (see 10–6, A and B).

Pencil in the shape of the hat as seen in top view: the crown, the gully around the crown, and the feathers. Shade in areas that need to be lowered (see 10–7, left). Now, having decided on the various depths of the crown, feathers, and gully, drill out the waste accordingly (see 10–7, right). Plan on having the crown about ¾″ lower than the topmost feather and the gully about ¾″ lower than the top of the crown.

After clearing a good deal of the waste and more or less establishing the various depths of the hat, take the gouge of your choice and start reducing and modelling the feathers. Don't aim for perfectly detailed realism; just go for big stylized forms. This particular part of the project is pretty

10–6   (A) Front view—note the nose area left standing proud. (B) Side view—with wig lines and the hat and face roughed out.

10–5   Use the gouge and mallet to reduce the wood at the hat brim.

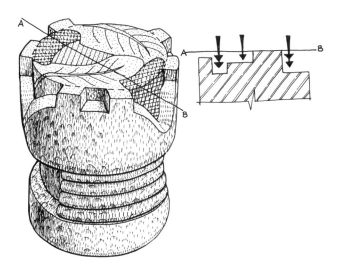

10–7 Left: Draw in the details of the hat as seen in the plan view—the brim and feathers—and shade in the areas of waste that need to be lowered. Right: Use the drill to swiftly sink the various depths of waste.

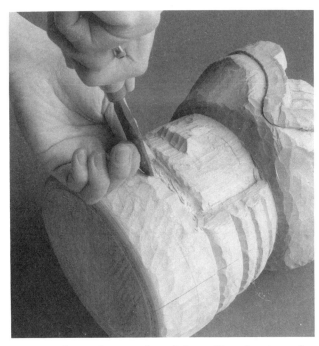

10–9 Shape the top edge of the ruff so that it angles into the neck cravat, leaving an undulating rippled surface.

hard going, as you will for the most part be trying to model end grain. It's not really tricky—just a hard slog!

Wood-carving tip: In carving the end grain of the feathers, it's best if you work with a slicing down-and-out cut. Be warned, if you try to cut directly down into the end grain, you will likely split the wood and/or get your tool stuck. It's much better

to approach it slowly, slicing little by little, than to risk disaster.

When you are satisfied with the top of the hat—the crown and feathers—run a line right around the hat, at a point about ½″ or so below the top

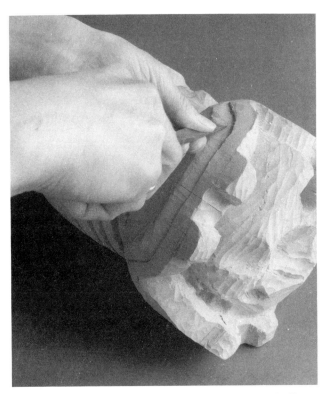

10–8 Slice across the grain with a series of shallow cuts, reducing all the waste below the stop-cut trench.

10–10 Front-plan view—showing the roughed-out forms of the hat brim and feathers.

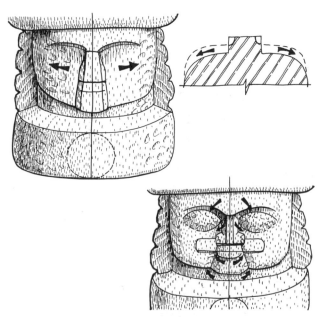

10–11 Top: Lower the brow and cheeks at either side of the nose. Bottom: Define the eye sockets, nostrils, whiskers, lips, and chin.

edge of the brim. Take a V-tool and run a stop-cut a little below the drawn line. When this is done, take a shallow-sweep gouge and reduce the sides of the hat so that they run in a smooth curve, up from the base line, out and around to their maximum fullness, and then back in a slow curve into the stop-cut trench (see 10–8 on page 113).

Finally, having used a pair of dividers to set out the medallion disc at the front of the ruff, cut away and angle the top of the ruff so that it runs in a slope up from the chest to tuck into the underside of the chin (see 10–9 on page 113). By the time you reach this stage, all the primary design areas should be clearly established (see 10–10 on page 113).

Roughing Out the Face

Having carefully drawn out the features that go into making up the face and shaded in the main areas that need to be lowered, stop a while and consider how important it is that you go very easy when you come to carve the nose, lips, chin, and forehead. Be aware of the simple fact that once you have cut back a certain area of wood, it can't easily be replaced. For example, if you make a false move and slice off the nose, then you've got a problem! Therefore, go at it with care and caution.

Wood-carving tip: If you do by chance make a mistake and slice off an important area—like, say, the nose—then either stick it back on with Super Glue or level off the area and build it up with a new piece of wood.

Using the tools of your choice, gradually lower the wood under the brow and the cheeks at either side of the nose (see 10–11, top), round over the cheeks so that they run into the wig, round over the rather pert chin, and define the eye sockets, nostrils, whiskers, and lips (see 10–11, bottom). Every few minutes along the way, spend time pulling everything together. Your order of work might run as follows: sharpen/hone your tools, check a detail off against your drawings, check that features are symmetric, check positions by triangulating features off one against another, adjust the carving in light of your observations, stand back and appraise your progress, and so forth. Don't be

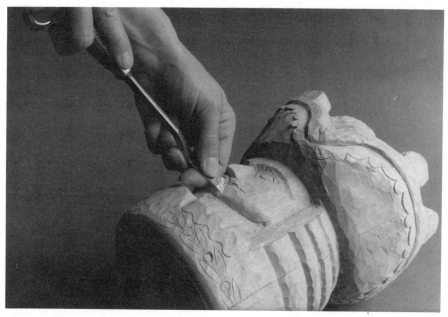

10–12 Hold the dog-leg chisel with both hands, and work with a slicing, paring movement. Cut across the grain, and model the chin and jawline.

tempted to take any single feature to completion; it's much better to keep everything moving forward at a nice, slow, and even pace.

Be extra careful with short-grain areas—especially the lips—that you don't lean on the tools against other features to the extent that you knock them off. In this respect, the dog-leg chisel is particularly useful, as it can be used to skim off areas that are restricted by other features. I find that a dog-leg is more easily controlled than, say, a straight or skew chisel. It's the perfect tool for shaping the jaw and the rather tricky area around the lips and whiskers (see 10–12).

Modelling

When you have roughed out the overall carving—the shape, position, and form of the dominant characteristics that go into making up the design—then comes the exciting stage of modelling. This is the phase that we like best. Gill thinks of it as being the time when the hard work of clearing the waste is over and the "real" carving can begin, whereas I think of it as being the time when the main risks are over and I can start to ease up and enjoy myself. Either way, the modelling stage is a pleasure.

With the carving more or less ready for the modelling, spend time assessing where you are at. Set the carving in a good light, tack up your drawings so that they are within view, and then stand back and be super-critical.

Having checked on proportions, generally made adjustments where necessary, and sanded areas that will need drawn details, take a soft pencil and draw out on the carvings the areas that need to be reworked and all the features that go into making up the design.

Wood-carving tip: We found that prior to drawing and carving fine details like eyes, it is best to prepare the area by sanding it to a smooth finish. It's easier to achieve accurate knife work on a uniform surface.

You might shade in one or two areas that need to be cut back and then draw in the details of the feathers, the decoration around the hat rim, the secondary lines within the wig and moustache, the details of the eyes and mouth, the ruff, the little bit of pattern around the base, and so on.

Wood-carving tip: If you can't quite see how two details look in relation to each other or how a particular feature looks in the round, then spend time making a full-size maquette.

Modelling the Hat Brim   When you have

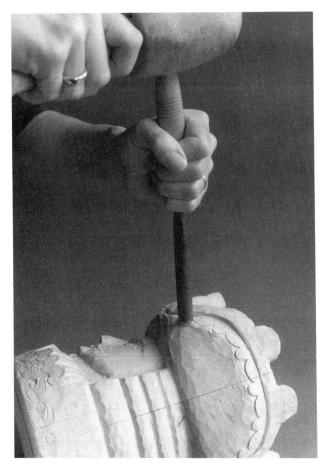

10–13   Gently tap the gouge into the wood so as to make a positive, but shallow stop-cut.

drawn in the fancy scalloped shape around the rim of the hat brim, take a shallow-sweep gouge—one that best fits the overall shape of the curves—and chop the drawn line in with a stop-cut (see 10–13). Sink the cut to a depth of about $\frac{1}{16}''$. Take a knife with a sharp point, and reduce the wood below the line to the depth of the cut. Then skim the surface of the sides of the hat back to the depth of the stop-cut, so that there is a sharp step-up to the scalloped design.

Modelling the Eyes   Having cut the brows and lowered the entire eye area, then comes the tricky task of cutting the two eyes. Start by drawing in a central line that runs from the forehead down to the chin. Take an eye-detail tracing from the master design—checking the symmetry and size—and carefully pencil-press-transfer the traced lines through to the wood. With the eye shapes in place, take your sharply pointed knife and set the drawn eye lines in with stop-cuts (see 10–14, top left on next page). When this is done, set the knife more or less down flat on the wood—so that the point is on the inside of the stop-cut line and the blade is flat on the eye—and lower the inside of the eye (see

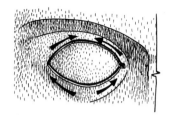
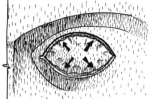
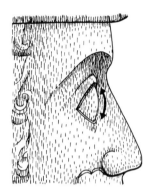

10–14   Top left: Set the drawn lines in with stop-cuts, and make the cuts slightly to the waste side of the drawn lines. Top right: Lower the inside of the eye. Bottom: Model the eyeball until it's smoothly convex.

10–14, top right on next page). Work with a careful, two-handed, paring cut. Pare around the inside of the eye line, until there is a sharp step-up from the eye to the lid and the eyeball looks smoothly convex (see 10–14, bottom).

Modelling the Nose and Mouth   First of all, take a good look at the working drawings and the various photographs and see how the stylized nose has a flat ridge, two sharply defined nostrils, and a square-cut underside that juts out over the mouth, while the mouth has a somewhat flat moustache-covered top lip and a full, pouty bottom lip. When you are clear in your own mind as to how the shapes relate one to another, make small stop-cuts for all the "valleys"—the line of the mouth and the creases around the nostrils—and then whittle them to shape with the point of the knife.

Wood-carving tip: If you are a beginner, you might well find that modelling the lips with the knife is a bit tricky. If this is the case, then follow up the initial knife-worked stop-cuts by using a small fold of sandpaper to rub the lips down to shape.

Modelling the Feathers   Having first carved the fancy scalloped trim that runs around the side face of the hat brim, take a knife and gouge and round over the rim edge—meaning the ropelike feature that decorates the topmost edge of the brim. Next, take the V-tool and set out all the lines that go into making up the design—all the individual strands that make up the rope and the pattern within the feathers (see 10–15). The pro-

10–15   Having drawn in the guidelines, systematically set the lines in with V-cuts.

cedure is much the same as carving a rope edging (see 10–16). You might want to refer to the instructions for the third project, Running-Rope Borders. The area between the little rosettes is somewhat difficult in two respects. First of all, you are

10–16   Roll the parting tool around the brim of the hat. Work from the high central area down and around towards the edge.

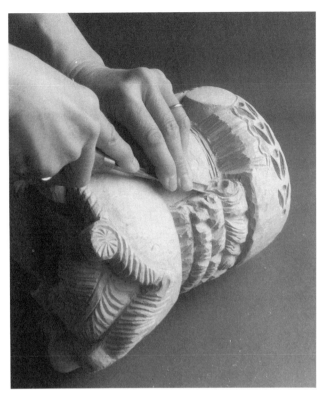

10–17 Use the parting tool to sink V-section trenches to mark out the curls and locks of the hair.

cutting with the run of the grain, with the effect that the tool tends to slip into the grain. Secondly, there is so little space in which to work. After experimenting with various tools, I settled for using a small knife.

Modelling the Wig and Whiskers When you come to model the wig and whiskers, use the V-tool, the small shallow-sweep gouge, and the knife in much the same way as you did for the ropelike details. In other words, first rough out the pattern with a series of V-cut furrows and then follow through by tidying up the details with the knife. Set the ends of the wig—meaning where it meets the face—in with the scroll-like features that suggest that the ends of the horizontal rolls are curled (see 10–17).

Modelling the Ruff When you have roughed out the collar, the sloping front, and the overall shape at the front of the ruff, use the V-tool and cover the surface of the ruff with decorative cuts. When this is done, use a deep U-section gouge to set out the pair of wavy lines that delineate the shape of the frilly details that run around the front at either side of the medallion. Set the stop-cut lines about ¼″ apart, and then swiftly round over and tidy up with the knife.

Draw out the stylized leaf-and-berry design around the front of the base, and clear the waste

with the knife and small scoop gouge. Aim for little concave holes for the berries and boatlike cuts for the leaves.

Finishing and Painting

Once the modelling is done, take a razor-sharp knife and a scrap of fine-grade sandpaper and go over the entire carving, cleaning out all the cracks and crevices and generally perfecting the piece. This stage takes a long time, so go at it nice and easy, all the while being very careful that you don't do damage to the fragile short-grained areas of the lips and nose.

And so you continue making a cut here, slicing a shade off there, tidying up a detail with a fold of sandpaper, and so on, until you consider the carving done (see 10–18, A, B, and C, on next page).

Wood-carving tip: It's always a bit of a problem deciding just when a wood carving is finished. As for myself, I am never absolutely satisfied that a carving is done; there are always areas and details that fail to come up to my expectations. If you are a bit unsure as to whether or not your carving is finished, then it's best put it to one side for a couple of days or even weeks and then come back to it with a fresh eye. I find that this breathing space helps me pick up on problem areas.

When you are happy with your carving, mix a small amount of plaster filler and use it in any cracks or cavities. Wait a while for the filler to dry; then swiftly sand back a bit, and lay on a thick coat of matt white emulsion paint. Next, if need be, sand back any nibs that may appear—especially on end-grain areas—and lay on another coat for good measure.

With the filling and sanding done, clean away all the dust and debris and move to the dust-free area that you have set aside for painting. Before you do anything else, refresh your eye by looking back at the working drawings and painting grids (see 10–2, A, B, and C, on pages 108, 109, 110). Then start by blocking in the main ground areas: black for the hat, yellow for the trim and wig, green for the back and shoulders, pinkish-tan flesh tone for the face, and so forth. When the ground colors are dry, then use a fine-point brush to pick out all the details: the red lips, the black eye details, and so on. Use a blush of watered-down red for the cheeks. Finally—and this is the part that I like best—paint on the gold details, give the whole carving a coat of clear varnish, followed by a coat of slightly sepia-tinted varnish, and PHEW! WOW! HURRAH! the project is done.

10–18   *The finished, unpainted carving—(A) front view, (B) side view, and (C) front-plan view.*

TROUBLESHOOTING AND POSSIBLE MODIFICATIONS

- If you have in mind to mount this carving on your boat, then be sure to use waterproof adhesive when gluing up and to brush on additional coats of varnish at the end.

- If you decide to use a section of a log, then make sure that it is free from ring shakes.
- On consideration, we should have given our admiral a slightly longer nose. He's okay, but he would be that much better if his proboscis were bigger. This is something to bear in mind when you work out your design.

Three-masted schooner

Inspirational designs (opposite)   Top left: A visual joke or pun, with the rudder head carved as one with a dog's head hat, Amsterdam. Top right: Rudder head of Mercury, Roman god of merchandise and merchants, with his winged cap, eighteenth century (Nederlands Historisch Scheepvaart Museum). Bottom left: Rudder head of Flora, Italian goddess of flowering plants, eighteenth century (Nederlands Historisch Scheepvaart Museum)—Floras are characteristically carved with plump bosoms and flowering garlands. Bottom right: Rudder head of a Flora figure from the ship Prins Hendrik, *eighteenth century (Maritime Museum, Rotterdam).*

11
Red Indian Chief Figurehead

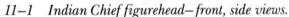
11–1   Indian Chief figurehead–front, side views.

In the middle of the nineteenth century, John Griffith, the famous American shipbuilder, declared that in much the same way as the face of a person says a lot about his character and qualities, there is something about the bow and the figurehead that conveys an impression of the whole ship.

Clippers were designed for speed. The raked curve of the bow meant that the figurehead needed to be slung under the extended bowsprit in a semi-horizontal position, with the body looking down at the waves and the neck and head arched back so as to face the horizon. And what could be better for a fast-thrusting clipper than to have a proud warrior for a figurehead!

The popularity of Indian figureheads had to do with the great American gold rush. As the land journey across America was very risky—on account of "red Indians" attacking on every side—

the preferred route was to sail by fast clipper around Cape Horn. Therefore, when shipbuilders were called upon to build ships for gold rush passage, it seemed only right and fitting to set the scene for the great American adventure to come by having red Indian figureheads.

THOUGHTS ON DESIGN AND TECHNIQUE

Take a look at the working drawings and painting grids (see 11–2, A and B), and note how, at a scale of two grid squares to 1", our Indian chief stands about 16" in total height—meaning 16" from the bottom of the base through to the topmost feather.

We have simplified the construction by taking four prepared sections of wood that are about 3¾ × 3¾" and cutting out the basic shapes on a band saw and laminating. The band-saw tech-

11–2A Working drawing and painting grid—front view. The scale is two grid squares to 1″.

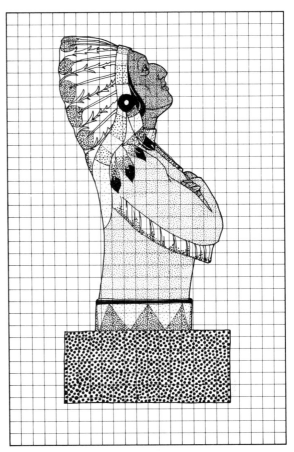

11–2B Working drawing and painting grid—side view. The scale is two grid squares to 1″.

nique makes the job a lot easier, with the front and side views being fretted out prior to carving.

Wood-carving tip: A good trick for beginners is to use your own face (and hands) as a model. Set a large mirror alongside the carving, and take calliper readings from your own features.

TOOL AND MATERIAL CONSIDERATIONS

Having noted that we built the blank up from four band-sawn sections, you might well run into problems if you need to use a single baulk of wood and/or you don't have access to a band saw. If you want to start with a large section of wood and you don't have use of a saw that is big enough for the task, then it's best to settle for clearing the rough with a large gouge. Certainly, it will be hard work, but it's one way to go. Then again, if you are happy to use four sections as described but you don't have access to a band saw, you can use a hand-held coping or bow saw.

As for wood, although we have decided to use jelutong, you could just as well use lime, holly, or just about any smooth-grained, knot-free, easy-to-carve wood that is readily available.

TOOLS AND EQUIPMENT

For this project, you need:
- four 16″ lengths of prepared 4 × 4″-square jelutong, with a finished size of about 3¾ × 3¾″
- a workbench with a vise or carver's chops
- a band saw with a narrow fine-toothed blade and the ability to cut 4″-thick wood
- a small fine-toothed flat-bladed tenon saw
- a carver's mallet
- two straight chisels: ¾″ and ¼″ wide
- a ¼″-wide parting tool
- two shallow-sweep gouges: ¼″ and ½″ wide
- a ¼″-wide bent, or curved, gouge
- a ½″-wide dog-leg chisel
- a small, sharply pointed knife
- a pencil and ruler
- a sheet each of work-out and tracing paper
- a pack of graded sandpapers
- a roll of masking tape
- a quantity of PVA adhesive
- a good quantity of Plasticine or modelling clay
- a number of modelling tools
- a selection of paintbrushes
- a can of matt white emulsion ceiling paint
- acrylic paint in black, red, brick red, blue, dark

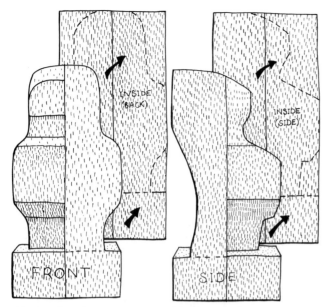

11–3 *Having cut out two blocks, use the cutouts to transfer the cutting lines through to the other two blocks.*

green, yellow, and various shades of light sandy brown
• a can of clear high-shine varnish

PROJECT STAGES

Drawing Up the Design, Cutting Out, and Laminating

When you have selected your wood, brought your carving gouges and chisels to a razor-sharp edge, and generally prepared for the task ahead, then draw the design up to full size and make tracings. Take your four 16″ lengths of wood, turn them about until the best faces are towards the front and side—so as to make a single section of about 7½ × 7½″—and strap up with masking tape. Being mindful that the join lines on the front face of the block are going to run straight through the nose, make sure that the best faces of the wood are looking to the front. With a pencil, label all faces and sides of the wood, so that you can put the block back together again.

Run a line around the block at a level of about 2¾″ up from the base. Set the front tracings on the block, and pencil-press-transfer the traced lines through to the wood. Repeat the procedure with one or the other of the side views. Make sure that the transferred lines are clear, and shade in areas that need to be cut away.

With the lines in place, and having labelled the blocks so that you know what goes where, remove the masking-tape strapping. Cut away the waste on the band saw from the two front and the two side blocks. When this is done, use the cutouts to transfer the cutting lines through to the other blocks and repeat the procedure as already described (see 11–3). It's all fairly straightforward, as long as you bear in mind that by the time each of the four blocks has been through the band saw twice, the cutouts will be pretty unrecognizable. Therefore, it's very important that you keep tabs on what goes where (see 11–4, A and B).

Wood-carving tip: When you pass each piece of wood through the band saw, keep all the parts numbered and put them back together like a puzzle. This procedure will help you keep everything organized and prevent you from throwing away the wrong pieces of wood.

Last of all, when you have achieved the four cutouts, smear mating faces with a generous amount of adhesive and clamp up.

Wood-carving tip: I used the bench vise for the clamping. Turning and turning it about, I glued up the two front blocks and put them in the vise, and then the two back blocks, and then finally I glued and clamped the double-block slabs. If you don't have a vise or clamps, first loosely bind the workpiece with nylon rope and then tighten the binding with wedges and/or a twist stick.

Making the Maquette

By maquette, we mean a working model or prototype. The idea is to make an image to copy, while at the same time working out potential problems. If you make a mistake with the Plasticine, all you do is remove it and continue until you get it right—it's not so easy with the wood!

Ideally, you should make a maquette as big as the carving itself; then you can set the two side by side and take calliper and divider readings directly. The more precise the maquette, then the better your chances of achieving a good carving.

Soften the Plasticine by warming it in your hands, and then mould it around a central core of wood. With the working drawings close at hand and a friend who is willing to pose, gradually model and shape the material, until you have what you consider to be a good likeness. Use the callipers and dividers to check the measurements off one against another.

Bear in mind that, apart from the crossed arms, the image needs to be more or less symmetrical. However, the crossed arms are particularly difficult, in that the two hands are held quiet differ-

11–4   Cutouts—(A) front view and (B) side view, with the waste cut away and glued up.

ently. The Indian's right hand is rolled over the chest with the fingertips tucked down between the chest and the upper arm, whereas with the left hand only the fingertips are in view.

Wood-carving tip: In terms of making maquettes, I always use Plasticine. It is sometimes possible to cut down on costs if you buy a large amount, especially if you buy directly.

Primary Roughing Out

With the maquette nicely modelled and the work-piece secured in the vise, start by using a knife and metal straightedge to mark the top edge of the plinth. Run the knife around the block several times, until the mark at the top of the plinth is cleanly and accurately set in with a scored line.

Take the ½"-wide shallow-sweep gouge and a mallet, and cut up and in from the scored line and across the end grain, so as to cut the top edge of the plinth to shape. Use the same procedure to finish the entire underside of the base. If necessary, dish the base slightly so that the carving stands fair and square.

Wood-carving tip: It's a good idea to sort out the base well before you start the delicate carving. At this stage, you can up-end the wood in the vise without fear of doing damage.

Being aware of the need to repeatedly use the callipers to check measurements off from the maquette, take the mallet and gouge and swiftly round up the waist, the sides of the arms, and the sides of the face. Establish the width of the nose with a couple of drawn lines, and then take the tenon saw and set the lines in with stop-cuts. Sink the cuts to a depth that you estimate is slightly less than the distance from the tip of the nose to the cheek. With the stop-cuts established, carefully gouge in from either side so as to lower the cheeks (see 11–5 on next page).

Now establish and cut away the waste from the arm crossover point, at the top of the brows and the forehead, behind the shoulders, and so on. When you come to chopping out the fringe on the underside of the arms, first draw in the line of the underarm, next set the line in with a stop-cut, and then slice in towards the grain and into the stop-cut, so that the waste falls away (see 11–6 on page 124). Aim to cut the face of the fringe back, so that it looks to be hanging from a central line that runs down the underside of the arm.

And so you continue working backwards and forward over the carving, repeatedly checking measurements off against the maquette, shading in areas of waste, reducing the waste, and so forth. Don't try at this stage to take any single detail to a

11–5 Round off the block and mark in the main features, while referring to the Plasticine maquette.

modelled finish; just settle for roughing out the main forms and levels.

Roughing Out the Nose, Mouth, and Chin

The nose, mouth, and chin are doubly tricky, in that, in addition to being extremely short-grained and fragile, they need to be left standing proud. Be warned: One small slip and you have an Indian chief without a nose! In fact, the wood at the very tip of the nose needs to be handled with extra care to the extent that you need to use the gouge with a restrained two-handed paring stroke—one hand holding and controlling while the other is guiding

and slicing (see 11–7). The same goes to a lesser degree for the brows, bottom lip, chin, and jawline. These areas are so short-grained that you need to minimize the shock to the wood by working with a delicate paring cut.

Roughing Out the Neck and Chest

Start by having a good, close, analytical look at the working drawings and the maquette. Note how the neck is narrower than the face, while the head is thrown back and the chin lifted so that the face slopes forward from the shoulders. Spend a lot of time working out how the various forms and planes

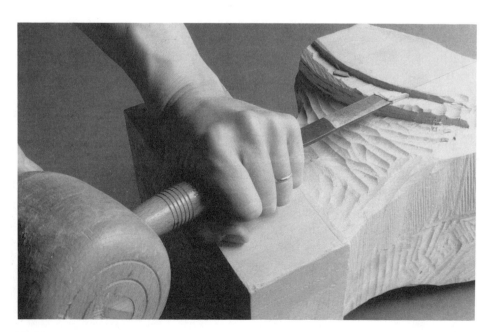

11–6 Lower the waste at the side of the arm down to the level of the fringe.

124

11–7 Use a light touch to define the length of the nose. Note that the tip of the nose is fragile and can be easily split away.

relate one to another. When you have a clear understanding of how the neck and chest need to be worked, take a soft pencil and mark in on the work-piece all the surfaces that need to be lowered.

The underside of the chin is particularly difficult, in that it is a sloping plane of end grain. The best procedure is to carefully draw out the features that need to be left in relief—such as the neck band, the strip of chest pattern, the necklace, and the top edge of the folded arms—and then to chop the drawn lines in with stop-cuts.

With the stop-cuts established, take the tool of your choice, say, a shallow-sweep gouge or a dog-leg chisel, and skim back the areas of waste to the required depth (see 11–8). Make shallow skimming cuts across the end grain on the chest, especially at the top edge of the beads.

Roughing Out the Hands

Start by looking at the working drawings and painting grids and at the maquette and your own hands. Stand in front of a mirror, and see how your hands look when your arms are folded across your chest. Consider how you can just about cover your face with an open hand.

Our Indian chief's hands are a bit too small. What happened was that we were so involved with fussing around with the modelling that we lost sight of the greater picture. By the time we had finished, the hands were well modelled but a bit on the small side. All I can say is, try not to become overly concerned with any single detail in isolation or . . . do as we say, not as we did!

Once again, draw in the lines of the design, shade in the areas that need to be lowered, sink the drawn lines with stop-cuts, and then lower the waste. When you have checked that the drawn details are correct—the set of the arms and the

11–8 Cutting across the end grain on the shoulders and chest requires a sharp tool and a lot of concentrated effort— it's slow work.

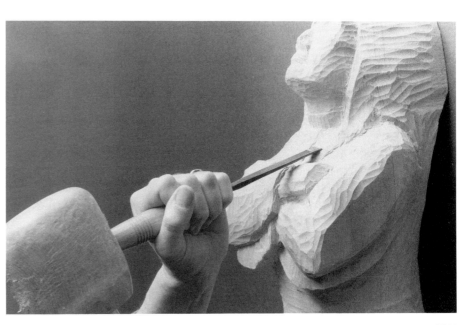

11–9   The completed rough—(A) front and (B) side views. Note the crossing over of the arms and fringe and the slope of the shoulders where the bonnet meets the back.

size and alignment of the hands—take a small shallow-sweep gouge and lower the wrist of the Indian's right hand, so that the cuff stands up proud by about ⅛". Run the underside of the hand down and around, and reduce the surface of the left forearm, so as to create the illusion that one arm passes over the other. Of course, if at any time you can't quite envision how the details ought to go, look at your own arms and study the maquette.

Now continue identifying and roughing out all the primary forms that go into making up the design (see 11–9, A and B).

Modelling the Details

When you have roughed out all the primary forms—that is, when you have cleared the greater part of the waste to the extent that the overall or preliminary shapes have been achieved—then comes the scary but exciting task of modelling. If you are a beginner, there's no sure-fire tip I can point out to ensure success. The best I can say is to keep your tools sharp and keep on referring to the master drawings and the maquette.

Spend time checking your measurements and drawing in guidelines, and then get down to work. Start by rounding over the corners of the base block. Then take the dog-leg chisel, and skim back

the top, shelflike edge of the base. It's end grain, so go at it slowly.

Wood-carving tip: If, when you are cutting or skimming back end grain, the surface starts to crumble, it generally means that your tools need sharpening. A sharp tool will leave end-grain jelutong looking smooth and polished.

Modelling the Belt

Using a knife and a metal straightedge, carefully define the top edge of the belt with a stop-cut. Cut in to a depth of about ⅛". When this is done, take the dog-leg chisel and skim back, or lower, the surface above the belt, so that it stands proud.

Modelling the Hands

Study your own hands, and remember as you are carving that the end grain can easily crumble away. Do not lean on the tool so that it pries against the wood. It's not that difficult, as long as you work with a two-handed stroke, all the while being prepared to pull back if you feel the tool overshooting the stop-cuts.

Wood-carving tip: The fingers of the Indian's left hand are very fragile, especially when each finger has been defined with a V-cut. Therefore, you might decide to settle for using shallow knife cuts to describe the fingers.

126

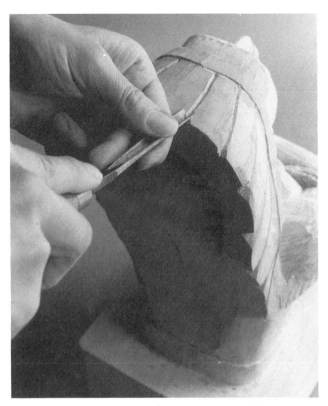

11–10   Use a V-tool to cut the feather divisions, working in from the back edge of the head.

Slope the surface of the hidden hand, so that it runs down to match the angle of the arm.

Modelling the Head and Feathers

Once you are happy with the overall proportions of the head—the width across the span of the cheeks and the angle of the chin to the neck—take the soft pencil and mark in both edges of the war-bonnet headband as it passes across the forehead and down each side of the head. Don't forget about the small area of visible hair at each side of the head.

Use the V-tool, knife, and shallow-sweep gouge to lower the wood at either side of the band, so that it stands up proud from the forehead, the hair, and the feathers. Skim away the sides of the cheeks, so that there is a step-up to the hair and another step-up to the headdress side tassels. Use a ¼" gouge to model the tassel as it curves around and onto the shoulders. With the wood stepping down from the headband to the area of feathers, first mark in the individual feathers and then set the lines in with the V-tool.

When you come to cutting the top ends of the feathers, take the V-tool, approach the headdress back-face-on, and chop from the feather ends through to the band (see 11–10). Make repeated chops until the groove between the feathers is

nicely established and the ends of the feathers look slightly rounded. Use a parting tool to texture the fringe. Swing the handle of the tool so as to achieve a flowing cut, and so that the tool is not "taken" by the grain.

Modelling the Eyelids

Take a small fold of fine-grade sandpaper, and sand the whole eye area until it's smooth to the touch. Carefully draw in the delicate, sharply ended, boatlike shapes that make up the eyes. Spend time making sure that the eyes are symmetrical, well matched, and aligned.

Sink the eyelid lines with nice, smooth, sweeping knife cuts (see 11–11, left on page 128), and then use the small bent gouge to lower the eyeball area by about ¹⁄₁₆ to ⅛" (see 11–11, right on page 128). Aim for slightly rounded eyeballs, all the while being careful not to split off the fragile edges of the lids. Finally, tidy up with the point of the knife and, if need be, a small fold of sandpaper.

Finishing

When you have modelled the overall shape of the feathers, the headband, the face, the neck and chest decorations, the hands, the fringe, and the belt, as well as all the other primary details, then comes the good-fun part of tidying up and finishing.

Invariably, the questions to ask yourself is: Just how much of a finish do I want? Do I, for example, want a smooth surface allover, or do I want to let the tool marks remain? Then again, do I want to give emphasis to selected areas by having tool marks juxtaposed with smooth areas? It's a matter of personal choice, and it needs a lot of consideration! We decided to go for a small amount of tooling on the face, the headdress, and the fringe, and then to rub everything else down to a smooth finish.

Start by going over the entire workpiece with a knife and fine-grade sandpaper. Clean out the creases and sharp corners, rub the war bonnet smooth, generally take care of any cavities and cracks with filler, and then give the carving a last swift rubdown.

Next, take a soft pencil and draw in all the spine lines and veins that make up the design of the feathers. Set the spine lines in with stop-cuts (see 11–12, top left, on page 128), and then take the ¼"-wide straight chisel and reduce the wood on either side of each feather so that the spine stands up proud. Angle the sides into the spine to exaggerate the feeling of depth (see 11–12, top right, on page

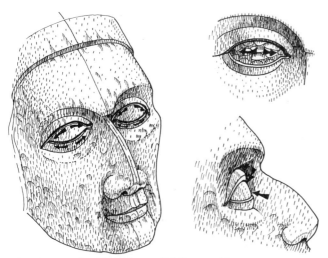

11–11   Left: Sink the eyelid lines with an easy, smooth, sweeping knife cut. Top right: Lower the eyeball area by about 1/16 to 1/8". Bottom right: Try to keep the eyeball a good rounded shape.

128). Reduce the wood on the top edge of each feather to create the illusion that there is a slight overlap (see 11–12, bottom left). Then use the parting tool to cut the little breaks and separation marks on the feather edges (see 11–12, bottom right).

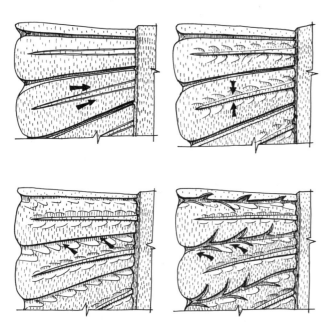

11–12   Top left: Set the spine lines in with stop-cuts. Top right: Angle the sides into the spine so as to exaggerate the feeling of depth. Bottom left: Reduce the wood on the top edge of each feather to create the illusion of a slight overlap. Bottom right: Cut the little curved breaks and separation marks on each feathered edge.

Use a knife and/or a V-tool to clean up the fringe, and use a knife to tidy up the individual beads of the necklace and tidy up the individual fingers, and so on. Work backwards and forward over the entire carving, until you are content with the overall effect.

Painting

When you consider the carving to be finished, wipe away all the dust and debris and move to a clean dust-free area that you have set aside especially for painting.

Start by giving the whole carving an all-over coat of matt white emulsion. When the emulsion is dry, rub it down with fine-grade sandpaper. Now study the painting grids (refer back to 11–2, A and B), and use a large brush to paint in the main ground areas: green on the base, sandy brown for the buckskin, and a rich brick red on the face and hands. Use a finer brush and yellow paint for the headband, the belt, and the neck and chest bands.

When the ground colors are dry, take a fine-point soft pencil and carefully draw in the lines that make up the zigzags on the belt, the triangles on the neck band, the straight divisions on the chest band and headband, the feather ends on the shoulders, and so on.

Then take a fine-point brush, and carefully block in the details. Use red on the belt, red for the beads and chest band, blue on the neck and head-band, red on the ends of the feathers, black for the thin lines around the eyes. Spend time getting it right.

Lay on a thin coat of sepia-tinted varnish, letting it collect in the cavities and hollows. Then wipe off the excess from the proud areas, so as to create a much-handled aging effect. Finally, give the whole carving a swift sanding, apply a couple of generous coats of clear varnish, let it dry, and the carving is done!

TROUBLESHOOTING AND POSSIBLE MODIFICATIONS

- If you have in mind to mount this carving on your boat, then be sure to use waterproof adhesive when gluing up and brush on additional coats of varnish at the end.
- If you decide to use a section of a log, then make sure that it is completely seasoned and free from ring shakes, splits, dead knots, and sappy areas.
- On consideration, in addition to larger hands, we should have given our Indian chief a much larger war bonnet with much longer feathers.

(Top) Project 1 Eagle's Head; (bottom) Project 9 Sea-Monster Rail End.

Project 14 Jack Tar Figurehead.

Project 10 Little Admiral Rudder Head.

(Top) Project 4 Quarter Board with Incised Lettering; (bottom) Project 15 Jenny Lind Figurehead.

D

Project 6 Scroll.

(Top) Side view of an Amphitrite (Cutty Sark Museum, London), probably from a nineteenth century barque, of exceptional quality; (bottom) Detail showing the very skilled carving.

F

Figurehead with detail inset, probably from a French merchant ship of the eighteenth century, circa 1760 (Cutty Sark Museum, London).

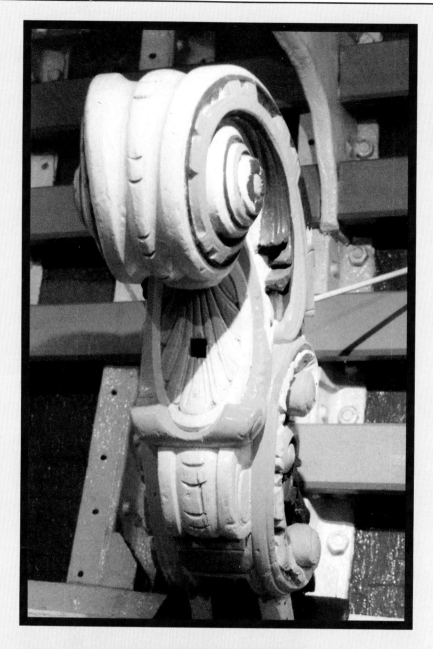

(Top) Billet head showing width and depth of the roll-over and twist-out at the top; (bottom) Side view of design showing skirt of scrolls and remaining leaves that would have continued down each side of the cut water (Cutty Sark Museum, London).

H

General Gordon (1833–1885) figurehead from a brigantine (Cutty Sark Museum, London). General Gordon was a popular figure in mid-nineteenth century England. He was killed at Khartoum shortly before it was relieved in 1885.

(Top) Hiawatha figurehead (Cutty Sark Museum, London) stands nearly ten feet high and is estimated at about half a ton; (right) Side view detail showing the "fluttering" cape and drapes.

Figurehead of the replica caravel the Santa Maria, *in which Columbus made his first trip to America (Barcelona). (See also color pages N and O.)*

*The helmeted figure of the giant Greek warrior Ajax from the
H.M.S. Ajax, 1809 (Maritime Museum Greenwich, London).*

Figurehead of Lord Nelson from the H.M.S. Horatio, *1807 (Maritime Museum Greenwich, London). Crowned with laurel, he has a sightless eye. The ship was broken up in 1865.*

Stern of the replica caravel the Santa Maria, *in which Columbus made his first trip to America (Barcelona). (See also color pages K and O.)*

Quarter gallery of the replica caravel the Santa Maria, *in which Columbus made his first trip to America (Barcelona). (See also color pages K and N.)*

(Top) Lion and coat-of-arms figurehead on the training ship Sir Winston Churchill *(at anchor in Fowey Harbour, Cornwall, England); (bottom) Carved figure similar to Dutch rudder heads (Cutty Sark Museum, London).*

12
H.M.S. *Blazer* Figurehead

The *Blazer* figurehead is particularly interesting, in that she was carved at the transition period, when full figureheads and bust figureheads began to go out of fashion, in favor of small shields, coats of arms, and billet heads. With her beautiful sophisticated face, streaming rays, and gilt finish, she is less than a figurehead, and more than a crest.

The H.M.S. *Blazer* may not only be the source from which the blazer got its name—meaning the lightweight sports jacket—but it's possible that her crew were the first to wear what we now think of as being navy uniform.

The story goes something like this: The H.M.S. *Blazer* was a three-gun paddle vessel launched in England in 1834. She was given the name of *Blaze* or *Blazer* to connote a ball of flaming light, like a meteorite or sun. The crew of the *Blazer* were unusual, in that they were all turned out in blue-and-white striped shirts and blue jackets—and this was at a time when there was no established uniform. Written accounts suggest that it is more than likely that the *Blazer* crew's outfit was the inspiration for naval uniforms now worn by seamen and the jacket that we think of as a blazer.

THOUGHTS ON DESIGN AND TECHNIQUE

Take a look at the working drawings (see 12–2, A and B), and note how, at a scale of two grid squares to 1″, the *Blazer* figurehead measures about 18″ long, 9″ wide, and slightly less than 8″ deep from the flat back through to the tip of the nose. Now take a look at the photographs, and note the way she is built up from six prepared 4 × 4″-square lengths of wood—three lengths wide and two deep.

It can be said that this project is, at one and the same time, both difficult and easy. On the one hand, the stylized rays allow for considerable license in terms of design and technique—if you make mistakes, they aren't going to show—and yet on the other hand, the face itself permits very little

12–1   Blazer *figurehead.*

leeway. The face needs to be carved with great care and attention to detail.

In terms of painting, all that's required is an all-over coat of gold paint. Okay, so the original *Blazer* figurehead is covered in gold leaf. We have settled for gold paint.

The face is characterized by an enigmatic smile, a glint in the eyes, and a serenity, all of which convey the impression that our beautiful, bright, blazing friend knows something that we don't. A gorgeous beauty no doubt, but not such an easy expression to capture.

All things considered, we feel that this is a good project for beginners who are looking for a challenge. The overall design is bold, the technique is

12–2, A   Working drawing—front view. The scale is two grid squares to 1".

12–2, B   Working drawing—side view. The scale is two grid squares to 1".

closer to relief than to three-dimensional carving, and the finished carving is stunning. It's a great project for beginners looking to prove their skills.

TOOL AND MATERIAL CONSIDERATIONS

Technically, this is quite an uncomplicated project to organize and set up. A relatively basic kit of gouges and chisels, a small easy-to-handle blank, and yellow and gold acrylic paint—what could be easier? We do suggest that you use a band saw to cut out the basic blank, but even that can be worked around. If you are prepared to spend time clearing away the bulk of the waste by hand—say, with a large gouge—then you can forget about using the band saw.

Wood-carving tip: If you don't plan to use a band saw, then there's not much point in building the blank up from small sections. Certainly, laminating does help prevent the finished carving from splitting and warping, but, in this instance, you could probably get away with using a single block of carefully selected wood.

Although we decided to use jelutong, this is not to say that you can't use just about any suitable wood that comes to hand. If it's relatively easy to carve, straight-grained, and free from knots and splits, then it will do the job.

TOOLS AND EQUIPMENT

For this project, you need:
• six 24″ lengths of prepared 4 × 4″-square jelutong, with a finished size of approximately 3¾ × 3¾″—this length allows for a good amount of waste
• a workbench with a vise and bench stop
• a band saw with a narrow fine-toothed blade and the ability to cut 4″-thick wood
• a carver's mallet
• a 1¼″-wide shallow-sweep straight gouge
• a 1″-wide shallow U-section bent gouge
• a ¼″-wide V-tool
• a ¼″-wide shallow-curve straight gouge
• a ¼″-wide U-section gouge

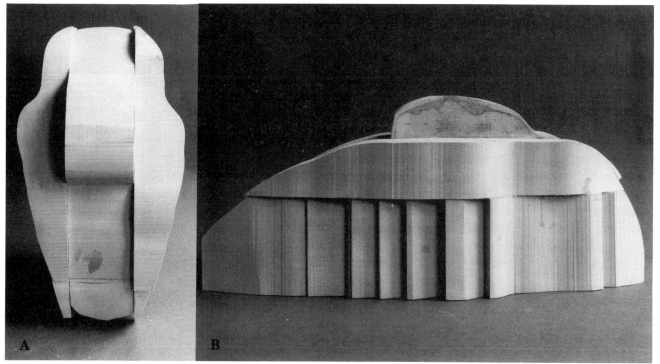

12–3, A and B   Front and side views of the glued-up six-block blank. Note the face profile on the side view.

- a ⅛″-wide bent gouge
- a ½″-wide dog-leg chisel and a hole punch
- a small, sharply pointed knife
- a pencil and ruler
- a sheet each of work-out and tracing paper
- a pack of graded sandpapers
- a sand bag and a quantity of PVA adhesive
- a good quantity of Plasticine or modelling clay
- a number of modelling tools
- a small amount of plaster filler
- a paintbrush that's about 1″ wide
- a can of matt white emulsion ceiling paint
- acrylic paint in yellow and gold
- a can of clear high-shine varnish

PROJECT STAGES

Drawing Up the Design, Making a Maquette, and Transferring the Design

When you've got everything together—yourself, the workshop, the wood, and the tools—draw the designs up to full size and make a tracing. Do this with both the front and side views; see the working drawings (12–2, A and B). Use the tracings to make a maquette. Don't worry too much about the streaming flames; just concentrate your efforts on the face. Pay particular attention to modelling the

details: the curve of the brow, the beautiful almond-shaped eyes, and the mouth. It's important to get the smile just right.

Once you have achieved what you consider to be a good set of drawings and a cleanly worked maquette, put them in view both out of harm's way. Now take the six lengths of wood, check them over for faults, and build them into a stack that is three blocks wide and two deep. Play around with the arrangement, so that the best length is in the middle of the front and potential faults—knots and splits—are at the outside edges where they will be cut away with the waste. Number and label the lengths so that you can easily reassemble the stack.

Use the tracings to press-transfer the front profile through to the top three lengths of wood; then remove the three lengths and repeat the procedure on the next level. Shade in all the areas of waste that need to be cut away. Having sorted out the front view on both layers, repeat the transferring procedure on the side face of the stack. Transfer the entire profile through to the two central blocks and the profile without the face on the outer blocks. If all goes well, the top-middle block should be the only one to carry the side-of-face profile. With all the guidelines in place, check to be sure that, once the waste has been cut away, the resulting cutouts will still be numbered and labelled.

Cutting Out the Profiles, Gluing Up, and First Cuts

Having checked and double-checked that everything is correct, run the wood through the band saw and cut away the waste. When this is done, clear away the debris, sweep up the dust, and reassemble the six-block stack (see 12–3, A and B). Smear a generous amount of adhesive on all mating faces within the stack, restack, clamp up, and leave to dry.

Wood-carving tip: If you intend to have the carving outside in all kinds of weather, then be sure to use waterproof PVA.

When the glue is set, refresh your eye by having another look at the working drawings and photographs and then draw in the central line of the face. Then take the mallet and gouge, and clear the main mass of waste. Be very wary that you don't cut too much wood away from the face. In fact, it would be a good idea to draw a circle around what will be the tip of the nose and leave this area alone for the time being.

Wood-carving tip: If you plan on hanging this carving on the wall of your cabin or house, then it would be a good idea at an early stage to turn the carving over and cut a ½"-deep scoop in towards the top. This way, you can fasten a screw eye in the dip, so that the carving will hang flush on the wall.

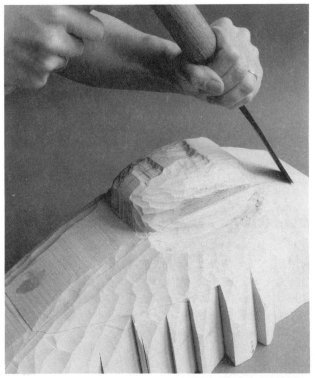

12–4   Carve the whole area outside the face so that it runs down at a slope.

Draw a guideline around the entire side of the workpiece—about 1" up from the back edge—and then use the gouges of your choice to cut and carve the area outside the face so that it runs down at a slope (see 12–4). Angle the sides of the carving in a smooth hill-like curve, from the outer edge of the face to stop short at the guideline 1" up from the base. While you are at it, round over the cheeks to the outer outline of the face (see 12–5).

Clearing the Rough

When you have worked over and around the face to the extent that you have cleared the most obvious areas of rough, take a pencil and, with one eye on the maquette and the working drawings, draw in as many guidelines as you think necessary. For example, you might draw in the folds that run down from the face to the ragged edges of the block, the main lines of the face, the lines of the brows, and so on. If you think it will help, swiftly shade in the areas that need to be variously dipped, modelled, and cut away.

With the guidelines in place, take the V-tool and make stop-cuts on the waste side of the drawn lines—around the face and down the main radiating furrows. Now, not forgetting to keep referring to your maquette and drawings, use the gouge to start clearing the waste (see 12–6). Use the large gouge for the main furrows and the larger areas of waste and the small gouge for the more complicated areas of the face. As with all the projects, don't be tempted to start hacking out great chunks of wood, but rather continually assess your progress with repeated calliper readings. Having carefully studied the side view, and not attempting at this stage to model the features, simply settle for clearing the larger areas of waste in small steps. Leave the nose, lips, and chin standing proud and the brow sloping away.

Modelling the Details

Once you have cleared away the rough to the degree that you have established the primary planes, redraw the main guidelines on the face and the radiating rays. Now comes the fun, though challenging, task of modelling the details. The challenge in carving has to do with not quite knowing how far to go. The first step in the process might be wonderful, the second step might be brilliant, but then the third step might be a disaster! The trick is knowing when to stop.

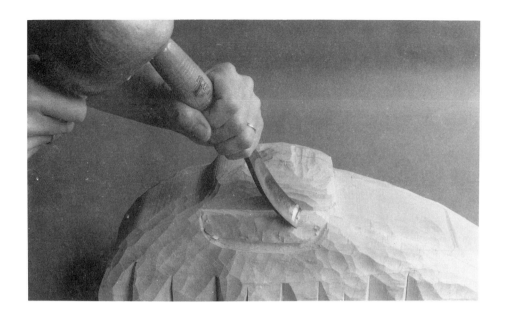

12–5 *Round over the face, cutting back to its outline.*

12–6 *Cutting the end grain at the chin—make sideways, downward, slicing cuts.*

Modelling the Rays

With the corona carefully drawn in, start by dividing the rays into the two types: the smooth ribbons and the grooved planes. If you look at 12–1, you will see that the rays extending from the middle of the top and bottom are made up from V-sections grooves, while the main ribbonlike rays are V-section ridges that stand proud of the grooves and textured ground.

Draw in the width of the primary ribbons—two at the top and two at the bottom—and lower the surrounding waste by between ¾ and 1″. The procedure is to first cut V-trenches on either side of the ribbons and then to lower the waste to the depth of the V-cuts. Repeatedly make the V-cuts and skim off the waste to the depth of the cuts, until the required depth is achieved (see 12–7). Don't try to texture the lowered ground at this stage; simply aim for a smooth surface.

12–7 *Use the dog-leg chisel to slice away the marks left by the gouge, and aim for a smooth surface that will be ready for V-tool texturing.*

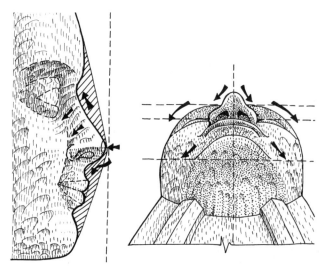

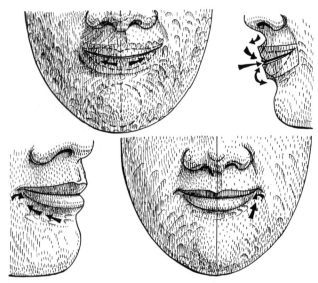

12–8   Left: Since the tip of the nose needs to stick out further than any other feature, lower the wood at the sides and curl the tip of the nose down into the lip area. Right: The work as viewed from under the chin, showing how the sides of the face fall away, the flare of the nostrils, and the curve of the lips.

12–9   Top left: Make a stop-cut between the lips. Top right: Model the top lip so that it curves down towards the bottom lip. Bottom: The bottom lip becomes narrower as it curves up at the edges to tuck under the top lip.

Modelling the Face

Before you begin to model the face, spend some time looking at the maquette and the working drawings and observe how the features relate to one another.

The Nose   When you come to modelling the nose, first draw in the central line and indicate the tip. Now slope the sides of the nose down into the cheeks. Remembering that the tip of the nose sticks out further than any other feature, continue lowering the wood at the sides until the nose falls away sharply where it runs and curls into the lip area (see 12–8, left). Model the nostrils so that they flare away from the tip of the nose—so that they curl out and down towards the cheeks. This is not an easy procedure. If you study the nose, as seen in side view and from under the chin, you will see that not only is the nose like a hill that curves down to the top lip, but, even more of a problem, the nostrils are set back behind the tip of the nose (see 12–8, right).

If you have any doubts as to how the various planes and curves of the nose relate to each other, refer back to the working drawings and the maquette.

The Mouth   By studying the working drawings and the maquette, you'll be able to see how the mouth curves around and back to make a "hill" while at the same time being slightly wider than the nose. Note also how important it is for the

mouth to curve around the face and not to project too far forward. Having carefully drawn in the shape of the mouth, make a stop-cut between the lips (see 12–9, top left) and then start skimming back with a small sharp gouge. Model the top lip so that it curves down towards the bottom lip (see 12–9, top right), and shape the bottom lip so that it tucks in at the corners. The bottom lip needs to be slightly lower than the top lip, while at the same time curled in at the ends, so as to create a gentle smiling expression (see 12–9, bottom).

The Eyes   Look again at the working drawings and the maquette, and see how the eyes need to be set back at a lower depth than the nose, while also being set at an angle so that they follow the contours of the face. The big mistake that most beginners make is having the eyes bulging out and looking forward, so that the carving appears goggle-eyed. You won't go far wrong if you are mindful that the eye is essentially a ball in a socket, the greater part of the ball being hidden from view (see 12–10).

Take the U-section gouge, and, working around the eye socket, cut a dip where the cheek finishes and the bulge of the bottom lid begins. Next, take a knife and cut a groove where the top lid meets the underside of the brow (see 12–11, top). Draw in the position of the eye, and use the knife to run a stop-cut around the almond shape. Model the ball by cutting from high to low wood—meaning from

12–10 *Use the ¼″ gouge to slowly and carefully round over the eye-socket area.*

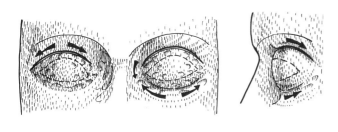

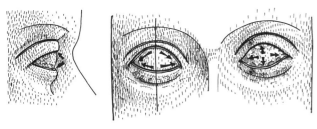

12–11 *Top: Cut a dip under the bottom lid, and finish with the small U-section gouge. Use a knife to cut a groove where the top lid meets the underside of the brow. Bottom left: Run a stop-cut around the almond shape of the eye, working from high to low wood—that is, from the middle to the sides. Bottom right: Lower the whole eyeball area, being careful not to damage the fragile eyelids.*

the vertical axis or central line of the eye down and out towards the pointed ends (see 12–11, bottom left). With the shape of the eye established, take a ⅛″-wide gouge and lower the entire eyeball area. Slice out towards the initial knife cut so as to form the edge of the eyelids (see 12–11, bottom right). Be careful, when you are lowering and shaping the surface of the eye, not to damage the now fragile lid.

When you are happy with the shape and depth of the eyeball, draw the iris in with a pencil line. Then run the point of the knife around the drawn line, so as to describe the edge of the iris with a slender V-section trench. Finally, use the punch to set in the pupil.

Wood-carving tip: As eyes are difficult to carve, you could spend time having a trial run with a piece of scrap wood.

The Chin and Cheeks Study the working drawings and the maquette once more. When you fully appreciate how the cheeks fall away at either side of the mouth—to slope down below the height of the bottom lip—start modelling (see 12–12 on next page).

Being aware that by the time you reach this stage the carving will be pretty close to completion, take a fold of fine-grade sandpaper and rub and stroke the details to a good finish.

The procedure here is as follows: look at the maquette, adjust a detail with a light touch of a small gouge and/or the sandpaper, stand back and assess your work, perhaps make another adjustment, and so on. Notice that, by this stage, some of the details will be within a hair's breadth of being finished. A cut too deep or too much sanding, and you might well spoil the entire piece. Keep the eyebrows sharp, the chin and forehead sanded smooth, the skin left slightly tool-textured. The contrast between smooth areas and areas that are tooled makes for a surface full of movement and interest.

Modelling the Rays Further

Having cut and carved the figurehead so that a good number of wavy ribbonlike rays or streamers are left standing in high relief, set them out now with central lines. When this is done, take a shallow-sweep gouge and skim back and angle the wood to each side of the central lines. Aim to create a ridge. Try to achieve strong curves that taper out towards the ends (see 12–13 on next page).

Finally, when you have grooved out all the secondary furrows, take a ¼″ V-tool and break the

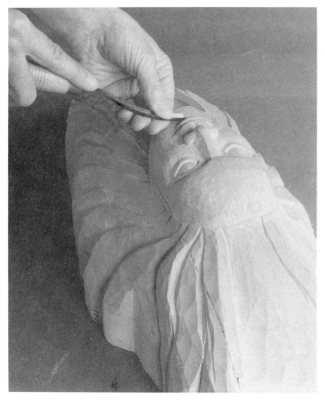

12–12   Use the bent gouge to lower the difficult-to-work gullies around the eyes, at either side of the nose, and under the bottom lip.

12–13   Create the angled sides to the ribbon rays by slicing away the wood at either side of the central line.

edges here and there to give a flamelike feeling of crackle and movement.

Finishing and Painting

When at last you are satisfied with the overall carving—and this is no easy state to reach—take the knife and clean up the various cuts and forms. Aim for a swift, crisp, spontaneous finish. Fill in any cavities or mistakes, and give selected areas a brisk rubdown with fine-grade sandpaper.

Now wipe away the dust, and move to the area you've set aside for painting. Remembering to let it dry and give it a light sanding between coats, lay on a coat of white emulsion all over, followed by a coat of yellow and then gold. Finally—and this is the stage that I like best—give the whole workpiece a couple of coats of clear high-shine varnish,

and the figurehead is ready to exhibit, show off to your friends, or even sell!

TROUBLESHOOTING AND POSSIBLE MODIFICATIONS

- If you have in mind to mount this carving on a boat, then be sure to use waterproof adhesive when gluing up and to brush on additional coats of varnish at the end.
- If you decide to use a section of a log, make sure that it is completely seasoned and free from ring shakes, splits, dead knots, sappy areas, and resinous ooze.
- If you can afford the gold leaf, then it's so much the better. Gold leaf will last 20 or 30 years and still be brilliant.

Clipper

13
Cat's Head Cathead

According to one of the first textbooks on shipbuilding—*Shipbuilder's Assistant,* written in 1711 by a certain Mr. Sutherland—the lion was the standard figurehead image. It's true that most English and European warships of the period, no matter what their name or country of origin, traditionally carried a lion figurehead as a symbol of aggression, speed, and power.

The use of lion imagery was so universal and long-lived that certain parts of the ship's structure came to be named after parts of the lion. For example, the two sections of the prow that swept up to the figurehead were known as "the sweep of the lion" and the "hair bracket." And the huge timbers that projected from either side of the prow—to act as a crane boom when hoisting the anchors up to the rail—were known as "lion's whelps," or, more commonly, as "catheads." It's interesting to note that by the late nineteenth century, lion figureheads had become long out of fashion, the shipbuilders by then favoring portraits of owners, historical figures, and the like; but the builders and seamen still continued to use lion terms for various parts of the ship.

The "lion's whelp," or "cathead," timber is of particular interest, inasmuch as the end of the beam—the outboard head—was nearly always decorated with the face of a cat or lion. The connection between the cathead structure and the cat's head image eventually became so fixed and taken for granted that even when cathead booms had become a thing of the past, the shipbuilders still continued to decorate the anchor-rail area with lion images.

THOUGHTS ON DESIGN AND TECHNIQUE

Take a look at the working drawings (see 13–2 on page 138), and note that, at a scale of three grid squares to 1″, the cathead is cut from a 2″-thick, 8 × 8″-square slab of wood. Also, note the naïve imagery, the simple stylized lines, the bold forms, and the way all the tool marks are left in, with the final carving being given a minimum of sanding and finish.

13–1   The finished cathead.

Consider how the carving is no more than a relief-worked slab. The appearance of roundness and depth has been achieved by the mane texture being wrapped over the slab sides, conveying the illusion that the lion is carved in the round.

This particular cathead draws its inspiration from a piece that was made in Portsmouth, New Hampshire. The original, made of pine and measuring about 14″ wide, bears a label that says, "This piece was carved by John H. Bellamy, 77 Daniel Street, January 1859." This carving is also described as being "a master carving—a wooden pattern used to make sand-cast, iron catheads." I'm inclined to go along with the notion that the carving was used for casting, inasmuch as it is unpainted and sharply lined, without there being any evidence of attachments. All this adds up to a carving that was never fastened to a ship.

TOOL AND MATERIAL CONSIDERATIONS

Although this is a project that can be managed with a minimum of tools, you do need to use a small-bladed band saw and/or a large scroll saw.

13–2 *Working drawings at a scale of three grid squares to 1". Top: Front view. Bottom: Cross section through the eyes.*

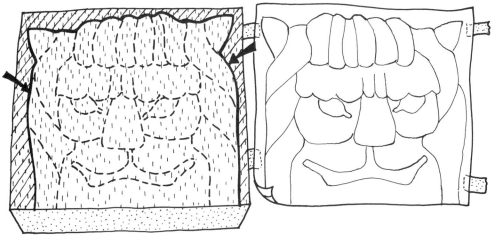

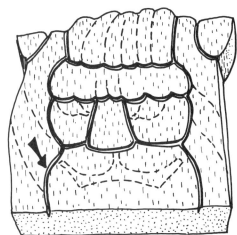

13–3 Top: Rework the main outline profile so that it is clearly defined. Bottom: Set the drawn lines in with ⅛″-deep stop-cuts.

As to your choice of wood, even though we used jelutong, I would, on consideration, recommend that you use a harder wood, like pine or maple. Yes, jelutong is wonderfully easy to carve, but you really need a wood that cuts with a hard, crisp finish.

TOOLS AND EQUIPMENT

For this project, you need:
• a 2″-thick slab of easy-to-carve wood that's 8 × 8″ square
• the use of either a band saw or a scroll saw
• two shallow-sweep straight gouges: ¼″ and ½″ wide
• a ½″-wide straight chisel
• a good sharp knife—we used a penknife
• the use of a workbench with a clamp
• a pencil and ruler
• a sheet each of work-out and tracing paper
• a brush and brown shoe polish
• a pack of graded sandpapers

PROJECT STAGES

Drawing Out the Design and Fretting

When you have checked the slab of wood over to make sure that it is in tip-top condition—no splits, knots, or sappy areas—set it down flat on the bench so that the best face is uppermost and the grain runs vertically.

Wood-carving tip: If you are going to do a lot of flat work on a bench, then you can't do better than getting yourself a clamp and a couple of bench stops/dogs—it's a perfect system for keeping work secure.

Now draw the lion design up to size, take a clear tracing, and pencil-press-transfer the traced image through to the wood. With the image in place, rework the main profile line so that it is absolutely clear and unambiguous (see 13–3, top).

With the transferred lines in place, run the wood through the saw and fret out the profile outline. If you are using a scroll saw, then there's no problem. All you do is run the line of cut a little to the waste side of the drawn line, follow carefully around all the curves and angles, and then exit. If you are using a band saw, it's a bit more tricky. With the band saw, it's best to run a series of straight cuts in from the edge of the wood through to the angles and then to remove the waste within the angles with a series of small bites.

Setting in the Stop-cuts and Roughing Out

When you have achieved a nice clearly cut profile, identify the primary troughs, or trenches, of the design and mark them in with a pencil. For example, you might mark in the line between the mane and the top of the brow, the line between the underside of the brow and the eyes, the lines on either side of the nose, and so on. Don't go over-

139

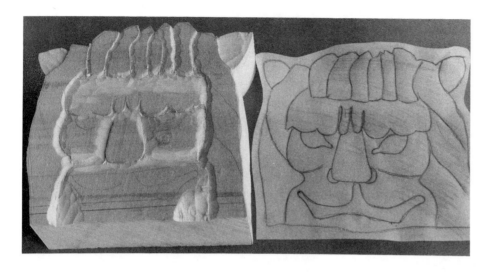

13–4 Use the tracing to ensure that the stop-cuts are correctly placed. As you proceed, the drawn guidelines will need to be reestablished.

board with this marking; just indicate the main troughs, or trenches. With the trough lines in place, take the mallet and the chisels and gouges of your choice and set the drawn lines in with stop-cuts. Chop straight down to a depth of about ⅛″ (see 13–3, bottom).

Now, with one eye on the tracing, and having carefully assessed the depth and width of the various troughs, take one or the other of your small shallow-sweep gouges and make low, slicing cuts at either side of the stop-cuts. Aim to create V-cuts. Bearing in mind that the angle and depth of each V-cut should relate closely to the part of the design that is being carved, work systematically over the slab (see 13–4). For instance, there is a slow flat angle from the top of the eyes through to the start of the mane and a steep angle on either side of the nose. Shape the cuts to suit the particular detail that you are carving.

Continue slicing at varying angles into the various stop-cuts, until the primary features begin to stand up in relief. While you are at it, slice back and lower the ears by about ⅜″ (see 13–5).

Having set in the main design lines with stop-cuts and cleared away the bulk of the waste at either side of the cuts, take a soft pencil and shade in the main areas of waste that need to be lowered and cleared. When this is done, take a small shallow-sweep gouge and start rounding up the main features (see 13–6). Not forgetting that the grain runs from the mane down to the jaw, try all the while to work at the most efficient angle to the run of the grain.

Be aware that if you want to put a brake on a cut, then you need to think ahead and set the limits by defining the area to be carved with a stop-cut line (see 13–7). For example, every time you lower the cheeks at either side of the nose, by making low slicing cuts that run towards the nose, you must be sure to control the cuts by ringing the nose with stop-cuts. Or, to put it another way, if the stop-cuts aren't in place and your low-slicing cut runs out of

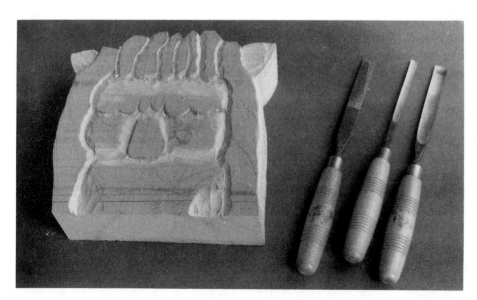

13–5 The completion of the initial cuts, showing the V-section trenches and the lowered areas.

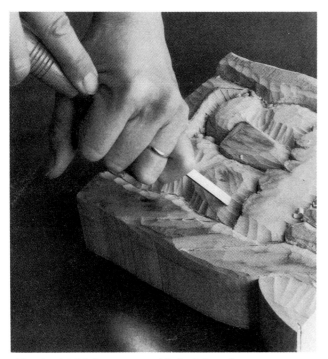

13–6 Hold the gouge with both hands—one guiding and the other pushing. Round the cheeks down and over towards the stop-cuts.

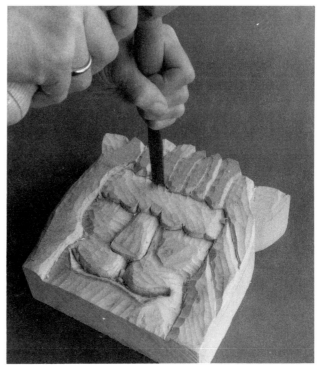

13–7 Make the stop-cuts with the mallet and gouge. Choose a gouge that suits the shape of the drawn line.

control, then the blade will run on through, the lion will lose his nose, and you will lose your temper!

Now continue chopping and changing your tools to suit the task, rounding over the individual waves that make up the top of the mane, rounding and separating the fringe, rounding the cheeks, chopping in the mouth, and so forth. It's all pretty straightforward, as long as you remember that all the tool strokes need to be unfussy and will be on view. The carving needs to look naïve and bold—more like a swift off-the-cuff cartoon than a highly finished piece. Okay, so you can't suddenly become a naïve carver, but you can, to some extent, work towards a swift, crisp finish. You won't go far wrong if you keep your tools sharp, think twice before making a cut, and keep the strokes broad. If nothing else, the cuts need to be smooth and clean.

Wood-carving tip: Get into the habit of stopping along the way to hone your chisels and gouges. I usually carve a little, then stand back to see the carving in its entirety, then hone the tool, then carve a little, and so on. It's a good idea to establish a comfortable working rhythm.

Final Modelling

When you have roughed out the basic relief to the extent of lowering the ears, shaping the mane and fringe, cutting back the wood on either side of the nose, and chopping out the overall shape of the mouth, then you are ready to start modelling the eyes.

Before you do anything else, go back to your tracing and make certain that the eyes are correctly placed and symmetrical in relationship to the central line of the nose and each other. Now take a pair of scissors and cut the tracing in half along the line at the bottom of the fringe. Set the bottom half of the tracing in place on the carving, align it with the nose and the fringe, and carefully pencil-press-transfer the shape of the eyes through to the wood.

Being satisfied with the position and angle of the eyes, take a small, sharp knife and set the drawn lines in with stop-cuts.

Wood-carving tip: Wood-carvers need knives of all shapes and sizes. I have two favorites: a small penknife and a crooked, or hooked, Northwest American Indian knife. You could start your own collection!

Sink the cuts in to a depth of about ⅛″. Now, being careful to keep a tight rein on your strokes, draw the knife around the stop-cut—so that the blade is leaning over the eye at a flat angle—and begin to shape the eye. Aim for a rounded eyeball that appears to run in a curve under the lid. Continue modifying the line of the eyelid and shaping the eyeball, until you achieve a convincing form. If your knife is sharp and you are careful not to let the blade run out of control and into the lid, you won't have any problems.

I have found that, as soon as the eyes are cut, the rest of the carving seems to fall into place. The moment the eyes have been established, the strengths and weaknesses of the rest of the carving tend to become more apparent. For example, once the eyes were finished, I could see that the top mane needed cutting back and the mane at the sides needed to have a bit more of a roll.

When you come to modelling the mouth, take a good long look at the drawings and photographs and note how the mouth is made up from a deep V-section T-cut that runs down from the nose. Consider the way the chops curve up and out from the nose to run in a smooth full curve down into the bottom of the mouth "valley," while the bottom

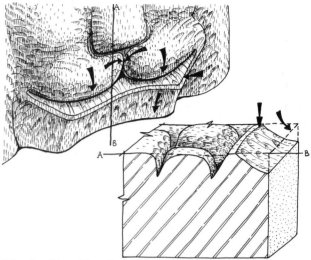

13–8   Top: Note how the mouth is made up from a deep V-section T-cut that runs down from the nose. Bottom: A cross section showing the bottom lip starting at a sharp ridge and angling down to a steep slope.

13–9   Cut the beard furrows, working systematically, and use both hands to control the cut.

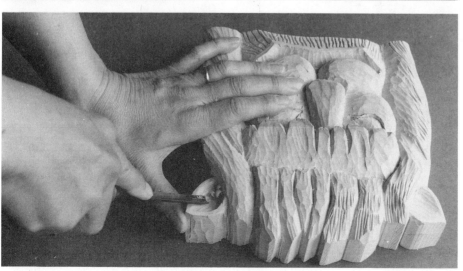

13–10   Use the thumb of your left hand to keep from prying the gouge down into the fragile end grain of the ears' outer edges.

142

lip starts at a sharp ridge to angle down in a steep slope (see 13–8, top).

The procedure for carving the mouth is as follows: repeatedly set the shape of the mouth in with a stop-cut—with either a knife or gouge—run the small shallow-sweep gouge from the sharp ridge down into the bottom of the stop-cut, and then round over the chops. Keep redefining the bottom ridge with a pencil line.

Having cut from the line under the mouth down in a straight steep slope into the mouth, take a pencil and draw along the underside of the ridge (see 13–8, bottom), so as to establish a plateau, or level area, that's a little under ¼″ wide. With the line in place, take a shallow-sweep gouge and cut the shape of the beard. Cut down at a good sloping angle from the chin side of the drawn ridge line. If you are doing it right, you should be left with a level area that defines the underlip—like a little track running along the top of a mountain ridge.

Take a small U-section gouge, and set the beard in with a pattern of furrows (see 13–9). While the small U-section gouge is at hand, set to work scooping out the ears. First chop a stop-cut straight down and level with the side of the mane, and then make sliding scooping cuts a little in from the edge of the ear and down into the depth of the wood to finish up at the stop-cut. Leave a ridge, or thickness, all around the outer edge of the ear. Plan on scooping the ears out to a depth of about ½″ (see 13–10).

Finally, use a ⅛″-diameter bit to drill out the pupil and whisker holes, cut the iris circles around the pupils, and the carving is done.

Finishing

Now give the carving a swift rubdown with the graded sandpapers and move to a dust-free area. Since we started out with a light cream wood and we wanted a dark effect, all we did was give it a couple of coats of dark brown boot polish and buff it to a dull-sheen finish. Of course, if your wood is already a dark color, you can simply give it a clear wax finish. Then again, if your wood is a light color and you want it to remain that way, you can just use a clear wax.

When the finishing is done, sign and date the back and set the carving out for all to see!

TROUBLESHOOTING AND POSSIBLE MODIFICATIONS

- The original cathead carving is about 14″ wide. At about 7 to 8″ wide, our carving is about half that size. If you decide that you want to go for a full-size carving, then it's best to go for a slab of wood that's about 4″ thick.
- Being aware that the grain runs from top to bottom through the slab, be careful not to make the ear tips so thin that they become too fragile and short-grained.

Whaler

14
Jack Tar Figurehead

Towards the middle of the nineteenth century—say, from about 1840 onwards—sailing ships began to change in design. Large ships gradually began to be made of iron or steel, while small ships became increasingly smaller and tighter in form. These changes resulted in much simpler decoration, with smaller and less elaborate trail boards and figureheads that were much reduced in size.

Little by little, over a 50-year period, the figureheads continued to get smaller, until eventually they were replaced by small billet-head scrolls or small busts. It became fashionable—especially on American whalers and schooners and on small naval ships—to model the bust from life. The bust

might be a portrait of the owner, the owner's wife or daughter, or an important statesman.

Our particular figurehead bust draws its inspiration from the Jack Tar figurehead made for the ship H.M.S. *Daring*, launched in 1844.

THOUGHTS ON DESIGN AND TECHNIQUE

Take a look at the working drawings and painting grids (see 14–2, A and B), and note that, at a scale of two grid squares to 1″, the Jack Tar figurehead stands 17″ high and about 10″ wide across the span of the shoulders. He is built up from nine 18″

14–1, A and B   Jack Tar figurehead—front and side views.

144

14–2, A   Working drawing and painting grid—front view. The scale is two grid squares to 1".

14–2, B   Working drawing and painting grid—side view. The scale is two grid squares to 1".

lengths of prepared 4 × 4″-square jelutong, all put together to make a 3 × 3″ block stack.

We found that building the basic blank up from 4 × 4″ sections was especially advantageous, in that we were able to clear away a good deal of the waste before gluing up. It is fair to say that this carving is pretty tricky. For instance, the hat brim is short-grained and fragile, the hunched-over shoulders are a problem inasmuch as they are difficult shapes to envision, the area between the collar and the neck is difficult to reach and you will be cutting into end grain, and the smooth curve of the collar is a subtle form that is arduous to achieve. And, yes, the bow on the hat looks difficult, but it actually can be made in a few minutes and then glued in place once the hat has been carved.

As for the painting, we layered the paint on in a number of thin washes and then rubbed through the layers at edges and wear areas. If you are looking for a challenge, this is a project for you!

Wood-carving tip: If you decide to carve the project from a single section of wood, be extra wary about end splits.

TOOL AND MATERIAL CONSIDERATIONS

Although this is one of the most difficult projects in the book, it can be managed with a relatively small tool kit. All you need is a modest selection of gouges and the use of a band saw.

We decided to use jelutong, but you could just as well use lime, white pine, or almost any straight-grained, knot-free wood that comes your way.

Wood-carving tip: If you decide to build the blank up from a number of sections in the way described, try to be sure that the main features—the nose and mouth—are free from joins. For example, if you look at 14–2, A, you will see that on the front view the joins occur, as planned, on either side of the face. It's easy to see that if we had decided to use an even number of smaller sections of wood—at, say, 2″ square—then one join at least would have occurred smack down the middle of the nose.

TOOLS AND EQUIPMENT

For this project, you need:
• nine 18″ lengths of prepared 4 × 4″-square easy-

to-carve wood—we chose jelutong—plus a small scrap of the same wood for the hat bow
- the use of a band saw
- a scroll or coping saw for cutting the bow
- a ½″-wide deep U-section straight gouge
- two shallow-sweep gouges: ¼″ and ½″ wide
- a ½″-wide straight chisel and a dog-leg chisel
- a V-section tool and a small, sharp knife
- the use of a workbench with a clamp, carver's chops, or a bench stop and sand bag
- a pencil and ruler
- a sheet each of work-out and tracing paper
- a pair each of dividers and callipers
- a good quantity of Plasticine
- a good quantity of PVA adhesive
- a pack of graded sandpapers
- a selection of broad- and fine-point soft-haired paintbrushes
- matt white undercoat emulsion
- acrylic paint in tan, yellow, grey, orange, brown, red, black, dark blue, white, off-white and gold
- a can of clear high-shine yacht varnish

PROJECT STAGES

Drawing Out the Design, Using the Band Saw, and Gluing Up

When you have checked to be sure that the wood is in good condition and set out your tools so that they are comfortably close at hand, draw the design up to full size and trace off the front and side views.

Then take the nine 18″ lengths of wood and arrange them down flat on the bench in a stack three lengths deep and three lengths wide. Spend time arranging the lengths so that the front and side faces are free from damage and faults. Number the lengths 1 through 9, and label the various faces and blocks, so that you know exactly what goes where. It's best to number each block at least twice—on the ends and side. Then you won't have any problem if one of the numbers gets cut away.

With everything organized, take your tracings and carefully press-transfer the front profile through to the wood. Don't worry at this stage about the details; just make sure that the main profile is clearly set out. Repeat the procedure on the other two layers. Then repeat the whole procedure with the side view. If all is correct, all nine lengths of wood will be marked out with some part of both a front and side view.

Once you have correctly set out the wood, move to the band saw and start the dusty and difficult task of cutting away the waste. It's only difficult in that, by the time each length of wood has been through the saw twice, the resulting cutouts will be more or less unrecognizable and almost half the wood will be scattered around the workshop as waste.

The best procedure, when using the band saw in the way described, is to tackle the stack one layer at a time and to very carefully relabel and reassemble the layers as soon as they have been cut.

Once the wood is well organized, take the lengths, one at a time, and smear a generous amount of glue on mating faces and clamp up (see 14–3, A and B). The easiest method is to bind the whole glued-up stack around tight with strong rope and then bang wooden wedges between the workpiece and the binding, until the whole works come together in a tight fit.

Building the Maquette

While the glue is drying, tack your drawings up so that they are in view and set to work building the Plasticine maquette. Warm the Plasticine until it is soft and workable, and then wrap it around an armature—we used nothing more fancy than a lump of wood—and model the form. If you have enough Plasticine, then model the whole figure. If not, settle for modelling what you consider to be the most difficult details. We modelled the front of the hat and the face.

Wood-carving tip: Ideally, the maquette should be as big as the envisioned carving. Okay, so building the maquette can sometimes be a major task, but once it's made, the carving will really take off.

Setting in and Roughing Out

Set the maquette alongside the working drawings, remove the rope and wedges from around the blank, clear away all the debris, and then get down to work. Draw in on the wood what you consider to be the primary features. We decided that we would cut the hat to size and then shape up everything else to fit.

Start by drawing in the line of the brim, as seen in side view, and then use a mallet and gouge to clear the waste. Repeat the procedure for the front view (see 14–4, A and B). When this is done, and bearing in mind that the brim is short-grained and consequently relatively fragile, use the tools of your choice to shape the crown and the top face of the brim. Use a compass to draw guidelines.

Be wary about cutting away too much wood. It's

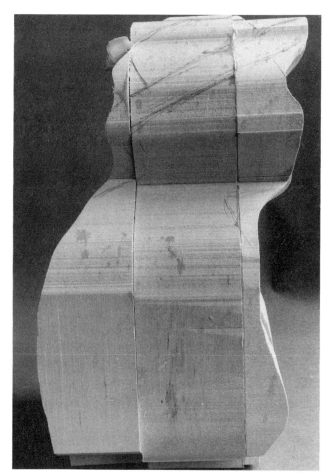

14–3, A and B   Front and side views of assembled and glued blocks, after cutting away the waste on the band saw.

all easy enough, as long as you remember that the hat has to remain round and the sailor's head has to more or less look as if it fits into the hat. Be careful not to get so involved that, say, you cut a beautiful hat that's a little too small and a beautiful head that's a little too big, so that there's no way that the two can fit together.

Having cut the top of the hat to shape and knowing that everything else has to fit and relate to the hat, mark in the line at the bottom of the brim and the secondary details. Draw in a central line for the nose and mouth, sketch out the shape of the collar, and so forth. With the main guidelines in place, take one or the other of your U-section gouges and proceed to cut back the waste from in front of the forehead and around the neck. The forehead area is easy enough, because it's more or less marked out by the width of the central piece of wood, but the neck is a bit more difficult. If you look at the working drawing and painting grid and the maquette in side view, you will see that the shoulders are hunched forward, the neck is stretched out, and the chest is sunk in.

Once you have established the hat, neck, and collar, the rest of the figure can be played around with for the best fit.

Bearing in mind that the true shape and size of the head and face are obscured by the mass of hair and side whiskers, set to work chopping out the neck. Use the U-section gouge to clear the main body of waste from the back of the neck and from under the chin, and then use the dog-leg chisel to slice out the valley between the neck and the rolled collar. Be mindful that at the front of the neck— under the chin and around the Adam's apple— the jutting-out angle of the neck means that the area between the chin and the throat is made up from end grain.

Once you have established the general shape of the neck, use a V-tool to cut in the edge of the collar and the neckerchief. Next, and bearing in mind that you have lots of wood to play around with, use the straight chisel and gouge to lower the triangular area of the shirt front. The procedure is as follows: mark out the area with a pencil line, sink the line with a stop-cut, and then lower the

147

14—4, A and B   Front and side views, showing the rounded hat and the main areas of waste cut away.

waste with the gouge and dog-leg chisel. You might well wonder why you can't simply chop out the layers all of a piece and get the job done. I think you are much more likely to achieve a sound carving if you tackle it layer by layer, all the while doing your best to try to see the whole carving.

So you continue lowering the side whiskers, rounding over the arms and shoulders, cutting the neck deeper and deeper, roughing out the face, and so on. Don't be in a rush, don't try to bring any single area to completion, and do keep checking dimensions by taking calliper readings from the drawings and from the maquette.

Modelling

When you have cleared away the main body of waste and more or less established the overall shape of the carving, then comes the not-so-easy task of modelling the details.

Modelling the Neck

Having studied the working drawings and painting grids (see 14—2, A and B) and the maquette,

and also looked closely at your own neck, take a shallow-sweep gouge and gradually deepen the valley between the neck and the collar (see 14—5). Especially notice the change of direction where the neck meets the shoulders and throat, the hollow at the bottom front of the neck, the protruding Adam's apple, and the column of muscle that runs down the side of the neck. Not forgetting about the end grain under the chin, lay the carving down flat on the bench and skim the gouge—we used a dogleg down the length of the neck, so as to finish up in the neck-collar valley (see 14—6).

Modelling the Face

Once you have roughed out the main features, drawn in a central line, and marked in the position of the nose, eyes, and mouth—use calliper measurements to get this right—start by using a gouge to cut back the whiskers. Chop them back until the sides of the face are revealed. While you are at it, thin down the sides of the whiskers and hair so as to establish the line of the hat brim.

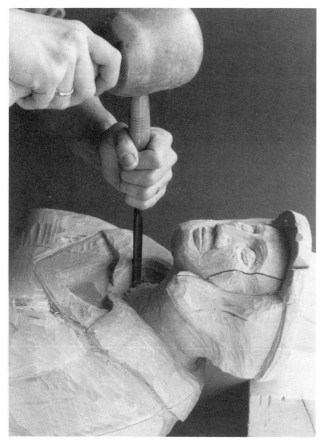

14–5　*When you come to the front of the collar, use the mallet and shallow-sweep gouge to chop across the grain.*

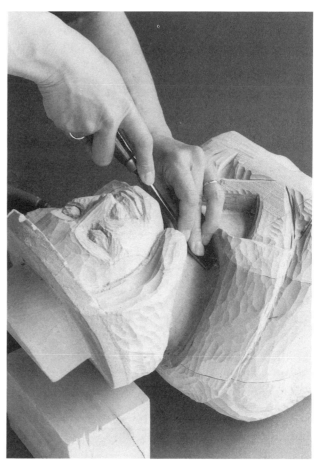

14–6　*The front of the neck is a tricky area to carve. Finish the surface with the dog-leg chisel.*

Carving the face is relatively straightforward, as long as you appreciate just how sharply the form falls back from the central line along the forehead, nose, and chin. The secret is to more or less leave the central line in place. This is important to bear in mind, because it's all too easy to keep carving away at the nose and lips too a point where you run out of wood.

So you continue skimming back the sides of the forehead, shaping the eyeballs so that they angle out to the side (see 14–7 on page 150), skimming the sides of the nose so that they run down to the cheeks, angling the top lips, shaping the sides of the chin, and so on (see 14–8 on page 150). If you have any doubts about the shape of the face, it would be a good idea to sit a friend down in an easy chair and study his or her features by looking down from the top of the head.

Our sailor is characterized by having a somewhat mournful expression, with heavy upper eyelids, eyebrows that slant down, and a heavy upper lip. However, there's no reason why you couldn't modify the features somewhat and model them after your own or a friend's. You won't go far

wrong if your tools are sharp and you take it a little at a time.

Modelling the Collar

Having pencilled in the line of the collar and the curve at the top edge of the shirt—something like a sweat shirt—first use a very sharp tool to sink the drawn lines with stop-cuts and then skim back with a shallow-sweep gouge and the dog-leg chisel. Try to achieve a soft and easy curve along the collar (see 14–9 on page 151). When this is done, undercut the front edge and run furrows up the folded neckerchief. Make stop-cuts to define the top edge of the arms, and lower the depth of the neckerchief (see 14–10 on page 151). If you have any doubts as to how the collar needs to fall, you might set up a little still life with a piece of heavy fabric and look at the roll, ripple, and fall firsthand.

Use a penknife to shape and cut the little detail where the collar rolls around and disappears behind the shirt, and a dog-leg chisel where the neckline of the shirt runs around under the "wings" of the collar (see 14–11 on page 151).

149

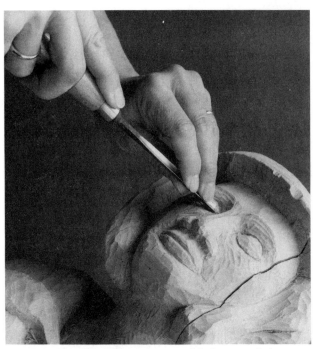

14–7 Use the ¼" gouge to model the rounded eyeball, working with very light, controlled movements.

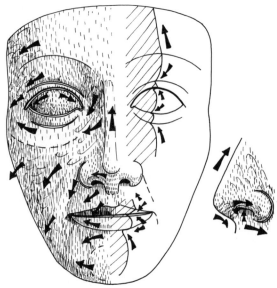

14–8 Skim the sides of the nose so that they run down to the cheeks. Angle the top lip so that it shelves inward, and model the bottom lip so that it curves down towards the chin. The tip of the nose is most prominent, with all the other details angling down and away.

Modelling the Arms and Chest

Folded arms are always somewhat difficult, because you have to create the illusion that one arm is tucked and folded under the other. Usually the problem is how to convincingly show both hands. We avoid part of this problem with our Jack Tar by having one hand completely covered up with the ends of the neckerchief. And, with the hand that is in full view, the form is simplified by having the thumb tucked down and out of sight.

Having drawn in the shape of the arms—as seen from front and side views—take a mallet and gouge and clear away the waste from the underside of both arms. With the overall shape of the arm roughed out, draw in an arm central line that runs from the shoulder, down the side of the upper arm, around the tip of the elbow, and along the forearm. Now take a mallet and shallow-sweep gouge and start to round over the arm. With the central line along the high wood, shape the arms so that the underside rolls into the side and waist and the top side rolls variously into the neckerchief and the chest (see 14–12). As the arms begin to take shape, you can start to model the neckerchief and the chest.

The chest area is an interesting challenge, inasmuch as you have to cut it back so that it appears to run in a smooth line, from the top of the arm, under the neckerchief, and through to the white shirt. The small triangle of the chest (refer back to 14–2, A) was particularly tricky and evasive. The chest didn't begin to reveal itself until I had lowered the top face of the left arm. At one point things were going so badly that I thought I had made a mistake somewhere along the line. But everything became clear the moment I started to reduce the underside of the neckerchief and the top side of the left arm.

Finally, with the arms more or less modelled, use a V-tool to slice out the stylized folds and creases.

Modelling the Shoulders

Bearing in mind that a good many figureheads are only carved at the front and sides, with the back left simply roughed out, you have to decide whether or not you want the back of the figure to be on display. You might feel, for example, that, because your figure is going to be fastened flush against the prow of your boat, or maybe stood in a niche where the back is hidden from view, there is no need to bother with the back. However, we decided to go for an all-around carving.

Run the line of the collar around the shoulders, and then step down to the back and shoulders. Use a shallow-sweep gouge to flatten the shoulder blades and to scoop out the spine valley between the shoulders. Tidy up under the arms, so that the crease between the underside of the upper arms

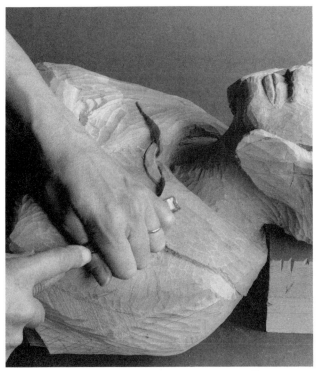

14–9 *Slightly hollow the surface of the collar, so as to create a natural fold where it turns over to come to rest on the chest and shoulders.*

and the side of the body is sharp. Then smooth out the crease at the top back of the arms, so that the upper part of the underarms runs in a smooth dip through to the shoulders and back.

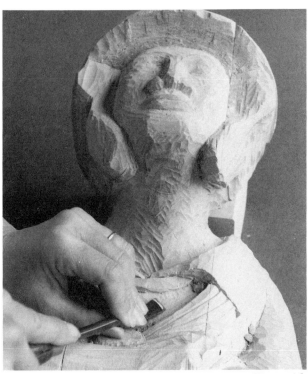

14–11 *Make sideways slicing cuts—controlling with one hand and holding and maneuvering the tool with the other.*

Modelling the Hair

If you refer back to the project pictures (14–1, A and B) and the working drawings and painting grids (14–2, A and B), you will see that the fullness

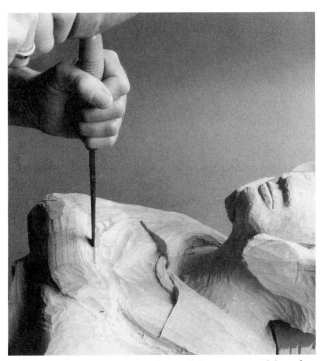

14–10 *Define the top edges of the arms and hand with a chopped-in stop-cut.*

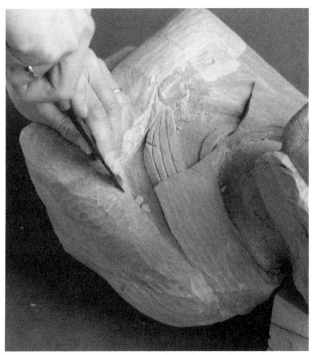

14–12 *Model the arms so that the surface rolls around and down towards the chest.*

151

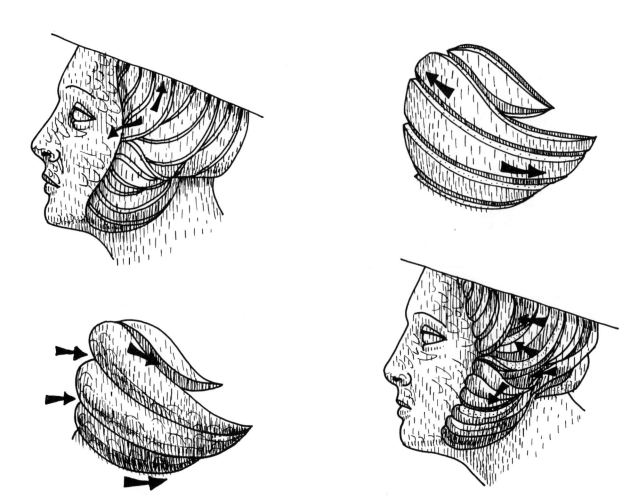

14–13 Top: Use the V-tool to cut the shape of the individual curls and locks. Bottom: Rework selected furrows, so that some hair masses appear to pass under and over others

of the hair has been exaggerated so that the hair becomes a support or bracket for the sides of the hat brim. Start by using a shallow-sweep gouge to bring the overall shape of the hair to a good finish. So, you can undercut the ends of the whiskers where they meet the chin and neck, cut in the valley that makes the curl on the right-hand side of the head, and so on.

When you have achieved the general shape of the hair, give the surfaces a swift rubdown with the sandpaper, draw in pencil guidelines, and then use the V-tool to cut in the shape of the individual curls and locks (see 14–13, top). Remembering that you are only aiming to carve stylized hairlike forms, chop out furrows that suggest the main masses of hair. When this is done, take the knife and rework selected furrows, so that some hair masses appear to pass under and over others (see 14–13, bottom).

Wood-carving tip: As this procedure is in many ways akin to cutting the shape of a coiled rope, it might be a good idea to take a look at the Running-Rope Borders project.

Modelling the Hat Bow

Take a scrap of 1″-thick wood, and draw out the bow as seen in the side view—see the working drawings (14–14, top). Clear the waste with the band saw or, better still, a scroll saw, and generally fret the bow out (see 14–15 on page 154). Use a gouge to lower the wood on the top edge of the bow "wings." When this is done, take a penknife and swiftly trim the cutout to shape. Finally, adjust the back of the bow so that it is a snug fit against the crown of the hat, sand it to a smooth finish, and glue it in place on the hat.

Further Modelling

Continue working backwards and forward, over and around the carving, until it all comes together. Pay particular attention to the eyes—the fullness of the bottom lids and their relationship to the curve of the cheeks (see 14–16 on page 154). Use a knife to trim and deepen the side of the eyeballs, so as to finish up with nicely rounded forms. Carry on until you are pleased with the overall effect. As

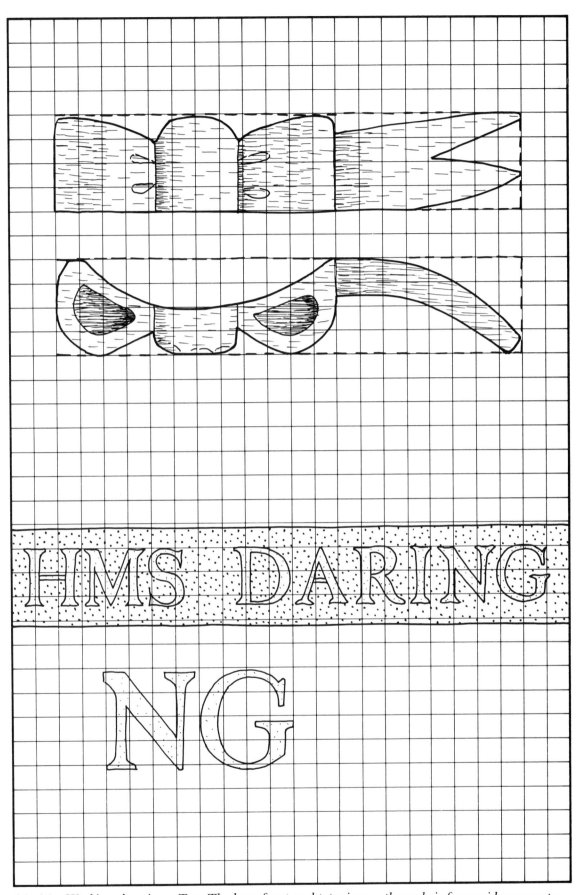

14–14   *Working drawings. Top: The bow, front and top views—the scale is four grid squares to 1". Bottom: The lettering for the hat and jacket—the scale is four grid squares to 1".*

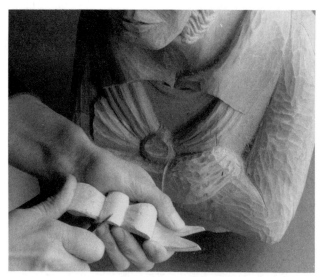

14–15 Use the penknife to round over the sawn edges, to achieve both front and side views.

14–16 Gradually pare away the wood in order to form the little shelflike ridge between the bottom eyelids and the cheekbones.

with all the other projects, if you have any doubts as to such-and-such a detail or any misgivings about the carving as a whole, put it to one side and go back to it another day.

Finishing and Painting

Take a scrap of fine-grade sandpaper and a sharp knife, and go over and tidy up all the surfaces. Clean out the crevices, rub off the rough areas and nibs, and generally bring the work to completion. Then brush away the dust and debris, and make use of the filler. Refer back to the working drawings and painting grids (see 14–2, A and B) before you start painting. Then rub the whole workpiece down with sandpaper, clean away the dust, and lay on a couple of coats of matt white emulsion.

When the white emulsion is dry, lay on a wash of tan paint all over. While the tan wash is still damp, use various thin washes—orange, yellow, grey, and red—to color the face, neck, and hands. Try to achieve a painterly effect, just as you might if you were painting a portrait. Have the lighter tones on the shoulders, forehead, nose, and cheeks, and the darker tones in areas of shadows around the eyes, under the cheeks, nose, and chin, and the throat. Paint the eyeballs white, block in the irises with grey-brown, paint the pupils and eyelashes black, tint the lips with red, and so on. When the flesh areas are dry, paint the jacket, collar neckerchief, and hatband with a wash of blue-black, the hat a mixture of yellow-green and orange, and the hair an all-over brown with streaks of blue-black. Paint the sweat shirt and the collar stripes off-white. Last, trace and press-transfer the letters in place

on the hatband and jacket, and line them with gold—see the working drawings (14–14, bottom on page 153).

Making sure that the workpiece is dry, take a scrap of fine-grade sandpaper and rub through at wear areas: the edge of the hat brim, the roll of the collar, the shoulders, and so forth. Wipe away the dust, and give the whole works a couple of generous coats of varnish. Finally, sign and date the base, and the job is done.

TROUBLESHOOTING AND POSSIBLE MODIFICATIONS

• If the hat brim starts splitting away, as it did with me, simply cut out the damaged areas—with a V-cut—make a wedge shape to fit the cut, and then glue the wedge in place.

• On close inspection, I saw that the original sailor's hat brim was built up from strips—either when it was first carved or as a repair. Therefore, if you made any mistakes with your brim, you could cut it all away, run a groove around the crown, and use ½"-thick wood to build a brim.

• On consideration, I think that either our sailor's head is a little too big or the hat is too small. What do you think? I told you that this project is a challenge!

• Acrylic paint will survive the ravages of all kinds of weather if it is protected with a couple of generous coats of yacht varnish. However, if you decide to use oil-bound paint, or enamels, or whatever, allow a couple of extra days for painting and then still give the finished work a couple of coats of varnish.

Inspirational designs Left: Sailor figurehead, 69" high, 1860, found in Maine. Top right: Sailor figurehead from the British sloop H.M.S. Cruizer, 1852, wearing the newly established uniform of the lower deck. Bottom right: Beckoning-sailor figurehead, from an unidentified ship, about 1850, Denmark.

15
Jenny Lind Figurehead

The inspiration for this project—the figurehead Jenny Lind, carved for the ship *Nightingale of Portsmouth*, registered in New Hampshire in about 1851—is, to my eyes at least, one of the most beautiful American female figureheads of the mid-nineteenth century. With her full figure, ringleted hair, slightly tilted head, and serene eyes, she is a wonderfully evocative and confident example of figureheads of the period. A three-quarter figure, now missing her arms, she was supposedly modelled after Jenny Lind, the famous Swedish opera singer who was affectionately known as "the Swedish Nightingale."

American three-quarter figureheads of this type, period, and character were designed and carved in such a way that they could be mounted on a bracket or shelf, with the scroll part of the carving running in a smooth unbroken curve to the part of the prow known as the cutwater. In this position, Jenny Lind would have stood more or less upright, most likely with her arms outstretched in a joyous welcoming pose.

The figurehead symbolized the heart and character of a ship. Give a ship a name and a figurehead, and it immediately took on a character and personality of its own. According to old accounts, sailors were very protective when it came to a ship's reputation. To cast a slur on a ship—its lack of speed, bad handling, or whatever—was akin to giving the figurehead a bad name.

As to the character of the *Nightingale of Portsmouth*, she must have been a wonderful ship—beautiful, successful, confident, and proud—just like her figurehead!

THOUGHTS ON DESIGN AND TECHNIQUE

Take a look at the photographs and the working drawings and painting grids (see 15–2, A and B), and note that, at a scale of one grid square to 1″, Jenny stands about 35″ high, and is 14″ wide across the span of the scrolls and about 10″ in depth. Also, note that she is built up from twelve 36″ lengths of

15–1   The Jenny Lind figurehead.

4 × 4″-square planed jelutong—four lengths wide and three lengths deep. We could have searched around for a single bulk of wood, but we decided to go for this laminated option for a couple of reasons. First of all, a laminated figure is less likely to move and split, and, secondly, it is possible to get by without a lot of sweat and slog by clearing a good deal of the waste on the band saw. In other words, if you draw the figure out on the stack of wood at the stage prior to gluing, then each of the 4 × 4″ sections can be run through a small band saw. Certainly, you have to label each piece of wood and make sure that you are clear in your own mind

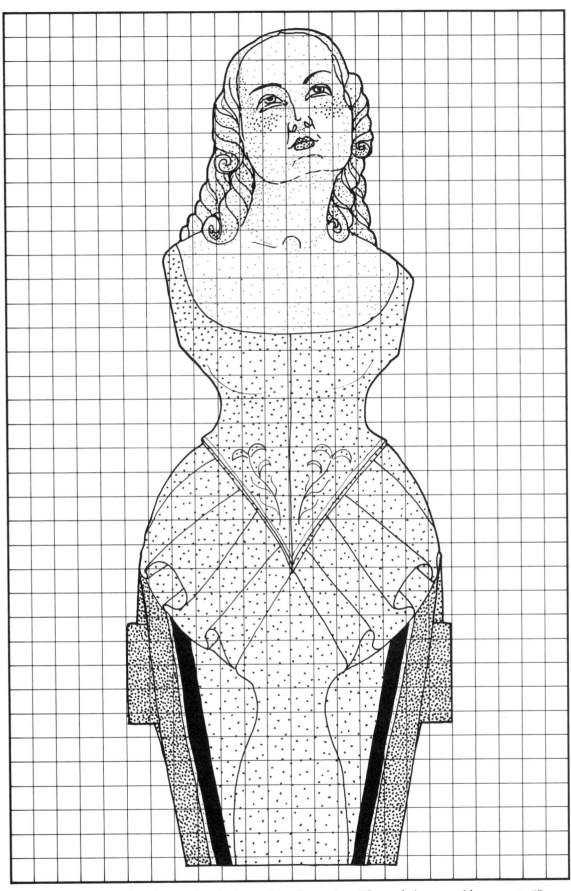

15–2, A   Working drawing and painting grid—front view. The scale is one grid square to 1".

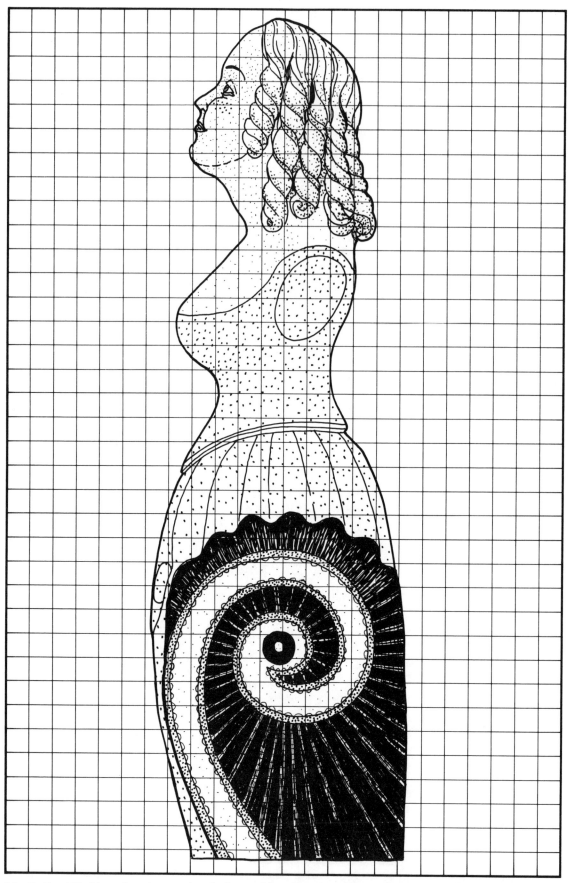

15–2, B   Working drawing and painting grid—side view. The scale is one grid square to 1".

15–3, A   The Plasticine maquette—front view. Note the tilt of the head.

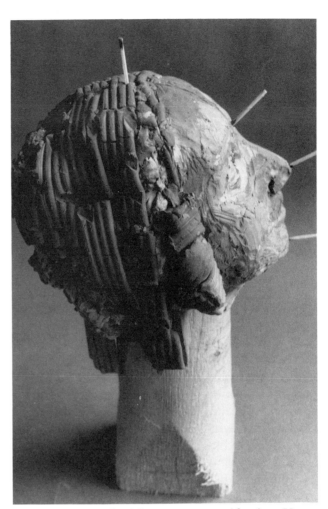

15–3, B   The Plasticine maquette—side view. Use match sticks to indicate the main reference points.

as to what goes where, but it's a wonderful time-saver if you get it right.

Note how this particular figurehead is made up from four primary elements, or areas of carving: the hair, the face and throat, the dress, and the scrolls.

Finally, it's worth noting that Jenny is a bonny lass—so big and heavy, in fact, that I needed a little help when it came to moving her around.

TOOL AND MATERIAL CONSIDERATIONS

Although this may appear to be a daunting project—altogether too big and intimidating for beginners—it is, in fact, a pretty simple piece of carving. However, you do need space, help when it comes to lifting her around, and a good range of tools.

If you decide to carve her from a single bulk of a much harder type of wood, then you will have to forget about using the band saw and probably have to use heavier tools.

TOOLS AND EQUIPMENT

For this project, you need:
- twelve 36″ lengths of 4 × 4″ planed and finished wood—we used jelutong, but you could just as well use an easy-to-carve wood like lime or white pine
- a large-width shallow-sweep bent gouge
- three shallow-sweep gouges: about ¼″, ½″ and, 1″ wide
- a slightly deeper U-section gouge that's about ⅜″ wide
- a spoon gouge that's about ⅜″ wide
- a V-tool
- a sharply pointed knife
- the use of a workbench
- a pencil and ruler
- a large pair of callipers
- a large sheet each of work-out and tracing paper—as big as the front and side views of the carving
- a large block of Plasticine

159

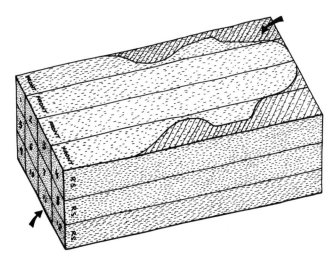

15–4 Having numbered and labelled the arrangement, set the wood down flat on the bench so that the front face is uppermost and press-transfer the traced profile through to the front four lengths.

- a collection of found stick tools for modelling
- three or four yards of strong rope for clamping
- a good amount of white PVA adhesive
- a collection of hardwood wedges for clamping
- a can of matt white emulsion paint
- acrylic paint in blue-green, red, pinkish tan, flesh tone, black, yellow, brown, sepia, and gold
- a couple of soft-haired paintbrushes: a broad- and a fine-point
- a pack of graded sandpapers
- a can of high-gloss boat varnish

PROJECT STAGES

Making the Maquette

When you have studied the design, drawn the image out to size, and made tracings of the front and side views, take the Plasticine and set to work building a maquette of the head. It's a very relaxing and satisfying procedure.

Special tip: If the Plasticine is very hard, break it into small crumbs and put it in a warm place to soften. Also, Plasticine is best removed from the hands with petroleum jelly.

With your working drawings and painting grids (15–2, A and B) close at hand for easy reference, and having first achieved the slight tilt to the head, concentrate on the primary features: the nose, eyes, and mouth. Add a bit here and there, take some away, stand back to admire your work, and check off measurements with the callipers, slowly building up the forms.

Although modelling the Plasticine is relaxing, this is not to say that it's easy! The best procedure, if you are making it life size, is to model the details from life. Therefore, try to find a female friend who will pose for you, and then step off the measurements and shapes directly.

Special tip: Your model needs to be a buddy. What's more, your model has to be able to sit quietly, while you run the callipers backwards and forward over her face.

Finally, when you have achieved what you consider to be a well-modelled head, spike the main triangulation points with match sticks—such as the nose, chin, and eyes—and set the maquette safely to one side (see 15–3, A and B).

Setting Out the Wood, Cutting On the Band Saw, and Gluing Up

When you have checked your twelve 36″ lengths of 4 × 4″ wood over to make sure that they are free from splits, warps, and knots, square off the ends

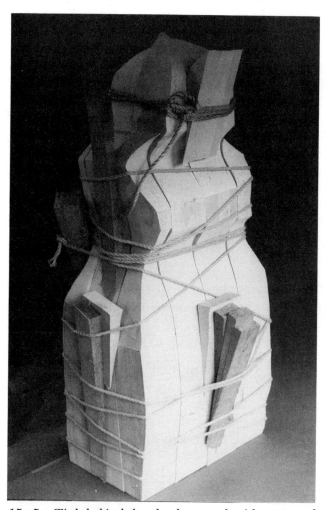

15–5 Tightly bind the glued-up stack with rope, and tighten up with wedges.

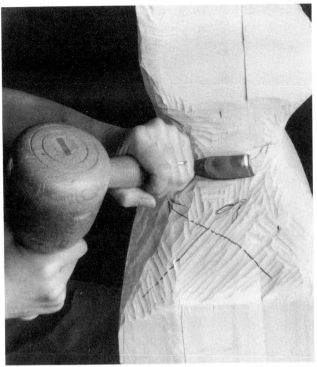

15–6 *Slice away the sharp corners of waste, working in a slow spiral so as to finish at the waist.*

and stand them up on the bench, so that you have a stack four widths wide and three widths deep. Spend time chopping and changing the arrangement, so that any corner damage is either going to be at the very middle of the figure, or at the outside where it will be cut away with the rough.

Having numbered and labelled the arrangement so that you know exactly what goes where, set the wood down flat on the bench—with the front face of the stack uppermost—and pencil-press-transfer the traced front profile through to the front four lengths of wood (see 15–4).

Wood-carving tip: The profile must be reduced to a simple easy-to-cut shape, so leave all the details on the generous size.

When this is done, remove the top four lengths and repeat the procedure right through the stack. With all the front views in place, reassemble the stack so that the side view is uppermost and set to work transferring the side image in the way already described. Make sure that the lines are clear, and shade areas that need to be cut away. By the time you have finished, all 12 lengths of wood

15–7, A *Front view—when you are rounding the forms, take calliper readings to ensure that proportions are correct.*

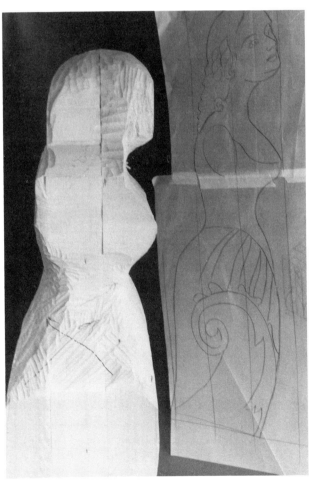

15–7, B *Side view—use the drawings as a reference.*

should be marked out so that you know precisely what needs to be cut away.

With all the guidelines in place, take the lengths of wood, one at a time, and run them through the band saw. The procedure is the following: cut away the waste as seen in one view, reassemble the waste, turn the wood over, and cut away the waste as seen in the other view. Do this with all 12 lengths of wood.

Wood-carving tip: By the time you have tackled all 12 lengths of wood, you will have a whole heap of waste and 12 difficult-to-recognize pieces of wood, so be sure to number the pieces and shade the waste areas.

With the workshop cleared of all the dust and debris, and having rearranged the wood in the original 12-piece stack, smear and spread glue on all mating faces and clamp up. The easiest way of working is to tightly bind the glued-up stack with rope and then to bang wedges between the binding and the wood. Continue until the whole stack tightens up and all the glued faces are butted hard against each other (see 15–5 on page 160).

Roughing Out and First Cuts

When the glue is dry and all the rope and wedges have been removed, then comes the exciting task of making the first cuts. I really enjoy this stage—the gouges are sharp, I'm fresh and ready to begin, and the wood is just asking to be cut!

With the workpiece arranged at a comfortable working height, the tracing tacked up on the wall, and the maquette and callipers within easy reach, take the mallet and your favorite large sweep gouge and get down to work.

Wood-carving tip: Be warned, if you work at the wrong height, your back will probably ache. Spend time figuring out the best working height. If it's any help, I find that my wood-carving bench needs to be about 6″ higher than my woodworking bench.

Make repeated passes, backwards and forward and around and around the workpiece, all the while slicing away the sharp corners of waste. Work up from the hips and down from the shoulders and bosom (see 15–6 on page 161). Go at it with smooth, gentle movements—tap-slice, tap-slice, tap-slice—all the while running around the figure in a slow spiral that finishes at the waist. If you go at it nice and easy, you will find that the slow spiralling movements not only help you define the full roundness of the hips and breasts and the

beautiful nipped-in curve of the waist, but they also map out the best line of cut in relationship to the run of the grain. The spiral route—from the breasts down and from the hips up—is the route that best avoids cutting into end grain. If you work in a slow spiral in a clockwise direction and then reverse the movement and travel in a counter-clockwise direction, you will be able to achieve a figure that is both symmetrical and well rounded.

Work around the figure as seen in the front view and then as seen in the side view, all the while checking off against the drawings (see 15–7, A and B, on page 161). If you have both the maquette and the drawings placed behind the carving, you will be able to keep checking them until you get the curves right.

Don't be in too much of a hurry; just take it nice and easy. Of course, if you find that the gouge is cutting up roughly, the wood needs to be approached in another direction, or whatever, then stop, reposition the wood, rehone the tool, and generally spend time assessing your work. Also, take calliper readings to ensure that the initial proportions are correct.

Modelling the Face and Neck

After cutting away all the sharp corners and edges, you'll be ready to start modelling the face and neck.

Wood-carving tip: Establish and keep a central line—this will help you balance the features.

Begin by establishing the primary areas: the line of the hair, the width of the face, and the position of the features in relationship to each other. Be mindful that the point of the nose is the outermost limit of your material (see 15–8, left). If you slice away the nose, you can't swiftly stick it back on again, as you can when modelling Plasticine; the best you can do is lower the cheeks. Therefore, it pays to cut the face back in a number of small, very slow, carefully checked stages.

Wood-carving tip: Yes, you can glue on a lump of wood to repair a mistake, but it's a long, drawn-out process that's best avoided!

Looking at your maquette from side view, measure the step-backs from the point of the nose to the fullness of the lips and then from the lips to the chin and so on. Assess how much wood you've got to play with, and then lower the various planes accordingly (see 15–8, right). Having noted how the neck slopes forward towards the chin, cut back at the point where the neck and body meet (see 15–8, right).

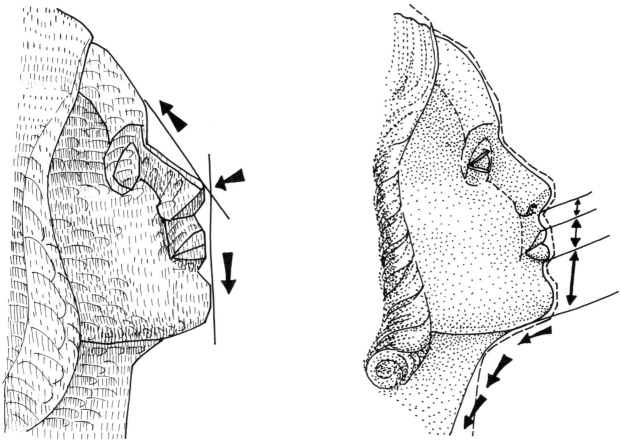

15–8   Left: Establish the primary areas—note that the ends of the nose and the chin are the outermost limits of the face. Right: Side view of the maquette, showing the step-backs needed for the lips and chin.

Don't be too slavish about carving the face in terms of our design; be prepared to carve the features to suit your own fancies. Certainly, the various features have to relate well with each other and be in proportion, but if you feel that you want to veer away from the drawings and model the carving after your mother, the girl next door, or whomever, then it's best to go in that direction. However, it's important to bear in mind that figureheads, by their very nature, should be naïve and vigorous in style, rather than sophisticated or bland. Experience has taught me that if I over-work the carving and make the features too small and tight, then the chances are that the sum total carving will lack conviction. The carving needs to be bold.

As you get closer and closer to the envisaged form, start using smaller tools and taking smaller, more controlled cuts (see 15–10, next page). To this end, put the mallet to one side and use the ¼″-wide gouge. Keep the tool moving backwards and forward around the face, neck, and shoulders, all the while being careful to cut with the run of the grain. Once you have chopped out the shapes of the nose and mouth, as seen from front view, then

start lowering the sides of the forehead, cheeks, nose, mouth, and neck so that these features fall back and become more rounded. Don't concentrate too much on any single feature; it's much better to try to work them all in turn. Working in this manner, you will be able to achieve a balance.

There are several potential problem areas. For example, when you are working on the nose, there will come a point when you will need to lower the cheek so that the transition from the nose to the cheek will be rounded and concave, rather than angular and stepped. I found that the easiest way to carve this area was to take a small deep-curve gouge and pry against the side of the nose with a careful scooping movement, so that the blade skimmed down the sides of the nostrils and then followed through across the cheeks and down to the corner of the mouth. It's not easy, so go at it very slowly (see 15–11, left on page 165).

If at any time you can't quite see how one feature relates to another, then either take calliper readings from the maquette or run your fingertips over your model's face to familiarize yourself with the various surfaces and curves firsthand.

The lips are particularly tricky, inasmuch as the

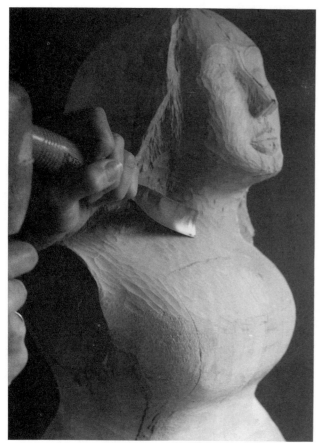

15–9   Working from the side, cut step-backs from the point of the nose through to the slope of the neck. The neck should thrust forward from the body.

15–10   Use smaller tools with two hands and make carefully controlled cuts, as you get closer to the envisioned form.

character and balance of the face tend to be governed by the shape of the mouth. A little too much down-curl at the ends of the mouth, and the face becomes sulky; if the lower lip is too full, the face looks pouty; and then again, too much upturn at the ends of the mouth makes the face appear to be grinning.

Wood-carving tip: The short grain on the lip and chin needs to be worked with an extra-light touch—use two hands and a very sharp tool.

When you come to carving the eyes, bear in mind that the eye is, in fact, a large ball that sits in a socket framed by the cheek and brow. The part of the eye that we see is only a relatively small part at the front of the total ball. And, although we have top and bottom eyelids, it is only the top lids that really shutter down to cover the eyeballs. What's more, the eyeballs are set well back in the sockets and angled slightly so that they look out at the side of the face (see 15–11, top right). The point is that, if you are going to successfully carve an eye—or any other feature—you need to be familiar with its structure and position.

I decided to forget about the small folds and creases of the eyelids and concentrate on the main curve that runs down from the brow to the eyeballs and the little flat area that shelves out from the eyeballs to the cheeks (see 15–11, bottom right).

I used a small spoon gouge to scoop out the waste at either side of the nose and the small shallow-sweep gouge for the eyelids. Once again, the actual technique of carving isn't especially difficult—although you have to make sure that you don't cut directly into end grain—but achieving a convincing form is more than a challenge.

Modelling the cheeks, chin, shoulders, and throat is relatively simple and straightforward, inasmuch as Jenny Lind is so nicely plump and rounded that you don't have to carve the bone structure. Use a broad gouge, and run the neck profile down in a smooth curve, from the chin, over and around the bosom, and on down to the waist.

Wood-carving tip: It's important to note that the neck doesn't spring vertically from the shoulders, but rather slopes forward to the chin.

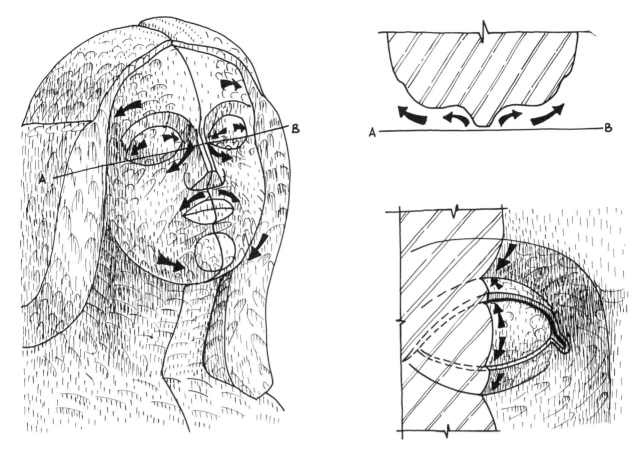

15–11   Left: Skim down the sides of the nostrils, across the cheeks, and down to the corners of the mouth. Top right: The eyes need to be set well back in the sockets and angled slightly so that they look out at the side of the face. Bottom right: The eye is a complex shape and needs to be kept rounded.

And so you continue making a cut, sighting the profile to check on the curve, making another cut, sighting, and so forth. Be mindful, when you are carving the face, that it's not so much the individual features that are a problem, but rather bringing all the features together to make a convincing and balanced whole.

Modelling the Dress

If you look at the working drawings and painting grids (see 15–2, A and B) and the photographs, you will see that the dress is made up from two elements: the smooth and rounded bodice, and the textured skirt. Note the way that the skirt curves out in a number of pleats and folds from the bottom of the pointed bodice to stop short just above the top and sides of the scrolls.

When you have studied all the elements that make up the costume, take a pencil and draw a central line that runs from the nose, down over the bosom and waist, and on through to the bottom of the figure. This line is important, so get it right the

first time around. With the line in place, use a pencil and masking tape to draw in the curve of the top of the bodice and the V-shaped terminal.

Having checked that the lines are well placed, take a V-tool and run a groove around the bottom of the bodice. Have the groove on the skirt side of the drawn line. If you start at the point in the middle of the front and work outward on each side so as to run over the swell of the hips and then through to the middle of the back, you will avoid cutting into end grain (see 15–12, left and central top on page 164).

Wood-carving tip: The function of the V-trench is to act as a brake, or check, on the downward thrust of the stop-cut. The V-trench ensures that the potentially damaging movement created when making the stop-cut is directed out towards the waste side of the drawn line.

Next, take a good-width shallow-sweep gouge and work around the figure, slicing up from the skirt and in towards the bottom-of-bodice stop-cut (see 15–12, top right on page 164). And so you proceed working around the skirt side of the bot-

165

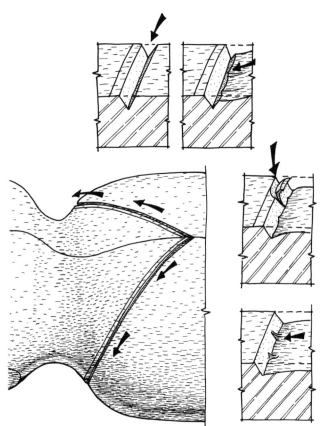

15–12   Left and top: Run a groove around the bottom of the bodice, making the cut on the skirt side of the drawn line. Central bottom: Chop down on the drawn line, so that the thin area of waste crumbles down into the groove. Bottom left: Grade the wood on the top of the skirt, so that the skirt springs out in a full, smooth curve from under the bodice.

15–13   Use the dog-leg chisel to skim and finish the ground, so that the skirt hem stands proud by about ½".

tom of the bodice, all the while cutting away the waste. With the V-cut in place, take a mallet and shallow-sweep gouge and chop a stop-cut along the drawn line, so that the small amount of waste between the drawn line and the side of the V-cut crumbles away. Do this all around the bottom of the bodice (see 15–12, central bottom).

When you have established a step-down from the bodice to the skirt, grade the wood on the top of the skirt, until the skirt appears to spring out in a smooth curve from under the bodice (see 15–12, bottom right).

Once the top of the skirt is finished, draw in the hem line. Use your tracing to ensure that the folds at either side of the front central line are symmetrical. Now, not worrying too much about the back of the figure, which can be left more or less flat, work around the entire carving. Continue, until the front runs in a smooth curve down to the base and the hips curve out towards the sides.

When you are satisfied with the overall profile, carefully shade in all the areas below the hem line

that need to be cut away and/or lowered and draw in the lines of the pleats and folds. Take the V-tool, and run a groove all around the underside of the hem line. Using the chisel and gouges that best fit the contours, carefully set in the drawn lines with a stop-cut. When this is done, use variously the shallow-sweep small gouge and the dog-leg chisel to lower and cut away the wood at the front of the skirt. In other words, slice away the wood to the waste side of the V-cut, until the fancy profile of the front hem of the skirt stands up by about ½" or so from the lowered ground (see 15–13). Don't try to gouge the waste out in one great thrust, but rather lower it layer by layer until you feel you're at the right depth. Be wary, when you are slicing up towards the hem of the skirt, that you don't overshoot and drive the blade into end grain.

The order of work is as follows: make the stop-cut, skim up towards the stop-cut so that the ground waste falls away, reestablish the shape with another stop-cut, and so on, until the edge of the skirt stands proud.

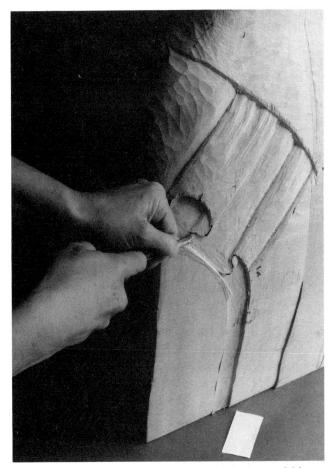

15–14 *Lower and shape the sides of the inner folds, to create the illusion of rippled and folded fabric.*

When you are ready to carve the folds, follow the same procedure as already described, only this time cut down to a depth of about ¼″. With the folds and ripples of the hem in place, take the V-tool and set in the fold and pleat lines that run from the hem to the waist. Lower and shape the sides of the inner folds, so as to create the illusion of rippled and folded fabric (see 15–14).

Wood-carving tip: Refer to the second project, Ribbon, or Banner, Stern Board, for a more detailed description of how to cut a stylized fold.

If by chance you do make a mistake when cutting the edge of the hem—it's very easily done— then be prepared to modify the contour to suit your changing needs. For example, if you study the sequence of photographs, you will see that because my chisel slipped and damaged one of the hem ripples, I had to reshape the hem on both sides of the central line. It's all fairly straightforward, as long as you stay cool and follow the progression of the work. The order is as follows: use a pencil to carefully define the area that you want to carve, set the drawn line in with a stop-cut, skim in towards the stop-cut until the waste falls away, reestablish the stop-cut, and so on. If your tools are sharp and you make sure that you don't chop into end grain, then you won't go far wrong.

Modelling the Scrolls

Having modelled the primary shapes and forms of the bodice and skirt, take the traced scroll— meaning the side-view tracing of 15–2, B—and carefully press-transfer the lines of the design through to the flat sides of the figure. Spend time making sure that the scroll midpoints are symmetrically aligned with each other and with the front-view central line.

15–15 *Use the mallet and large gouge to remove the waste wood from around the scroll.*

15–16 *Lower the waste from around the spiral scroll, so that the background follows the form.*

15–17 *Use the dog-leg chisel to skim the ground to a smooth finish.*

With the two scrolls carefully aligned and drawn out, shade in the area that needs to be cut away and lowered. When this is done, take a mallet and V-tool and cut a trench all around the scrolls on the waste side of the drawn line. Set the drawn line in with a crisp stop-cut. With all the preliminary cuts in place, use the tools of your choice to lower the shaded areas of waste around the scrolls. You have a lot of wood to clear away, so go at it quite forcefully. Not forgetting to repeatedly define the shape of the scrolls with stop-cuts, carefully lower the waste to a depth of about 1½" (see 15–15 on page 167).

Now, if you look at the working drawings and painting grids and the various photographs, you will see that the scrolls—as seen from side view—are set at an angle so that they slant in towards the front of the figure. The overall effect is that Jenny is mounted on a huge scroll that appears to run the full width of the figure. If you look at the front view, you will see that the scroll increases in width as it travels up from the base, or, to put it another way, the scroll is widest across the middle. Notwithstanding this complicated explanation, the scroll is delightfully easy to carve.

With the carving set on its side, and having lowered most of the ground from around the scroll, start in the middle of the scroll and skim off the face, so that it runs in a continuous slope from the middle down to the end. Deepen the background waste, so as to narrow the front of the carving (see 15–16). If you've got it right, when the

15–18   *Cut straight down to texture the sides of the scroll and create an interesting contrast.*

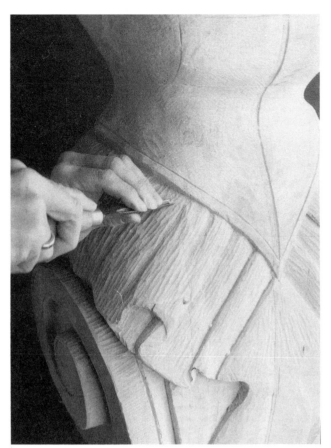

15–19   *Work systematically over the entire skirt area, using the direction and flow of the tooling to describe the form.*

figure is on its side, the scroll should have a high spot in the middle that slopes down to the base. Or, to put it another way, if you were an insect and you were to start in the middle of the scroll and walk to its end, you would be walking downhill on a road that got wider.

The easiest procedure is to lower the waste from the sides of the figure—first one side and then the other—to slope the scrolls as you go, and to keep standing the figure upright and checking off the shape of the scrolls against each other.

Skim off the face of the scroll and the surrounding lowered waste (see 15–17), and decorate the scroll with V-cuts that are set about ¼″ in from the side edge.

Finally, when you have achieved what you consider to be a scroll effect and have carved the hem line so that there is a convincing arrangement of ripples and folds, then take the small U-section gouge and texture the whole skirt, the edges of the scroll (see 15–18), and the lower-waste area around the scroll. Use the direction and flow of the tooling to describe the shape of the skirt and give movement to the various planes and slopes (see 15–19).

Modelling the Hair

If you look at the photographs and the various drawings, you will see that, although at first glance the hair appears to be a complex arrangement of coils and ringlets, it is, in fact, no more than a stylized pattern of rope twists. Refer to the third project, Running-Rope Borders.

With the rough shape of the hair blocked out, establish the overall pattern of the ringlets by setting them in with V-cuts. In other words, having first drawn in the width of each individual ringlet and the strands within each ringlet, use a V-tool to set in the drawn lines. Use a shallow-sweep gouge to widen and deepen the divisions (see 15–20 on page 170). Continue until the individual ringlets look to be more or less rounded—like fat coils of rope. When this is done, use the tools of your choice to shape the individual strands that make up the twisted formation within each of the coils (see 15–21 on page 170). Refer to the third project. It's all fairly straightforward, as long as you take note that you have to relate to the run of the grain by changing the direction of cut for each side of each strand.

169

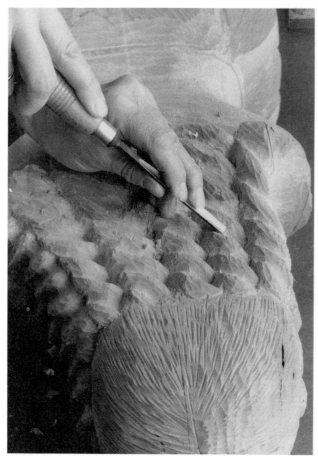

15–20 *Widen and deepen the curls before you attempt to add texture.*

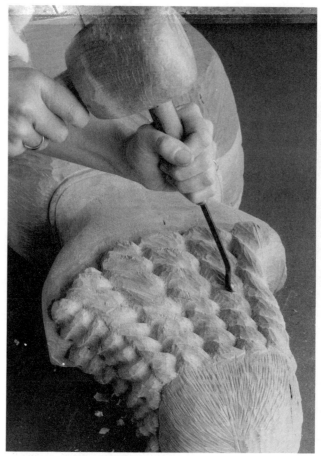

15–21 *Use the tool of your choice to separate each lock, so that the hair flows over the shoulders.*

Detailing and Finishing

Having modelled all the individual areas that make up the figure—the face, bodice, skirt, and so on—then comes the exciting task of pulling everything together.

When you consider the carving to be ready for detailing, you can either put it out of sight for a couple of weeks and come back to it with a fresh eye or simply get on with the job. We feel it's best to leave it be for a week or so.

Now, hone one or two selected tools to a razor-sharp edge and start the process of detailing. This involves cutting and lowering the almond shapes of the eyes, scooping out the nostrils, cutting in the line between the lips, and so forth.

Wood-carving tip: By "selected tools," I mean tools that you consider to be most appropriate for the task at hand and those that you enjoy using. I usually clean up with a selection of knives, a shallow-sweep fishtail gouge, and a small U-section gouge.

Work backwards and forward over the entire carving, generally sharpening up the angles, skim-

ming off the surfaces, and bringing the work to completion. Pay particular attention to any of the lines that help describe the form. For instance, by carefully positioning and cutting the neckline so that it is slightly stepped along its length and dipped at the breasts and shoulders, it is possible to enhance and exaggerate the forms (see 15–22). The line helps to create weight and tension. And so it is with the hair line, the decorative V-cut at the bottom of the bodice, the hem line, and the decorative lines between the scrolls and the front of the skirt.

Use the point of a penknife to slice out the corners of the eyes, to clean out the angle between the top of the scroll and the bottom of the skirt (see 15–23), and so on.

Take a sheet of fine-grade sandpaper and rub selected areas down to a super-smooth finish. Concentrate on the face; the neck, throat, and bosom; and the bodice. If need be, fill any splits and cavities. Finally, give the workpiece a swift rub-down to remove rough areas and nibs.

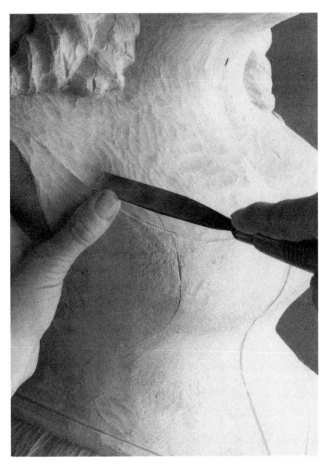

15–22   Use your thumb to guide the tool, being very careful not to damage the neckline of the dress.

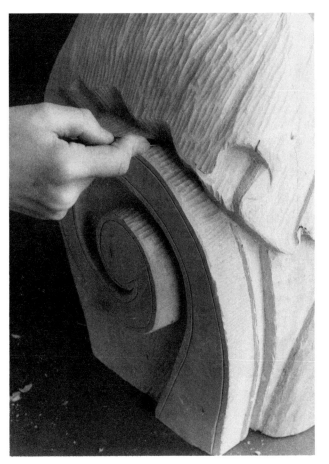

15–23   Use the point of a sharp tool to clean the jagged bits of waste left in the crevices.

Painting

When the carving is done, brush away all the dust and debris and move to the area set aside for painting. Start by giving the entire carving a couple of all-over coats of matt white emulsion. Be generous and rub down between coats. When the base coat is completely dry, look at the working drawings and painting grids (15–2, A and B) and then lay on the main areas of ground color: blue-green for the bodice and skirt, black for the lowered area in and around the scrolls, yellow for the hair, red for the sides of the scrolls, and a pinkish-tan flesh color for the face, neck, and throat. If you think that the ground colors are a bit thin or patchy, apply another coat.

Use a fine-point brush to apply the gold on the face of the scrolls and for the decorative line at the bottom of the bodice. Then trace off the bodice decoration, and paint it gold (see 15–24 on next page).

When the yellow hair is dry, use the colors of your choice to streak and darken the various coils and strands. Darken the hollows, so as to exagge-rate the depth and create shadows. Continue adding washes and streaks, until you have what you consider to be a pleasing effect. There are two schools of thought when it comes to painting figureheads—especially the face. One school says that it's best to go for hard blocks of flat color, while the other prefers to aim for realism and a more painterly finish by applying graded tones. So, for example, when you come to the face, you can either paint the flesh a flat pinkish-tan and the lips red and then highlight the details with, say, black, or you can lay on the basic colors and then continue adding washes and tones. We prefer the latter approach.

While you are waiting for the basic flesh color of the face, neck, and shoulders to dry, mix a small amount of thin red wash for the cheek tint. Dab the red wash on the blush area, and then use a soft-haired brush to grade the cheek blush in with the surrounding flesh tone. Repeat this procedure with a sepia wash on the top lids, under the chin, at the throat, and in the dips in the shoulders and the breasts. Paint the irises brown, the pupils black, and so on.

Wait for the paint to dry, and then give the whole works a couple of coats of clear varnish. Finally, mount the carving on a shelf so that it is well above eye level—as it would be if it were on a ship—and then sit back and enjoy the viewing!

TROUBLESHOOTING AND POSSIBLE MODIFICATIONS

- If you like the project but want to make a smaller carving, then simply reduce the scale accordingly.
- If you intend to display the figurehead outside— say, on your boat or maybe in your garden—then

be sure to use a waterproof glue when you are building up the block. Also, be especially generous with the varnishing, and cover all surfaces, including the back and base.

Inspirational designs (opposite)   Top left: Mother-and-child figurehead, 1840–1850, Denmark. Right: Figurehead from the American ship Creole, *1847, Brooklyn, New York (Museum of Fine Arts, Boston). Bottom left: Figurehead from the American whaler* Eunice H. Adams, *built in Newport, Rhode Island, in 1845.*

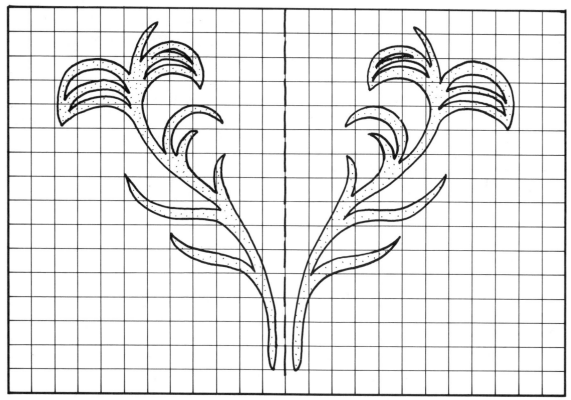

15–24   *Pattern for the bodice design. The scale is four grid squares to 1".*

Three-masted schooner

Bibliography

Bailey, S. F. *Cutty Sark Figureheads*; Shepperton, Surrey, England: Ian & Allan Publishing, 1992.

Brewington, M. V. *Shipcarvers of North America*; New York: Dover Publications, 1962.

Costa, Giancarlo. *Figureheads*; Hampshire, England: Nautical Publishing Co., 1981.

Frere-Cook, G. *The Decorative Arts of the Mariner*; London: Jupiter Books, 1966.

Hamilton, Georgia W. *Silent Pilots: Figureheads in Mystic Seaport Museum*; Mystic, Connecticut: Mystic Museum Publications, 1984.

Hansen, Hans J. *Art and the Seafarer*; New York: Viking Press, 1968.

Laughton, L. G. Carr. *Old Ships' Figureheads and Sterns*; London: Halton-Truscott Smith Publications, 1929.

Noughton, Peter. *Ships' Figureheads*; London: David & Charles, 1976.

Pinckney, Paul. *American Figureheads and the Carvers*; New York: W.W. Norton & Co., 1940.

Stammers, M. K. *Ships' Figureheads*; Aylesbury, England: Shire Publications, 1990.

Taylor, David. *Figureheads, Maritime Collection*; London: National Maritime Museum Publications, 1992.

Museum Collections

United States
Buffalo Historical Society, Buffalo, New York.
Bourne Whaling Museum, New Bedford, Massachusetts.
Carnegie Museum, Pittsburgh.
De Young Museum, San Francisco.
Hampton Galleries, New York.
India House, New York.
India Wharf Rats Club, Boston.
Kendall Whaling Museum, Sharon, Massachusetts.
The Mariners Museum, Newport News, Virginia.
Masonic Temple, Philadelphia.
Museum of the City of New York.
Museum of Fine Arts, Boston.
Mystic Seaport, Mystic, Connecticut.
Peabody Museum, Salem, Massachusetts.
Penobscot, Maritime Museum, Searsport, Maine.
Seamen's Church Institute, New York.
U.S. Naval Academy Museum, Annapolis Old State House, Maryland.

United Kingdon
American Museum in Britain, London.
British Museum, London.
Clipper Ship Cutty Sark, Greenwich, London.
Glasgow Museum and Art Gallery, Glasgow.
Horniman Museum, London.
Manx Museum and National Trust, Isle of Man.
Marlipuis Museum, Shoreham-by-Sea.
Maritime Museum, Southampton.
Maritime Museum of East Anglia, Great Yarmouth.
Museum of Maritime and Local History, Deal.
National Maritime Museum, Greenwich, London.
Poole Maritime, Poole.
Royal Naval Museum, Portsmouth.
Royal Navy Dockyard, Chatham.
Royal Navy Dockyard, Devonport.
Royal Navy Dockyard, Portsmouth.
Science Museum, London.
Town Docks Museum, Hull.
Valhalla Museum, Tresco, Scilly Isles.

(Museums outside the United States or the United Kingdom are cited within project captions when examples have been drawn for the "inspirational designs.")

Index

Metric Conversion

Inches to Millimetres and Centimetres
MM—millimetres   CM—centimetres

Inches	MM	CM	Inches	CM	Inches	CM
⅛	3	0.3	9	22.9	30	76.2
¼	6	0.6	10	25.4	31	78.7
⅜	10	1.0	11	27.9	32	81.3
½	13	1.3	12	30.5	33	83.8
⅝	16	1.6	13	33.0	34	86.4
¾	19	1.9	14	35.6	35	88.9
⅞	22	2.2	15	38.1	36	91.4
1	25	2.5	16	40.6	37	94.0
1¼	32	3.2	17	43.2	38	96.5
1½	38	3.8	18	45.7	39	99.1
1¾	44	4.4	19	48.3	40	101.6
2	51	5.1	20	50.8	41	104.1
2½	64	6.4	21	53.3	42	106.7
3	76	7.6	22	55.9	43	109.2
3½	89	8.9	23	58.4	44	111.8
4	102	10.2	24	61.0	45	114.3
4½	114	11.4	25	63.5	46	116.8
5	127	12.7	26	66.0	47	119.4
6	152	15.2	27	68.6	48	121.9
7	178	17.8	28	71.1	49	124.5
8	203	20.3	29	73.7	50	127.0